Tog on Software Design

Bruce Tognazzini

With a foreword by Robert Glass
and illustrations by Marsh Chamberlain

Addison-Wesley Publishing Company

Reading, Massachusetts • Menlo Park, California • New York
Don Mills, Ontario • Wokingham, England • Amsterdam
Bonn • Sydney • Singapore • Tokyo • Madrid • San Juan
Paris • Seoul • Milan • Mexico City • Taipei

Many of the designations used by manufacturers and sellers to distinguish their products are claimed as trademarks. Where those designations appear in this book, and Addison-Wesley was aware of a trademark claim, the designations have been printed in initial capital letters or all capital letters.

The author and publisher have taken care in preparation of this book, but make no expressed or implied warranty of any kind and assume no responsibility for errors or omissions. No liability is assumed for incidental or consequential damages in connection with or arising out of the use of the information or programs contained herein.

Library of Congress Cataloging-in-Publication Data
Tognazzini, Bruce.
      Tog on software design / Bruce Tognazzini.
         p.   cm.
      Includes index.
      ISBN 0-201-48917-1 (alk. paper)
       1. Computer software — Development   I. Title.
QA76.76.D47T64   1996
005.1'2 — dc20   96-38790
                                                CIP

Copyright © 1996 by Bruce Tognazzini

All rights reserved. No part of this publication may be reproduced, stored in a retrieval system, or transmitted, in any form or by any means, electronic, mechanical, photocopying, recording, or otherwise, without the prior written permission of the publisher. Printed in the United States of America. Published simultaneously in Canada.

Sponsoring Editor: Martha Steffen
Project Manager: Sarah Weaver
Production Coordinator: Deborah McKenna
Text illustrations: Marsh Chamberlain
Cover design: Suzanne Heiser
Text design: Greg Johnson, Art Directions
Set in 10.5 point Stone Serif by Greg Johnson, Art Directions

1 2 3 4 5 6 7 8 9 –MA– 0099989796
First printing, December 1995

Addison-Wesley books are available for bulk purchases by corporations, institutions, and other organizations. For more information please contact the Corporate, Government, and Special Sales Department at (800) 238-9682.

Find us on the World-Wide Web at: http://www.aw.com/devpress/

To my mother, Page Solomon,
and my wife, the real Julie Moran

A portion of "Nehru Jacket Computers" (Chapter 10) was originally published in Farrand, A.B., et al., "Common Elements in Today's Graphical User Interfaces: The Good, the Bad, and the Ugly," proceedings of INTERCHI, 1993 (Amsterdam, The Netherlands, April 24–29, 1993). ACM, New York, 1993, pp. 472–473.

Portions of "Magic and Software Design " (Chapter 34) were originally published as Bruce Tognazzini, "Principles, Techniques, and Ethics of Stage Magic and Their Application to Human Interface Design," proceedings of INTERCHI, 1993 (Amsterdam, The Netherlands, April 24–29, 1993). ACM, New York, 1993, pp. 355–362.

Portions of "Designing with Video Prototypes" (Appendix B) were originally published as Bruce Tognazzini, "The 'Starfire' Video Prototype Project: A Case History," proceedings of CHI, 1994 (Boston, MA, April 24–28, 1994). ACM, New York, 1994, pp. 99–105.

C O N T E N T S

Foreword

*A*re you ready for the future? *Tog on Software Design* is a refreshing and amusing look at how computer technology—and society itself—will be transformed over the next decade. It is a book aimed at everyone whose life is touched by computers (which is probably all of us).

Tog begins with a look at coming changes in our lives at work, at school, at home, and on the road, touching upon many of the important issues that will shape tomorrow. He then explores the path the computer and communications industries must follow over the coming decade if they are to be a positive force for change, enriching people's lives as well as building economic wealth.

Tog presents the details of his team's previously-secret advanced computer design project at Sun, code-named Starfire. You will see how new, high-productivity interfaces can and will enable people to interact with each other and their computers with an ease almost unimaginable with today's needlessly complex systems. Finally, he details techniques and approaches software designers, programmers, and managers can apply today to make their own products—and companies—successful now as well as tomorrow.

We are in a period of accelerating decentralization and reformation of government, business, and schools. The whole economic fabric of the world will be rewoven in the next five to ten years. Government will no longer be able to control the information its citizens see or generate. Many current laws and concepts will be swept aside. Our centralist model of information will crumble. Freedom of the press will explode beyond the confines of the traditional clique of those with the money to own a press. Copyright laws will be overhauled, with royalty payments becoming automatic, but minuscule. Information will be available to everybody, everywhere, instantly and continuously.

Software of the future will be predominantly object-oriented, making it much easier to build integrated, tailor-made user environments. Reusable code will result in an increased pace of software evolution as turn-around time for new products drops radically. Users are struggling now to keep up with changes and releases. The increased rate of change will force developers to make their products more compatible with user habits, more reliable, and more stable. The quality movement that transformed the automobile industry is already making inroads in the software industry today. In the future, quality will become a necessity to successful competition.

In reading *Tog on Software Design,* I found Tog to be, as usual, his funny, visionary self. I met him about seven years ago, and was totally taken by his prophetic view of the world. He is uniquely qualified to take us into the future. He built his first computer in 1957 at age 12 and has been an integral (and vocal) part of the personal computer industry since its inception. His enlightening ideas and viewpoints are reflected in the Macintosh and are shaping future Sun operating systems. His first book, *Tog on Interface,* influenced a whole generation of software designers. *Tog on Software Design* now propels us into the new millennium. Sit back, relax, put your feet up, and prepare yourself for an enjoyable read. Welcome to the future.

Bob Glass
Los Gatos, California
September 1995

To the Reader

Welcome to the new millennium. In ten years, society will be in the midst of a great transformation, and mature object-oriented systems will be among us. The book first explores what business, school, home, and travel will look like in ten years, as seen through the eyes of leading futurists. It then details the steps the computer industry needs to take now to deliver the intimately integrated systems the coming decade will demand. Finally, the book offers a good measure of tips and techniques developers can begin applying today.

Who Should Read This Book?

People who deal directly with software design. Human interface experts, graphic designers, programmers, architects, writers. We've been designing a lot of dialog boxes and buttons over the last ten years. We're about to be called upon to redesign the most fundamental underpinnings of our systems.

Managers and marketers in the computer industry. You are the ones making the decisions. Your choices in the next few years will determine the fate of your company. The industry will be transformed in the ways outlined here. You will decide how fast. In this book, you will discover material to help you plan for the future, along with some grounded, practical advice on how to organize and manage your software design talent.

People in related fields, such as communications and information. You will soon merge with the computer industry. Whether you run a newspaper, own a neighborhood bookstore, or build and market new videophone systems, you will discover how the coming revolution will affect your livelihood and your life.

Computer buyers and users. You have a stake in the future of this industry. This book is a vision of what computers could look like in ten years. You are the ones who can demand that it happen.

Students. Whether you are studying computer science, psychology, or design, you are perhaps the most important audience of all, for you will be implementing the future.

Acknowledgments

This book is the outcome of Sun's three-year Starfire project. I am deeply grateful to all those who worked on the project, both within Sun and outside it. First, I thank the original members of the Vision Team, headed by Frank Ludolph. Rafael Bracho, Dave Geyde, Don Gentner, Jim Glenn, Jay Guyot, Harry Hersh, Ellen Isaacs, Earl Johnson, Rick Levine, Steve Martino, Kevin Mullet, Elizabeth Mynatt, Ed Patterman, Darrel Sano, Julie Sarbacker, John Tang, Nicole Yankelovich, and Ricky Yeung not only laid the foundation for the Starfire vision but generated the scenarios that pepper this book and added their writing and design talents.

Some of the most clever ideas that found their way into the project were developed by our Virtual Attendee Screen Team—Dave Geyde, Don Gentner, Ellen Isaacs, Amy Pearl, Darrell Sano, John Tang, Annette Wagner—and our Industrial Design Team led by Phil Yurkonis—Alison Armstrong, Michael Antonczak, Nancy Aaron, Craig Hartley, and Adam Richardson.

I was helped in forming the ideas for this book and seeing the overall project to fruition by additional Sun people: Jakob Nielsen, Whitfield Diffie, Bob Sproull, Rick Levenson, Rick Levine, Laura Davis, Kimberley Mar, Lynn Bailey, and Maria Marguet.

Without the help and support of my management—Bob Glass, Ed Zander, and Steve Mackay—both the Starfire film and this book would have been impossible.

Many people worked hard to breathe life into the Starfire vision. I thank our stars: Judith Borne, who played Julie Moran with the perfect blend of vulnerability and strength, and Jonathan Fuller, the nicest guy in the world until the camera turned on and he transformed himself into the "yuppie scum," Michael O'Connor. Thanks to Gina St. John, who injected her vibrant personality into the role of Natalie; Derrick Partridge, an Adrian who would stand out in any crowd; and Shawn Morningstar, who turned the little side story of an inadvertent privacy invasion into a literal show stopper.

Alex Funke, our Academy Award–winning cinematographer, gave an enormous amount of his time for our little industrial film, and Michael Carp's skillful motion control cinematography brought Julie's office computer to life. Daniel Todd scrounged up resources from nowhere. Marty Cusak built a palatial set on a hovel budget, and Mario Celestino kept us all in line and on time. I thank as well Darrell Sano, responsible for so much of Starfire's graphic design, and Ken Matusow, our unsung third unit cameraman who made the "Making of Starfire" possible. Most of all, I thank my producer and codirector, Tony Barreca, whose fierce talent and drive ensured an effective, quality film.

A number of people outside Sun have strongly influenced the direction of my work, not only on this project but throughout my career: Bill Atkinson, Bill Buxton, Andreas Dieberger, Hugh Dubberly, Dan Fitzpatrick, Bill Gaver, Eric Hulteen, Allan Kay, Brenda Laurel, Riley McLaughlin, Doris Mitch, William Newman, Don Norman, P.J. Plauger, Jef Raskin, Gitta Salomon, Abby Sellen, Andrew Singer, Mark Weiser, Pierre Wellner, and especially Doug Engelbart, who began it all.

Thanks to Martha Steffen, Jean Seal, Deborah McKenna, Sarah Weaver, Keith Wollman, and Steve Stansel from Addison-Wesley for making this book happen. And to Kent Borg, who ferreted out errors on my part that even my editors couldn't find!

Thanks to my friends of the Club Med Round Table—Tom Weston, Annie and Sam Lamott, Terry Richey, Sarah Patterson, Diane Hamlin, Mary McGowan, Jerry Callaway, Meg Averett, and Pat Nisson—who over the course of writing this book kept me in good spirits and good spiritual condition. To Molly O'Neill, who offered encouragement when I most needed it and Paul and Max Ohlinger, Dr. Bob Smith, and Bill Wilson, for keeping me happy, joyous, and free.

Finally, I thank my kids, Joshua and Rebecca, who not only added their own talents to the Starfire film but once again lived with a shadowy figure hunched over his word processor for many months and once again offered nothing but support and encouragement.

Bruce Tognazzini
Woodside, California
October 1995

Introduction

*A*ll hell is about to break loose. The computer revolution that has come before is nothing compared to the cataclysmic tidal wave of change that we are about to visit on human society as phones, fiber, and computers converge. In the next ten years, the world will become wired. National boundaries will cease to exist as information—good, bad; legal, illegal; useful, trivial; hard science, soft porn—flashes around the world.

Governments are struggling valiantly to contain and control the beast, but it is far too late. Such muddle-headed ideas as the clipper chip are meaningless. Sure, the government can force its citizens to spend millions on encryption chips that the government alone can break into,[1] but the bad guys will only preencrypt the information themselves, so that when the government does break in, they will find nothing but gibberish.

For the next several years, individuals will enjoy the benefits of secure private encryption, while large banks and institutions, under the watchful eye of the government, will comply with a weak encryption standard decipherable by talented children. Ultimately the government will be forced to relent.

The government of Singapore banned *Wired* magazine from their island after *Wired* published a somewhat unflattering article by William Gibson, "Disneyland with the Death Penalty." Almost immediately, *HotWired,* the augmented Internet version of *Wired,* appeared in its place and has been operating with impunity in Singapore ever since. Traffic on the Internet cannot be selectively stopped without stopping the Internet itself, and if anyone were to attempt to halt the Internet now, much of the world's economy would come to a standstill.

Intellectual property laws are being left in disarray as graphic designers and artists generate new art from old, snipping bits and pieces into a new creative whole, often without the niceties of royalty payment. Some of what is going on is outright thievery, but we are also

....
1 Well, actually, they and around 100,000 bright and determined 17-year-olds, who will instantly share the details of their discovery with millions of people around the world, so that everyone can break in.

seeing the emergence of a new and powerful form of expression, as works grow, change, and divide, with each new artist adding to these living collages of color, form, and action.

Soon cyberspace will become the money pump the corporations have dreamed of and the hackers fear.[2] However, people will not be paying $1,000 or $2,000 for the rights to a snippet of someone else's photograph. They will pay 1¢ or 2¢. The profit will come from several billion people snipping snippets, instead of the few dozen with pockets deep enough to afford today's enormous fees. As the revolution continues, our society will enjoy a blossoming of creative expression the likes of which the world has never seen.

While the news is filled with the antics of the young computer cat burglars on the FBI's Most Wanted list, some of America's largest software companies are sneaking across networks, rummaging through America's boardrooms and bedrooms, further rending the tattered curtain of America's illusion of privacy. Security is as much an illusion as privacy, as naive, idealistic hackers automate their activities and release them, copyright free, to an awaiting world of less talented thieves and charlatans. Orwell's prediction of intrusion is indeed coming true, but government is taking a back seat to the activities of both our largest corporations and our next-door neighbors. The trend will be reversed as the network is finally made safe for both business and individuals, but it will be accomplished by new technology, new social custom, and new approaches to law. The old will not work.

The last computer revolution, in the 1980s, produced a completely unexpected result: desktop publishing, the final chapter in the history of printing. Today, thousands of "zines"—magazines with an attitude— struggle in the absence of any reasonable distribution system to carry their idiosyncratic messages to the world. Within a couple of years, this last flourish of the printer's art will have left the real world for the wonders of cyberspace.[3] Writers will no longer need to curry the favor

---

2 Cyberspace, popularized by cyberpunk science-fiction writers and embraced by virtual reality enthusiasts, refers to the electronic world inside our computer systems and networks. A picture on your desk is in real space; the same image, whether glowing on your computer screen or flashing across the network on its way to a different continent, is in cyberspace.

3 As we were going to press, I received a letter to subscribers from the publishers of XO, a high-quality, glossy, mainstream magazine that has just elected to go exclusively CD-ROM because they are sick and tired of having to deal with recalcitrant or ill-equipped printers and because their readers will be able to see the photos that grace their pages "with digital clarity, the same way we see them on our editing screens, before they're muddied by a 300-year-old paper and ink process!" CD-ROMs are only temporary. Once effective electronic readers arrive, we will receive our newspapers and magazines exclusively online.

of a publisher to be heard, and readers will be faced with a bewildering array of unrefereed, often inaccurate (to put it mildly), works.

Today, few people would want to read an entire book such as this on a 72-dot-per-inch, fuzzy computer screen, but within only a few years, electronic readers thinner than this book, featuring high-definition, paper-white displays, will begin the slow death knell for the tree mausoleums we call bookstores.[4]

Bookstores are not the only social institution under threat from the growth of cyberspace. Every retail business, from small stores to shopping centers to even the large discount superstores, will feel an increasing pinch from mail order, as people shop comfortably and safely in the privacy of their own homes from electronic, interactive catalogs.

Our lives at work are already beginning to undergo radical change. More and more corporations are embracing telecommuting, freeing their workers from the drudgery of the twice-daily commute and society from the wear, tear, upkeep, and pollution of their physical vehicles. They will flit around cyberspace instead, leaving in their wake only a trail of ones and zeros.

Even schools, by the turn of the century, will be dragged kicking and screaming into the present, finally coming to accept that their job is to help students learn how to research, how to organize, how to cooperate, create, and think. Dry-as-dust, committee-created, and politically safe textbooks will be swept away by the tide of rough, raw, real knowledge pouring forth from the cyberspace spigot.

Information Superhighway

The phrase "information superhighway" is no longer cool—and for good reason: it is not even close to accurate. Cyberspace is no more a highway than the U.S. Interstate Highway System is a choo-choo train.[5] Cyberspace is an ephemeral web woven of glass and silicon, ether and ideas. It is at once the concrete reality of your nearest phone pole, the

---

4 Books will not disappear entirely. They will, like movies and radio, find a new, more specialized niche. Many bookstores will likely survive as well, moving from their neighborhood corner to the ephemeral webs of cyberspace.

5 Attempting to pigeon hole new technologies with old, inappropriate names is not new. Choo-choo trains were originally called iron horses, and cars were labeled horseless carriages. (One can only assume a car being drawn by a train would have been referred to as a horse and carriage.)

abstraction of an electromagnetic wave hurling itself from 22,300 miles in space, and the mysticism of the minds and spirits of millions of people scattered across the earth, tied inextricably together through the power and expression of knowledge and wisdom.

Some will find that definition just a bit sickening in its romantic lyricism, but let me assure you that my only failing is in capturing the full majesty of what cyberspace will soon become. It will be an alternative universe that will be just as sensory, just as real, just as compelling as the physical universe to which we have until now been bound.

Today's legislatures still dream of setting up a highway patrol and tollbooths along the information superhighway's length, ready to keep their citizens in line and extract taxes from them.[6] How disappointed they will be when they eventually discover the truth, for a new electronic economy will likely soon rise, based on a system of barter and anonymous electronic currency that not even the finest nets of government intrusion will be able to sieve.

The Haves and Have Nots

When electronic calculators first came out and cost $500, "rich" children were not allowed to use them at school because it might give them an advantage in their education that other students might not have. Those objections soon collapsed as calculators began showing up as prizes in cereal boxes. Cybercereal is just around the corner. The poor and minorities will not long be excluded from cyberspace. Short term, it's a problem. Long term, it will become a nonissue, as programmers might say.

We do face the real prospect of millions, perhaps billions, of have-nots shut out of cyberspace, but this threat has little to do with economic status, country of origin, race, creed, or color. Instead, it has everything to do with age, gender, education, culture, and attitude. If cyberspace today were to have a dead-honest advertising slogan, it would read: "Built by Boys, for Boys!" Margie Wylie has written: "Far from offering a millennial new world of democracy and equal opportu-

....

6 In 1995, Illinois was attempting to tax its citizens for their receipt of television signals from satellites orbiting 22,300 miles in space. Estimates were that it might cost as much or more for information providers to collect, remit, and account for the tax as the amount of the tax itself.

nity, the coming web of information systems could turn the clock back 50 years for women." The 18- to 39-year-old males of above-average intelligence and education who have built today's cyberspace have built it for themselves.[7] Large parts of it reflect the delicate ambiance of a automobile junkyard. We must make fundamental changes in the direction of computer design if the true have-nots of cyberspace are not to be those rare individuals who do not feel instantly comfortable clattering over mounds of metallic twisted wreckage—in other words, most people.

People today want to embrace all manner of new technology, if only we can provide an easier, softer way. The first direct broadcast satellite system was launched in mid-1994. Its first-year sales exceeded 1 million units, easily outpacing the first-year volume of radio, television, VCRs, music compact disc players, and personal computers combined. The cable companies that watched as their customers began fleeing forty years of high prices, mediocre technology, and cavalier service dubbed it the "Deathstar."

The direct broadcast satellite industry did more business in its first six months than the older, large-dish satellite industry did in its first decade. Why? The new systems are simple and approachable. Even more people edged out onto the World Wide Web in its debut year, escaping a similar tyranny of technological complexity and confusion.

We are now poised to embark on a new chapter in computer science. The three major operating systems in use today, DOS/Windows, Macintosh, and UNIX, were all launched in the seventies. They are old, tired, and creaking under the weight of today's tasks and opportunities. A new generation of object-oriented systems augmented with Web-based applets stands in the wings.

The industry will have a choice of porting over the same tired, limited applications and interface technologies or taking advantage of the powers that these new systems will bring. We have some reason for concern. When the industry moved from Teletype printers to video displays, the designers mimicked every drawback and defect in the original mechanical technology. Today, more than 15 years after the widespread availability of bit-mapped displays, the tired, old teletype look of MS-DOS is only now fading from the scene. If North America is to remain the world's leading economy, we cannot afford to allow 15

....
7 See Chapter 23, "Boytoys."

years to pass before fulfilling the promise of object-oriented and applet technology.

Careening Toward the Future

A hook-and-ladder fire truck has two steering wheels: one in front to set direction and one in back to avoid killing and maiming people along the way. In my last book, *Tog on Interface,* I was speaking only to software designers. I have come to realize that they are too often at the back of the truck, personing the tiller. In front is a committee—high-level managers, low-level system engineers, government policy makers, marketers, buyers, and users—all grasping at the wheel of a vehicle that is hurtling toward the future.

If we are to achieve the promise of the future, we must stop using the front steering wheel of our fire truck like the floating pointer of a Ouija board as we all fight to steer at once. We need to replace random twists and turns with long-term strategies and coordinated directions.

The convergence of phone, fiber, and computer is providing us with the opportunity to design and develop the most powerful machine in human history, a network of tightly integrated computing environments. This machine will be built by hundreds of thousands of people working at tens of thousands of companies around the world.

Today, you can hardly pick up a newspaper without reading about a new industry alliance with the aim of building a proprietary communications structure, be it on land, sea, air, or outer space. They must not be built in isolation. These structures, both hardware and software, must be tied together if we are not to be doomed to babble.

As our fire truck speeds along, we may want to consult the occasional road map. This book is just such a map. Like maps of antiquity, it will eventually prove incomplete, inaccurate, and crude, but I offer it in the hope that it might help us to stay the course until we catch sight of the fiery blaze ahead.

As our fire truck speeds along, we may want to consult the occasional road map. This book is just such a map. Like the maps of antiquity, it will eventually prove incomplete, inaccurate, and crude, but I offer it in hopes it might help us to stay the course until we catch sight of the fiery blaze ahead.

From Fire to Ice

Much of what you are about to read came to light during the course of a secret, three-year project at Sun Microsystems called "Starfire." The purpose of Starfire was to explore where the world and industry will be a decade hence, then design and build a prototype of the kind of computer system that people will want to use. We quickly abandoned efforts to build our prototype on one of today's computers—it was just too limiting. Instead, we built the critical pieces of our prototype in cyberspace, then breathed life into them through the miracle of Hollywood special effects. The result was a 13-minute, 31-second film called, appropriately, "Starfire."

Film is an excellent medium for communicating mood and tone, as well as displaying the details of animated visual design, while print is superior in facilitating an intellectual understanding. The Starfire film, as sparkly as it may be, was intended to be the tip of the iceberg. This book is the other 90 percent.

In Part 2, you will find the complete, annotated Starfire script. Should you never see the film itself, this script will help set the stage for the balance of the book. However, reading dry words on a page is no substitute for sitting back, relaxing, and watching the characters bring the Starfire vision to life. We have therefore arranged for Sun Microsystems to reproduce the film on video, at cost, and distribute it to the readers of this book. At the back cover of this book, you will find ordering information for the film. If you call now, it should arrive just about the time you reach the Starfire chapter. I hope you will get yourself a copy. It will cast a bright light on the material that follows.

PART 1

Trends

An interplanetary spacecraft bound for Jupiter is not aimed at Jupiter but at the place Jupiter will be when the spacecraft reaches the planet's orbit a few years thence. Only by understanding the future, only by properly predicting Jupiter's position, can a successful rendezvous occur.

The computer and communications industry has its own rendezvous with the future. In ten years, not only will our own world of computers and communications have changed, society will have changed as well. Only by understanding where society will be in ten years can we successfully converge.

Many changes in society will come about because of forces already on the march in the world today: the collapse of the USSR and, with it, the Cold War; the rise of free world trade; and the economic consolidation of Europe, coupled with the decentralization of much of the rest of the world. Other shifts will be caused by changes in and convergence of the communications and computer industries. The typical interplanetary probe lacks the gravitational assets to perturb Jupiter's path. Our industries have the potential to throw society into an entirely new orbit.

Part 1 of this book explores the changes society will soon experience in business, in education, at home, and on the road. It suggests the convergence point at which software design and our society of users will meet a decade hence. With that point established, in ensuing sections we can then explore what responsive systems in the next decade might look like and the steps we can take today to prepare the way.

CHAPTER 1

Business

*T*wenty years ago, you stood in long lines at the supermarket while the only working checker laboriously punched in the price of each item. Ten years ago, three checkers were working, and they had only to pass each item over a laser scanner. Now, all the checkers are in action, you pay for your package of Taste-Free Super Protein Drink Powder with an ATM card, and before you've left the store, the market has sold your name to every health club in town.

Twenty years ago, getting your oil changed was a major and unpleasant event in your life. Ten years ago, some folks would have had you on your way in a little over a half-hour, except they didn't have your size oil filter in stock. Today, the happy-faced attendants have you in and out in less than 15 minutes, and even before you've driven off, the home office has received a message via satellite telling them to resupply that branch with the model filter you used, plus six new quarts of oil.

Twenty years ago, sending a document across the country took the post office two to five days, if it ever made it. Ten years ago, Federal Express delivered it in less than 24 hours. Today, your fax machine, computer, or personal digital assistant will offer it up in a matter of seconds, at a cost lower than the old airmail.

Twenty years ago, you shopped at the neighborhood strip mall or drove into the city to the big downtown department stores. Ten years ago, you found yourself at Wal-Mart or that fancy new fashion mall just outside town. Now, you go to the Price Club and buy for less than at your supermarket, or curl up at home and order through an 800 number from a slick color catalog designed especially for you, based on that 96-ounce can of Taste-Free Super Protein Drink Powder you bought last month.

Speed, flexibility, quality, personalized service, and trust will be the keys to success in the coming decade. Companies tied to the industrial revolution model of rigidity, uniformity, and employees-as-suspects are being forced into change. The first wave of computers eliminated a lot of mindless, thankless, blue-collar jobs, but most of those workers are coming back, better trained and able to control the very machines that replaced them. Now, as companies move toward lean, nimble organizations, 70 percent of those being laid off are white-collar workers—middle managers—and they aren't coming back, ever (Perelman 1992).

The first large American corporations were the railroads. They had to be big, and, back then, they had to run on time. Coordinating the railroads required a high overhead of managers who could overlook the system and pass timely reports back up the line, with each level in the hierarchy culling through and concentrating the information from below. Information systems can do that job as well or better, and deliver the results at the speed of light.

Sam Walton, the founder of Wal-Mart and the world's largest retailer, didn't have to wait weeks or even days for his managers to report back up as to how his week had gone. He could stroll over to the satellite communications center and watch as the sales figures from all over the country rolled in. "I can see the total of the day's bank credit card sales adding up as they occur. I can see how many stolen bank cards we've retrieved that day. I can tell if our seven-second credit approval system is working as it should be and monitor the number of transactions conducted that day," he said. Every Saturday around 3:00 A.M., he would have on his desk his financial statement for the week that ended at midnight, just three hours ago, and if he didn't like what he saw, he could walk over to his own TV studio, get on the satellite, and have a little chat (Walton and Hey 1992). Walton had a flat organization and great communication.

Managers used to expend a lot of energy keeping their workers in line, particularly after Frederick Winslow Taylor wove his magic into the workplace around the turn of the century. He developed a system that called for workers who would show up exactly on time; perform dull, repetitive tasks without question or complaint; and go home quietly at the end of a very long day. His "scientific management" techniques exacerbated the growing rift between management and worker by neatly excising any possible pride or pleasure workers might have felt in their jobs, turning worker and management into hardened adversaries. Workers soon took any opportunity to shirk their responsibilities and sabotage the company's efforts. Hard-line managers cracked the whip to keep the "lazy creatures" in line.

Our balance of trade with the Japanese taught us in no uncertain terms exactly how much this corporate warfare was costing us. Today many companies are forming cooperative relationships with their workers: everyone works toward common goals of quality and high productivity, and both management and employees share in the rewards. Managers in these new and restructured companies are seen as leaders and coaches, not as spies and slave drivers. Factory workers are allowed—no, encouraged—to learn several jobs, so they can avoid having to put the same nut on the same bolt for the rest of their lives. Workers once again are using their minds, not just their hands. People work in teams, with peer pressure maintaining a level of commitment and service that no amount of external discipline could have ever achieved. A single manager can now oversee dozens of workers instead of a few. The management hierarchies of old, sometimes reaching 15 levels, are collapsing into five, four, or even three.

In industrial revolution companies, information flowed only in one direction, upward, and management information services departments saw that everything flowed smoothly. Today, the "M" in "MIS" is disappearing, as information becomes a two-way flow. By the year 2000, "the newest and lowest-level employees will be expected to know more about the company that employs him or her than many middle managers and most supervisors knew about the company they worked for in the 1970s and 1980s" (Boyett and Conn 1991).

Even more shocking than divulging closely held corporate secrets to the former enemy within is the emerging practice of sharing secrets with one's suppliers and customers. Davidow and Malone (1992) write, "Like all industrial transformations, the new business revolution is forcing a revision of traditional corporate arrangements toward what Harvard professor Benson Shapiro calls, 'the new intimacy.' As the rapid gathering, manipulating, and sharing of information become a preeminent process, and as company boundaries grow increasingly fluid and permeable, established notions of what is inside or outside a corporation become problematic, even irrelevant."

Layoffs continue at large companies, but small to mid-sized businesses are growing, enough to take up the slack and more. Large companies depend on these new companies to supply them with parts and to distribute finished goods and materials.

Just-in-time delivery, a cornerstone of the Japanese revolution, was the buzzword of the early eighties in America, as big companies demanded their small-company partners fill their latest whims within days, hours, or even minutes. It didn't work. The big corporations succeeded in reducing their warehouses only by making their smaller suppliers increase their own. Today these same corporations are forming close ties to their suppliers, cooperating with them in the development and sharing of information that will help everyone do a better job. Manufacturers let their suppliers know their plans months and even years in advance, so their suppliers can ramp up accordingly. Retailers such as Wal-Mart allow companies like Procter & Gamble to monitor in real time how P&G's products are moving, enabling them to spot trends and avoid shortages.

Supplying the information needs for our emerging economy goes well beyond data collection and accounting. All CEOs will soon demand the kind of instant access Sam Walton enjoyed. All employees will need to be able to track various categories of sales and product information. Research and development will need local security layers that enable them to collaborate with their peers without fear of intrusion yet allow them when appropriate to share their findings with the rest of the company.

Information services departments will be called upon to develop systems for capturing corporate memory in social simulations. (See "Simulation" in Chapter 21). In old-line companies, employees who had been there for 30 or 40 years kept their firms from making the same mistakes twice, or three times, or four. People in Silicon Valley now last only around five or six years at a given company. They are leading the trend. If future companies are to avoid repeating the mistakes of the past, their employees' experiences must be caught in an electronic amber.

Employees will need to be able to share information directly with partner suppliers and customers, swiftly and securely, and they will need direct access to industry information, through services analogous to Lexis and Nexis (online legal and news and business information services).

Still, this is not enough. Employees will need to connect to the open world of cyberspace if they are to achieve maximum creativity and full productivity. Tomorrow's workers will need access to their colleagues around the world, to vast online libraries, and to video, audio, and data feeds from network news services offering everything from this minute's news to archived video history. This may seem obvious to those of you used to working in high technology, but much of the world is lagging way behind. MIS managers' perceived need for control in the seventies and eighties led to powerful workstations running a few sparse, corporate-approved applications in information-parched environments protected by impenetrable[1] firewalls of security. It was little wonder that Macintoshes started coming in the side door.

Software architects and designers are working to replace the single corporate firewall with encryption and local zones of security, and to replace the chaos of today's Internet with an environment that will allow secure communications and transactions. The corporate information services of tomorrow will be as decentralized as the management structure itself.

Today most workers can order up research materials only through corporate library gatekeepers. Workers will be moving to direct, online access, causing pressure on information providers to abandon their 1960s interfaces in favor of efficient, accessible, human-centered designs. The cost of information will plummet as the volume finally increases.

Information services managers are running scared at the prospect of this decentralization, and over the short run, they have good cause. More and more workers are demanding full access to the Internet and the World Wide Web. Today's Web is filled with propaganda and low-grade information and is far more a playground than a serious information tool. Two things will soon change: First, the quality of information on the Web will increase immeasurably as soon as people start to charge for it. Second, the same workers who might fritter away their time at work now will all soon enjoy the Web at home, eliminating stealing time from their employers as an all-but-unavoidable cost of such recreation.

....
1 Except to 17-year-olds with Radio Shack computers and a lot of determination.

A Company of the Future

It's a week before Christmas. Your boss comes in and announces a two-week vacation for everyone, with pay. Oh, and just one thing: pack up everything in your office; whatever won't fit in a one-half-cubic-foot area, throw out or take home.

With some trepidation, you return two weeks later and discover the reason for this directive. Your telephone is gone. Your computer is gone. Your filing cabinets are gone. In fact, your entire office is gone. In its place, you have a locker much like the one you had in junior high, where you can keep all your personal possessions. Opening the door, you find within it a small black case with a handle on top where you can keep any paper files you need, along with floppy disks, pens, pencils, and other personal supplies. You also find a portable Apple Powerbook computer.

Now you move on to explore what else might have changed. Where the building had been jammed with a vast rabbit warren of cubicles and offices are now wide-open spaces. A huge library with lots of tables, comfortable chairs, and couches where people can go to research or do other work. A common room 100 feet long and 75 wide with exercise machines, pool tables, punching bags, and soda fountain booths where people can relax, play, or talk in groups. A kitchen with cappuccino machines and microwave ovens, and long counters covered with freshly baked bagels and muffins. Another room, perhaps 50 feet on a side, is given over to nothing but carnival Tilt-a-Whirl cars, providing quiet, private seating for small groups. And conference rooms, conference rooms, conference rooms.

Most amazing, even with all this, there is still room left over for cubicles—but only for half the people.

The surroundings are warm, intriguing, and inviting, but you haven't noticed. You're too worried about whether you're one of the lucky ones that will be getting a place to work.

This is not some fanciful dream of the future. It happened in 1994 at the Venice, California, office of Chiat/Day, the advertising agency of Energizer Bunny fame. Jay Chiat explained to the people assembled that January day that just because half their offices were missing didn't mean everyone didn't have a job. Rather, the company had become distributed and mobile. He showed them that adorning every possible work surface was an almost invisible new feature: little holes leading to the corporate network. Whether people were in a private cubicle, lounging in a soda fountain booth, or hanging around in a Tilt-a-Whirl car, they could jack in and be part of the company.

From then on, he explained, no one would own a private work space. Where there had been offices for all 330 people, there were now around 150 open cubicles, each of which could be signed out by anyone for the day. Someone who needed to do some scanning could pick out a cubicle with a scanner. Someone who needed to do a lot of dye-sublimation printing could pick out a cubicle near the printer. Anyone might decide to work in the library or at a soda fountain table. Or they might even choose not to come into work at all and telecommute instead.

Jay Chiat let his people know that he had enough trust in them, enough belief that they too shared the company's dream and vision, that he felt completely comfortable letting them decide where, when, and how they should get their work done. And, by the way, he said, don't worry about the number of cubicles.

Chiat's employees were no fools. They'd gone a few rounds of musical chairs before, so at 6:30 the next morning, there was a line of people around the block, waiting to grab a cubicle. After a few weeks, though, they began to settle down. Different groups acclimated themselves in perhaps predictable ways. True, the accounting people checked out a different cubicle every morning, but they always seemed to end up clustered as close together and as close to their old space as possible. The creative types flitted from Tilt-a-Whirl to soda fountain to home to park, wherever their muses might guide them.

Chiat/Day people now communicate by radio telephones they check out in the morning and return to a charger at night. With their portable computers jacked into the company network, they are as connected to each other—in some cases, more connected to each other—than they were when each had a private office and a dedicated computer.

Chiat/Day used to be in two buildings. Now all employees are in one, at a substantial real estate cost saving of around 35 percent. They love their new freedom, and Chiat/Day was happy enough with the new way of working that six months later they changed their Manhattan office over to the same system.

Chiat/Day is in the vanguard, but many other companies are not far behind. Most Silicon Valley companies are already much like

Chiat/Day, but without quite as much flair. The typical business model of one worker, one office, one desktop computer does not work today; in a decade it will be fading into the past.

"The Factory Floor": A Scenario

(Sometimes it's possible to find real companies of the future, such as Chiat/Day. Other times, designers turn to scenarios to define the people, tasks, and environments of the future. See Appendix A.)

In 1992, SunSoft launched the Starfire project to develop and promulgate an advanced computing/communication interface. We developed a number of fictional scenarios to help the team focus on the future needs of real people. You will find scenarios sprinkled throughout this book. The one that follows, set in a Pacific Northwest automobile assembly plant, we created during our initial exploration of the needs of business.

We used "The Factory Floor" scenario to explore the facilities that will be needed to support concurrent engineering. Davidow and Malone (1992) wrote, "The central notion behind concurrent engineering is that everyone affected by design—engineering, manufacturing, service, marketing, and sales personnel, as well as suppliers and customers—should participate as early as possible in the design cycle." Concurrent engineering is a key element in quality processes. It replaces the serial engineering, or "waterfall," method of having each group along the way add its contribution and then throwing the results "over the wall" to the next people in line.

As we tune in, the manufacturing group is finding it impossible to mate the metal overbody of its prototype car to the "green" composite underbody made of CFC-free foam.

The calculations for the underbody size had been done at an outside engineering firm in Phoenix, so Jim Moran placed a call to Liz Simpson, his contact in Arizona.

"Hi, Liz."

"Hi, Jim. You look a little worried."

"Yes, well, Liz, I'm afraid we have a bit of a problem up here."

Liz formed a rather drawn-out "yeeessss?" and Jim hesitantly began explaining.

"We made four prototype bodies three days ago, and everything seemed to be okay. All three passed parameter testing just fine. We assembled a car with the first underbody on the first day, and the car is perfect. Yesterday, however, when the assemblers went to fit the panels on the second body, they just barely fit, and today..."

"Yes?"

"They were way too big and didn't fit at all."

"And there's only one mold...."

"Yes. That's the weird part. The size is perfect going into the curing stage but different coming out. Our expected shrinkage factor has disappeared."

"Uh, well, okay, Jim, let me see your data from the first day's measurements."

Jim opened the relevant spreadsheet.

"Looks okay. Do you have any measurements from two days ago?"

"No, Liz, but we did retest the remaining two parts yesterday, when the assembly almost failed."

Jim slid yesterday's test results onto his workspace, but before he could open the results, Liz dropped them onto her 3D rendering application. Liz then superimposed the model of the original part on this new model built two days later. The part had grown. Jim, following her lead, then added their remeasure from today, created when the underbody had grown so large it would no longer work at all. The outline of the new image covered both the older ones.

"Jim, I'm going to try to get Jill Claiborne from Engineering on the line."

A long silence ensued once Liz had explained the expansion problem to Jill.

Jill Claiborne was a top-notch engineer with a knack for explaining the unexplainable. Blind since birth, she relied on her computer to

translate a visually oriented world into the auditory and tactile feedback she could perceive.

Jill asked Jim if he would mind repeating the measurements right now. Jim pressed his intercom button and got the floor supervisor on the line. The underbody was still on the testing rig, and the floor supervisor motioned to a couple of his workers to run the test again.

As soon as the testing started, a new spreadsheet model appeared on Jim's notebook, and he immediately dragged it to the 3D rendering icon. The model began to take shape on the three linked computers.

As Jill listened to the three data sets, it was clear that the latest model showed the underbody was slowing its growth. Playing a hunch, she used her Web browser to visit the U.S. Department of Commerce, where she pulled data on weather changes in the factory area. When she plotted the various parameters against the changing shrinkage factor, humidity stood out, tracking closely the differences in the shrinkage of the foam. She then asked Jim to feed in data from his factory's environmental system on actual humidity on the factory floor. The two curves now overlapped perfectly. Jill recommended two new drying ovens for the underbodies, showing that when she added their higher curing temperatures to the simulation, the growth disappeared.

While he listened, Jim privately opened his just-in-time-delivery catalog from the oven vendor and found that the company did, indeed, have two ovens in a San Francisco warehouse. He could have them overnight. He selected the items and applied his digital signature. By the time Liz was through with her explanation, the ovens were on their way.

K–12 Schools

If an unfriendly power had attempted to impose on America the mediocre educational performance that exists today, we might have viewed it as an act of war.

National Commission on Excellence in Education, *A Nation at Risk,* 1983

My stepson, Josh, a straight-A student now in the ninth grade, had always enjoyed school until last year. Then he began the same litany of complaints that our parents had to listen to: "Why do we have to learn this stuff? It's boring. I'm never going to use it." He's right, and we all know it. We just haven't known what to do about it. After all, memorizing the date of the Battle of Hastings and calculating how many pieces of pie Johny ate based on when the train left Chicago is what got us all into college.

Kids come into the world happy sponges, eager to seek out every bit of knowledge and learning they can possibly soak up. Then we send them to school, where they are to expected to sit quietly for the next 12 to 16 years. They do not go to learn; they go to be taught. They do not go to explore, discover, invent; they go to memorize data about explorers, discoverers, and inventors. They do not go to gain an understanding of the events that have shaped our history; they go to read bloodless texts and memorize dates. They go, most of all, to pass the tests. Passive learning. It impedes skill development, destroys motivation, and generates the discipline problems that reinforce the teachers' belief that kids have to be closely controlled for their own good.

The same forces that have revolutionized the factory stand today at the gates of our public schools, fighting to get in. Edward Fiske (1992) notes, "It is no longer possible to run an effective system of public instruction under the old values of centralized authority, standardization, and bureaucratic accountability any more than it is possible to run *any* large institution effectively in this fashion."

The very businesses that brought clocks to the schools 100 years ago, demanding that the schools teach discipline, repetition, and punctuality to prepare workers for the rigors of mass production, today are demanding something much more sophisticated—basic literacy—and the schools are failing.

We spend more money on our children's education that any other country in the world, and yet the average American student entering college in this country would not even be allowed out of high school in most other developed countries (Carlson and Goldman 1994). Why are we in this sorry state? Dr. Lewis J. Perelman (1992) charges that, "U. S. public schools and colleges are technologically stuck in the Middle Ages for the same reason Soviet collective farms were: a complete lack of accountability to the consumer and total insulation from competitive market forces."

Two trends are about to break apart this rigid monopoly. First, we have begun to return control of all parts of government to lower and lower levels. A return to community-operated schools, along with increasing numbers of charter, pilot, and privately managed schools, will act to break apart the rigidity that has built up as state governments have taken all control. Second, the move to some form of a voucher system, enabling children to escape from the confines of the public school system altogether, is well underway.[1]

Free enterprise has lurked around the perimeter of the education system, slopping up whatever dollars might be available for trade schools, but business cannot compete head to head with a publicly subsidized school system. As vouchers and private management become more commonplace, business is moving in.

Free Market Forces

Competitive market forces will cause schools to cut expenses and raise quality, following much the same path taken in the last 20 years by American business. "Schools in a market setting will be strongly

....

[1] Contrary to public perception, the main impetus for vouchers is coming from poor black parents in the inner city. They want their children to escape schools that have become little more than institutions for learning pharmacological sales techniques and advanced weaponry. The growing Catholic Hispanic population is adding to the voices of demand. Carlson and Goldman (1994) suggest that within 20 years, Catholic schools will be out of business unless they receive some manner of support.

encouraged to optimize—to do what they are good at, to learn to do it better, and to set goals that are both high and realistic. The reason? They will be rewarded for it," writes Louis V. Gerstner, Jr., chairman and CEO of IBM (Gerstner et al. 1994, p. 56). In business, this has taken the form of automation of both production and information collection, a returning of responsibility to the workers, and the elimination of much of middle management. American elementary and secondary schools are about to undergo the same revolution.

Administration

Most public school systems are operating like the railroads of 100 years ago. Just as in business, the primary task of middle managers—administrators—in schools has been to keep the workers—teachers—in line. All decisions, down to the smallest level of detail, have been made at the highest levels.[2] Layer after layer of management has ensured they are carried out to the letter, leaving teachers as little more than mouthpieces.

In private enterprise, the first to go are those who do not produce. The Chicago school system today has 3,500 administrators for a half-million students. The Catholic schools in America teach nearly a quarter million students, and they have exactly 35 administrators (Gerstner et al. 1994). With all the current rules, regulations, and rigmarole, Chicago needs 3,500 people. As educational and administrative decision making reverts to the teachers and students, the need for administrative overhead we have today will disappear, and the exodus of middle managers will begin.

Dade County, Florida, which includes Miami and 25 outlying municipalities, is already well into the process, with schools in the district converting to decentralized, shared-responsibility management on the average of one school every nine weeks. They expect all 271 schools, with 18,000 teachers and 300,000 students, to be fully decentralized by 1996.

Most decisions are now made by the teachers, parents, students, and school principal. When decisions need to be discussed on high, schools communicate directly with the top administration, bypassing regional

....
2 Texas even has a state law dictating exactly how many minutes each teacher will spend on each subject each day (Fiske 1992).

centers filled with middle managers who are quickly becoming superfluous (Fiske 1992). Other school systems around the country are following.

Education Alternatives, a Minneapolis-based for-profit company, took over Baltimore's ten worst schools in 1992 and turned bombed-out, graffiti-laden facilities punctuated with bullet holes and littered with broken glass into clean, well-lighted schools surrounded by trees and plants and suffused with a pleasant atmosphere conducive to learning. In the first year, they increased in-classroom spending by 30 percent, bought 1,000 new personal computers, supplying four per classroom, and even turned a modest profit.

Most of the savings came from reduction of administration costs. The president of Education Alternatives, David Bennett explains, "The sad reality is that, in most school districts in this country, 50 cents out of every dollar is spent outside the classroom. If you're serious about increasing pupil performance, you just simply have to spend more of the dollars you have *in* the classroom." Today, the schools' accounting is handled by the automated and efficient services of KPMG–Peat Marwick, while janitorial services are provided by another for-profit concern, Johnson Control World Services, both at substantially lower costs than in the old system (Hotakainen 1993).[3]

This shift toward administrative reduction and management automation is the same that swept industry. Today, American business supplies each worker with around $50,000 worth of capital equipment—computers, multiline phones, office furniture, and so forth. In the high-tech industries, this can rise as high as $300,000. The total capital equipment bill per American teacher is $1,000, fifty times less, an amount that barely covers desks and chairs (Perelman 1992).

I've talked to a lot of students who have complained that when their schools finally got computers, their teachers grabbed the lion's share, leaving few for the students. This is understandable. Teachers are desperate for equipment that will increase their productivity. In this, the richest country in the world, 125 years after the invention of the telephone, most teachers do not have a phone in their classrooms.[4]

....

3 In true entrepreneurial spirit, the new janitors receive merit pay tied to their "customer satisfaction indicators," sending shivers through the rest of the academic administration community.

4 I recently ran across a posting in the American Federation of Teachers bulletin board from a teacher with a brand-new computer and modem but no phone line to connect them. She described her failed attempts to weave her way through the bureaucratic nightmare and was plaintively asking if anyone could help her.

Teachers have become so used to having no access to technology that 84 percent of them recently reported that the only technology they consider absolutely essential to their jobs is the photocopier, and many of them have little access to that (Negroponte 1995; Fiske 1992).

The next ten years will finally see a major budget shift from paying functionaries to investing in capital equipment. The 630-student Boston Renaissance Charter School, which opened September 14, 1995, was the fourth of some 200 schools expected to be opened by the for-profit Edison Project, headed by former Yale University president Benno Schmidt.[5] The school stresses "civility and civic responsibility," echoing the recent Carnegie report *The Basic School* (Boyer and the Carnegie Foundation 1995), while at the same time covering a solid educational curriculum. Following the path of Education Alternatives, the Edison Project has cut administration to the bone, freeing its people to experiment with new approaches to education and providing them with the funds to supply computer links for every student between home and school (*Boston Globe,* March 26, 1995).

The computer and communications industry will need to be prepared to supply administrative technologies that will help school systems cut their expenses while improving overall communication. The same suppliers feeding downsizing businesses today will be in good position to take charge of this emerging market. However, they will need to understand that this is an entirely new, computer-phobic user population that has not had 15 years to get used to the dreadful interfaces of today's corporate computing environment. The companies that succeed will have plunged head first into human-centered design, offering systems that are approachable and explorable and encourage self-learning.

The Classroom of Tomorrow

Today the majority of our children come to school to be taught, not to learn, just as the factory worker of old came prepared to take orders, not to think. We have been teaching our students content instead of teaching them how to access information. We have substituted memorization of the Preamble to the Constitution and the Gettysburg

....
5 The Edison Project was founded by Chris Whittle, who was the first to bring television advertising into the classroom via his Channel One service.

Address for a lifetime ability to discover and explore all the great political documents of history. We should not abandon the teaching of facts, but we must add a far greater emphasis on teaching our children how to obtain knowledge.

In the classrooms of tomorrow, children will come to explore, discover, invent—to learn. Today, workers operate in teams instead of strapped to a single machine. Tomorrow, our children will be unchained from their desks, free to plan, research, and build, working in teams, just as they will be expected to do when they leave school and join the work force.

Professor Roger C. Schank of the Institute for Learning Sciences at Northwestern University is fond of pointing out that all he learned about education was taught to him by the Department of Motor Vehicles. The DMV offers two tests: "One, can you drive a car. Two, can you memorize a book of irrelevant facts and keep them in your head long enough to spit them back on a multiple-choice test. The schools have eliminated one of those tests! The acquisition of skills is what [education] is all about. Can the student do it?"[6] The student of today doesn't have to do it. With passive learning, he or she can sit there for 12 years parroting back data and passing all tests with flying colors, all the while developing few transferable skills. That will change radically as we move our schools back to being places of learning rather than lecturing.

When the conditions are right, the power shift from teaching to learning is nothing short of amazing. Seymour Papert, the MIT master of artificial intelligence research and father of the Logo language for children, tells of the time they arranged for every student at a Texas elementary school to have a computer both at home and school. They had installed Logo on every student's computer, but the teachers had decided to teach it differently depending on grade.

The most delightful feature of Logo is the "turtle," a creature you control through the Logo language, asking it to move forward so many steps, turn left so many degrees, and so forth. The teachers had decided that they would show the first graders how to move the turtle forward and backward a few steps at a time but withhold knowledge of turning, which required understanding not only what a degree is but knowing the numbers between 0 and 360. (These kids knew how to count only to ten.)

....

6 From an address given at the Technology, Entertainment, and Design 6 Conference, February 24, 1995.

As Dr. Papert put it, this "resulted in an unstable social situation." Only a few weeks into the school year, a little boy came running into the classroom at lunch's end, red-faced and out of breath. He gathered all the other students around him and began whispering to them earnestly. The group broke apart as all the students shot to their desks and started pounding on their keyboards.

Dr. Papert went over to the first little boy's desk and asked him what was going on. Maintaining unwavering attention to his screen, the little boy replied, "I've just talked to one of the third graders. It turns out there is a way to turn the turtle. It is some kind of a secret code having to do with numbers. We don't know what it is yet, but we're working on it."

Within two days, every one of those first graders knew exactly what a degree was and knew and understood the numbers between 0 and 360. How many days or weeks would that have taken in our current nine-teenth-century schools? ("All right, Class. Put your pens down and look at me! I'm going to write a 'three' on the board in front of the 'four' that is already there. Who can tell me what the number is now? No, Sally, it is not twenty-four. Billy, sit up! You're not paying attention!")

The Logo incident is not a story about technology, although technology played a role. It is about teachers who, with not a little courage, gave up their traditional roles as taskmaster to let the children run free and explore. In most schools I have visited, computers are kept in a special room under lock and key, with the students allowed to carry out only certain approved activities. Any deviation from the rules is grounds for banishment—from the room or even from the school. If you ask the students why all the rules, they will tell you, "They don't want us to have fun," or, "They want to limit our freedom." When you ask them why the teachers are so strict, they shrug and say, "I don't know; that's just what teachers do."[7]

The real reason for all the security is that the teachers are terrified of what the students—the enemy—might do. The students know more than the teachers do about the machines, making the teachers feel out of control. Instead of channeling the energy of the bright students who might, with some encouragement, learn enough about the computer systems to help improve them, the teachers lock up the computers and punish those who want to explore, discover, and invent.

....
7 Actual quotes from students who wish to retain their anonymity.

A few sociopathic children should not be allowed within 20 miles of the school's computers, but they are the exception. The student versus teacher polarity that is the real cause of the restrictions exactly parallels the now-fading worker versus boss relationship in the industrial revolution factory. The factories are changing to a cooperative system, and the schools will follow.

Cougar Valley and Silver Ridge Elementary, in Silverdale, Washington, represent the wave of the future in American education. They are dedicated to making the teachers "managers of instruction, not presenters of information," and have created an open, freewheeling environment with lots of computers to enable kids to work at school with all the efficiency they will find at their jobs. These students don't spend their time filling out questionnaires on what the teacher said yesterday; rather, they work on projects that encourage them to fight for knowledge.

When Silver Ridge first opened in 1992, some of the teachers were quite taken aback at the results. One teacher gave the children a three-day assignment to research a dozen different countries, requiring they find a great deal of demographic and other information. They returned from the school's largely electronic library exactly 10 minutes later with all required data stored on a floppy, completely disrupting the lesson plan. The teachers soon learned that their students' time would be spent applying information, not gathering data.

Most teachers only dream of their charges having such free access to technology. While American business invests in the productivity of their workers, we supply our students with tools that have remained unchanged since the invention of paper, a root cause of the inefficiency of today's schools. Perelman found that "even rather ordinary computer-assisted instruction—CAI—produces about 30 percent more learning in 40 percent less time and at 30 percent lower cost than conventional classroom instruction." More advanced technology and technique will surely double and redouble student productivity. American businesses have noticed these advances; they spend *300 times* as much on computer-based instruction as do American schools, and they are not in it to lose money. Perelman (1992), in discussing General Motor's successful diagnostic/training systems for service dealers, proclaims, "Mr. Goodwrench actually has more to tell us about the future of education than Mr. Chips ever imagined."

Why have schools been so slow to change? Administrators and teachers have powerful lobbying groups; calculators, telephones, and computers don't. Public institutions tend to be people-heavy, and educators tend to resist change.[8] As schools become market driven, their appetite for high technology will skyrocket. Will this money be squandered on high-priced equipment of little real value, or will it be channeled into areas that will produce strong results?

Research and Development

President Clinton (1994) said, "I am absolutely convinced that there is not a single, solitary problem in American education that has not been solved by somebody, somewhere." The questions are, who are those somebodies, where are they hiding, and what can we learn from them? The answers will be found only through formal research and development.

America spends 2.5 percent of its gross national product on research and development efforts. High-tech industries spend anywhere from 10 to 30 percent of their revenues on it. American schools spend 0.025 percent of their revenues on it, or around $5 per student annually from kindergarten through college (Perelman 1992). With private enterprise being allowed in the door, this too is changing.

Education in Touch

Schools in the next decade will be clamoring for new hardware and software solutions virtually identical to those required by business, and for the same reasons. They will need to communicate and administer, and teachers and students will need the same access to cyberspace—to friends and colleagues, to the library, to news services.

Classroom projects will spread beyond the confines of a single room to blanket the country and the world. A case in point is the Monarch Butterfly Project launched in the American Federation of Teachers forum on America Online in 1994:

----

8 We need only recall an earlier educator, Socrates, who decried in *Phaedrus* the arrival of writing: "If men learn this, it will implant forgetfulness in their souls. They will cease to exercise memory because they rely on that which is written, calling on words that can't speak in their own defense or present the truth adequately."

Subj: Call for Collaboration　　　　　94-09-13 01:30:44 EST
From: GeraldAxe

Subject: Monarch Butterfly Tagging Project

Call for collaboration: We are going to capture and tag Monarch Butterflies as part of a University of Kansas research study to identify and monitor Monarch migration patterns . . . .

Students will learn science research skills by working in groups to record data; learning how to capture, tag and release study subjects without harming them; how to make data collection devices (such as butterfly nets); how to record data on a map, looking for patterns and drawing inferences; reinforce geography skills; and learn the value and methods of telecommunicating to conduct research. This project is suitable for grades 3rd and up.

Teachers and students across the country quickly became infected with Monarch fever. Here's a sampling of three of the postings that followed:

Last week my two science classes, the 4th and 5th grades of The College School in St. Louis, spent time in class preparing nets to catch monarchs for tagging. This was a wonderful project. We had roughly 15 yards of inexpensive muslin that the kids cut into 40" by 26" rectangles before trimming further into net sewing shape.

Many sewed by hand, but I also brought in my sewing machine. It was such a nice project to see them hunched over a machine, carefully feeding the material in to make hems and seams. Most had never sewn with a machine, and the mechanical operation was fascinating to them.

It was a real opportunity to talk to the boys and the girls of the class about the beauty of sewing and making things yourself. Granted, it went slowly, but the time was well worth it for each group to make their own nets.

❖ ❖ ❖ ❖ ❖

The following message was written by the students in Sue Beaudet's fourth-grade class at John F. Horgan Elementary School. The report was written in a whole group format.

On September 30, 1994 Mrs. Beaudet's 4th grade class went on a field trip, because we were involved in Monarch Watch. We went to Beavertail State Park in Jamestown, RI, to catch, tag and release Monarch butterflies....

We were able to tag 29 Monarchs in 2 hours. We ran out of tags or we could have tagged more. They were everywhere. They were on Goldenrod flowers and on orange flowers. They were hard to see when they were in the bushes.

We noticed the Monarch's wing colors are darker on the inside wing than on the outside wing. We had to approach the Monarchs slowly or else they would fly away.

When we released them they flew in a south-westerly direction.

❖ ❖ ❖ ❖ ❖

We sent away for Monarch kits from the University of Kansas and started to learn about Monarchs. It was really exciting, because all of the teachers put a lot of effort into the project. The teachers learned hand in hand with the students. We coordinated the program with quick meetings before school and after school. We also used our local telecommunications service, Learning Links, to get information from Chip Taylor and Julie Ellis from the University of Kansas.

We tagged the Monarchs we raised ourselves. The kids and the teachers had a difficult time letting go of the butterflies. There were many of us that shed a tear or two on the release day.

The most exciting aspect of the program was that students and teachers at Horgan school became real scientists. We learned how to learn together. I feel that the teachers will be open to many more hands on experiences in the future.

Today, a robot at Cal Tech is online on the Internet. Students from around the world can sign up to spend several minutes manipulating its arm, searching through debris for buried treasure, all the while watching the results in slow-scan video. Soon elementary school children will be able to get time on the largest astronomical telescopes in the world. Yet in 1995, only a third of our nation's public schools have any access to the Internet. Vice President Al Gore has pledged to see that rise to 100 percent by the year 2000 (Suryaraman 1995).

The American Federation of Teachers bulletin board is exploding with project ideas. These early experiments—and that's all they are—will open a floodgate of change and generate enormous economic pressure. The communications and computer industry in the next ten years will at last be given the funds they need to revolutionize education in America.

A Return to the One-Room Schoolhouse

The classroom of tomorrow is alive and well today at Open School in Los Angeles. This elementary school of 360 children is divided into six "pods," each with two teachers and 60 kids. The pods consist of two generous rooms with a wide-open portal between. Each pod typically has students in three different grades, and students stay in a given pod from one to three years. Much of the course work each year is centered around that pod's project.

When I visited, one of the pods was working on a city of tomorrow. Students had started the year with a large landscape contained on a table around 6 feet wide and 12 feet long, resembling the land under perhaps 40 square blocks right around the school. During the course of the year, they were struggling to convert that bare land into a working city, with homes, apartments, office buildings, schools, hospitals, fire and police stations, rapid transit—all the essential buildings and services of a modern city. They had recontoured the land to make room for a reservoir and recreational park. They were fabricating buildings and arguing about placement and view corridors. They were making the same kinds of decisions city planners face every day.

Along the way, they were studying the history of their city and their state. They were learning about climate, geology, meteorology, bureaucracy, and law. They discovered the trade-offs of a single, centralized hospital versus neighborhood clinics. They found out they would be in serious trouble if they built the only fire station on the edge of town. They were writing reports and composing environmental impact statements. They were covering all the scholastic processes and materials that we shove down most other students' throats today and more, but they were learning gleefully and gratefully.

The atmosphere in an Open School pod is like that of the one-room school house of old, with barely controlled pandemonium as older kids teach young, and students work feverishly in small groups on their own special projects. Of course, the schoolhouse looks a little different. Most of those old-time schools didn't have large-screen TV sets, or VCRs, or video disk players, light tables, projectors, or one computer for every two children. Open School does. Because there is instant and constant access to computers, the computers are not special. They are tools used as casually as a pen or pencil. They are integrated fully into school life.[9]

When you have sat in one of these classrooms, it is hard to leave without a sense of despair at your own childhood lost. These kids are getting the education out of which we were all cheated. In the next ten years, the teachers of America, along with the people of the computer and communications industry, will see to it that no generation is ever cheated again.

....
9 The children's primary education programs are their word processors and their drawing packages, not multimedia CD-ROMs. In fact, the only student I ever saw at Open School looking bored and isolated was a young girl using a multimedia package. It and it alone represented the schooling of old, delivering its material slowly and methodically, while the girl sat there passively, occasionally pressing a button.

Colleges and Universities

Our higher education system has always been a competitive market, eager to seek out ways to contain costs and improve education in the process, resulting in the finest colleges and universities in the world. Not only do they use technology, they are the fountainhead for much of the technological revolution of this century and among the world leaders in their level of computerization. Still, they have a long way to go. Perelman (1992) reported that coming into this decade, American colleges and universities averaged only one publicly available personal computer for every 45 students. Private ownership is not making up the loss. In even elite private colleges, only 30 percent of students own a computer. This situation is better than what I found at the University of Rome when I visited there in 1987—fewer than 35 computers for 60,000 students and 12,000 teachers—but it is a far cry from the real need of one or more computers for each student.

Colleges and universities also have better networking than our K–12 schools, but the best network access is typically reserved for students in computer science. In the next decade, we will see institutions of higher learning embracing the same technology as business and other schools.

Higher Education: A Scenario

Abdul Abba is a junior at Hudson University. The summer is nearly over, and Abdul is deciding what courses he should take next semester. As he sits propped against the cushions on his bed, he leisurely browses through Hudson's online catalog.

One course that catches his attention is in the Political Science Department: Politics of Pollution taught by Professor Mary Smith. He is attracted to her description, as well as attached student comments about the course: "hands-on experience," "full of adventure," "truly collaborative learning experience." A few of the student comments have associated with them video clips of portions of last semester's classes.

He plays back one such snippet and likes what he sees and hears. The fact that these digital clips exist at all indicates to him that Professor Smith allows her lectures and her electronic white board notes and drawing to be captured for synchronized digital playback on the computer. If he oversleeps or is late for class, he knows he can always lie in bed and watch the class while it's happening live or replay the experience later in the day.

Abdul is impressed with Professor Smith's first class. She starts off with a dynamite presentation displaying still images of the world's worst pollution problems as leading environmentalists and politicians discuss their significance. After a series of video clips from news broadcasts, she ends the presentation by focusing on issues of pollution facing Hudson University's immediate community.

In a semester-long project that will make up the bulk of the work for the course, the class must come up with three solid recommendations for the governor on how to clean up the state's polluted waters. These recommendations must be feasible, possible within the constraints of the current budget, and, most difficult of all, alienate as few constituents as possible.

The class will interview politicians, environmentalists, public officials, possible polluters, and waste disposal companies. All class members will have access to the data collected by other students. At the end, the class will select the three entries they will submit.

Several weeks into the course, Abdul and his study partner, Violet, are off on their third interview. Meeting with Carlie Staples from University Hospital has both of them nervous. In preparing for the interview, Violet explored a number of environmental databases around the country looking for any references to University Hospital. The local Greenpeace database contained a small note in one article saying that although the evidence was sketchy, University Hospital was suspected of illegally dumping some of the medical wastes that have been showing up on area beaches.

Abdul wanted to confront Carlie directly, but Violet thought that would be a bad idea. During the interview, they went through the class-developed, standard questionnaire, with Abdul capturing the responses with voice recognition, while Violet videotaped (with Carlie's permission).

Frustrated by Carlie's bureaucratic answers to all their questions about how and where medical wastes were being disposed, Abdul couldn't resist openly confronting her about the Greenpeace accusation.

Carlie grew still for a moment, then motioned for them to turn off the camera and the computer. "So that's what this is about. Look, we know there's a problem going on around here. As far as we know, this medical waste is not coming from this hospital. The hazardous-waste disposal company we've been using has impeccable credentials, and our waste disposal manager, Frank Graham, has put in tight controls.

"We don't think this waste is ours, but if it is, we want to know about it. I'll cooperate with you fully in your investigation. I'll get you started by sending you down to talk to Frank right now. But in return, I ask one favor: if you find out it's our waste that's involved, tell me first."

After a polite if unrevealing interview with Frank Graham, Violet and Abdul hatched a plan to spy on the waste disposal site. Graham had told them the waste was picked up on Tuesdays at noon, but the students figured any bad guys would likely transfer the hazardous waste at night, when few were around to watch. Violet proposed they start a stake-out at 11:00 that very night. Abdul barked at his computer, "Appointment with Violet, 11 P.M."

"Roger Wilco," responded the computer.

Violet rolled her eyes. "Abdul, couldn't you just have taught it to say 'OK'?"

Two days later, Professor Smith initiated a video call to both Abdul and Violet. She told them that Frank Graham had called to report they had both exhibited rude behavior during the interview and had asked that they not be sent around again. Neither Violet nor Abdul was surprised at Graham's move—not with what they had to show Professor Smith: digital photographs that Abdul and Violet had taken of illegal dumping the night before.

Professor Smith complained the pictures were too dark to prove anything, but once Violet had selected the photos, zoomed in on the license plates, and said, "Enhance," there was no mistake: the truck being loaded at the hospital dump site at 11:17 P.M. was the same truck captured at 12:06 A.M., dumping waste into the water several miles away.

The three of them went to University Hospital the next day armed with the students' tightly woven multimedia report they had built the previous night, collaborating over the network. They confronted Carlie Staples with the evidence, including Frank Graham's unusual response to their visit. Carlie thanked the students for fulfilling their promise to her, then asked them to sit on their information for a few days while she carried out an internal investigation. Meanwhile, she'd like to copy the report, including the enhanced photographs, to her own computer. Abdul and Violet transferred the report and reluctantly agreed to wait.

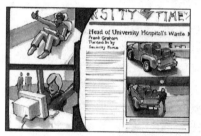

A few nights later, Violet's agent reported the news they were waiting for. The word *arrested* in the headline caught her attention. She immediately connected across campus to her partner. "Abdul, look at this!" she exclaimed as she dragged the story onto their shared work surface.

Together they read:

Head of University Hospital's Waste Management Arrested
Frank Graham Turned in by Hospital's Own Security Force

CENTRAL CITY—Today the head of University Hospital's waste management department was arrested for allegedly masterminding a scheme to siphon money from University Hospital by dumping raw medical waste into the ocean. The hospital thought it was paying out money to a prominent hazardous waste management concern when in fact Mr. Graham and several as yet unnamed co-conspirators were dumping a large portion of the waste into the ocean from the back of a pick-up truck, then pocketing the money.

The scheme came to light when two students from the local university began an investigation, turning over their findings to the hospital.

The article continued, but what now caught their attention were two computer-enhanced photographs accompanying the article—the very photographs they had taken!

The next day they would not soon forget. With their permission, Carlie Staples let the press know who the two local heroes were, and they soon found themselves on every local television news show. They even fielded a phone call from the producers of the David Letterman show, asking that they show up the following Monday so Letterman could grill them thoroughly on their views about garbage.

That evening, they completed their class presentation, including the AP story and, in a moment of understandable pride, clips of their television interviews.

The Automatic Plagiarizer

Abdul and Violet maintain ethical standards that are above reproach. Other future students may be more desirous of taking advantage of certain technological shortcuts. As a final example of the changes computers will visit on education, let me suggest to you my personal favorite: the Automatic Plagiarizer (pat. pending).

When I was a lad, we wrote our term papers the old-fashioned way. We assembled them from passages gleaned from *The World Book Encyclopedia, The Illustrated Classics,* and other sources, shifting the vocabulary just as much as necessary to throw our teachers off the scent. When it worked, it was great; when it didn't, it was disaster. One student in our school attempted to crib an entire term paper from an article in the rather obscure *California Historical Society Quarterly.* This journal was so obscure, in fact, that only two people had ever read it: he and his teacher. The teacher hadn't read it prior to perusing the student's paper, mind you, but once having recognized a vocabulary level far beyond that of the offending student, the teacher took time out of his otherwise busy schedule to spend three days down at the county library, ferreting out the original source.

Would that the teacher had stopped there, but he didn't. Instead, he announced a lecture for all the school to attend entitled, "On Comparative Historical Perspective," during which he alternately read from the historical journal and the student paper, claiming to want to show how differently two historians viewed the same event. Within seconds, the entire school not only recognized that the student historian's views were more than passingly similar to the journal historian's, but we knew who the culprit was. He was the one doing his best to dig a hole through the concrete subfloor into which he could sink out of sight forever.

This incident was the unhappy result of low technology. Fortunately, a solution should soon be at hand. Students should soon be able to buy an application that will do their plagiarizing for them. The application will first ask the student purchasers to feed into the application a sample of work they actually did on their own, should they possess such a document. The plagiarizer will then be prepared to digest thoroughly an article from the *California Historical Society Quarterly* or any other source that might be found kicking around the electronic Library of Congress. After a few moments of munching, it will spit out a neatly typed document chock-a-block with cleverly disguised statements such as, "So the dude goes, 'Yo, Dude, I'm like totally bummed that I have like, only, one life to, like, lay on my country.'"

Certain bugs may need to be worked out.

Students will herald the automatic plagiarizer as nothing more than the pocket calculator of the next century, a simple student aid. Their more moss-backed teachers may adopt a contrarian position. Like so many other areas of emerging technology, electronic documents and reader control will force us to reexamine and extend our ethics—or give up trying.

CHAPTER 4

Home

*I*n the early part of this century, people sat out on their front porches on warm, summer evenings, calling out to friends and neighbors as they passed. People lived in communities, knowing who their neighbors were and what they were up to. Radio brought little alteration, except that people might leave their front door open, so the sounds of "One Man's Family" or "The Shadow" might brighten their evening. Then came television, and everything changed. Today you can walk down those same streets and never see a soul. The only signs of life are the telltale bluish glow of the TV sets within.[1]

The social isolation that has resulted has brought about a new form of instant intimacy. Television shows have devolved from formal stage presentations and movies down to a peek into that interesting neighbor's window down the street (an augmentation of the same peek we used to take in person). You can now watch people just like yourselves losing their pants at a wedding, revealing graphic details of their marital infidelities, or being shot or arrested, all in living color right on your TV.

Today we are engaging in the myth of a set-top box that will connect to the family TV set, around which everyone will cluster, watching in rapture as Dad traverses a labyrinth of baseball statistics or Mom

....
[1] Television was not our only effort to destroy community. Traffic engineers helped things along by codifying a requirement that suburban streets be 50 feet wide, to enable two fire trucks to pass each other at 50 miles per hour. "Andres Duany, a Miami architect who specializes in designing new towns, maintains that the traffic engineers have thereby depleted human interaction and fellowship from modern America. He calls them the 'devils'" (Howard 1994). Today our communities, dotted with fortress houses, are so far removed from the intimacy of old that even were TV to disappear, we would find it difficult or impossible to return to those thrilling days of yesteryear.

pays the bills.[2] Interactive services do not invite partnership. In the coming decade, the single blue glow of the living room TV will be replaced with a separate glow for every member of the family. This has already happened at my house, where we have moved our computers into the living room, so we can be together while we work and play on our own. With the advent of continuous speech recognition and vocal conversation on the Internet, we may finally be driven into separate rooms, spending time with each other through our viewports and offering greetings as we pass through the hall.

Cyberspace and Community

America is staying home. In the 1980s, futurist Faith Popcorn labeled the phenomenon "cocooning." Now she is suggesting we have entered into an even more isolated phase, "burrowing," as we go beyond physical withdrawal into emotional withdrawal as well: "Some of us are too overwhelmed or exhausted by the stress of life to bother to return... even the phone calls of friends we really want to talk to" (Popcorn 1992). The next stage she predicted is "clanning," whereby we cluster like birds of a feather into clans of anywhere from 20 to 20,000 members. That trend is full upon us today, and cyberspace is facilitating its growth.

In Seattle is a small card club where folks gather for an evening to play a few rounds of bridge. It is not a fancy spot—just a comfortable place in a not-so-good part of town where around 40 people can get together at 7:00 each evening for some good conversation while they pursue their favorite obsession. I spoke with one of the former regulars a short time ago. He hadn't given up bridge, he assured me; he had just switched to the Internet, where you can stir up a foursome at any time, night or day, without venturing forth from your personal burrow. He went back to visit the club shortly before we met. It was virtually deserted. The action had all moved to the net.

The net has been a community for a few select members of our society for 20 years. Now everyone else is joining in. Currently the net

....
2 Today only the physical prowess of the Man of the House keeps the family at bay as he indolently clicks his remote. The situation has already worsened to the point where women openly discuss capturing possession of the remote control as one of the pleasures of widowhood.

is increasing people's isolation. Internet bridge clubs do not engage in idle chitchat; they sit in their houses, staring at text, punching at keyboards, restricted to typewriter telegraphy. The coming convergence with phone and fiber will change all that. Tomorrow's electronic communities will see each other, hear each other, touch each other. Although even the most optimistic view of virtual reality finds us far short of true face-to-face, physical intimacy in the near future, the emotional connection we will enjoy in a decade will be worlds ahead of what we experience today.

Not everyone is pleased by this development. Lee Sproull and Sara Kiesler (1991) have this to say about e-mail:

> Ordinarily when people communicate, they aren't just exchanging information: they are projecting an image of themselves. This knowledge can make them shy in front of others, especially those whose respect they most desire. Ephemerality and plain text in electronic mail reduce the fear of appearing foolish in front of others. By removing reminders of a possibly critical audience, electronic mail induces people to be more open.

The newspapers continue to be filled with sci-fi stories of video on demand and 500 channels of TV. Both are already here. You can get practically any tape you want at your neighborhood video rental store, keep it for three days at no extra charge, and watch it as often as you want. Those of us with movable home satellite dishes receive more than 500 channels already.[3]

Home shopping, sports, and gambling are where the television industry sees money to be made. Home shopping, broadcasting 24 hours a day on our nation's cable systems, is targeted squarely at women. Like many of the televangelical shows, the shopping networks act as surrogate family and friends. These shows are as intimate as a morning chat with a neighbor over a cup of coffee. After a while, the susceptible develop a strong emotional connection with the hostesses, dreaming of the opportunity to speak live with them on the air while purchasing. To ensure sales will be closed, the shows pull the merchandise after a fixed number of minutes, creating a false scarcity that motivates the

....
3 Even with 500 channels, sometimes there just "isn't anything on," but you never know it. By the time you finish traversing the sky, that half-hour is over and the next has begun.

customers to buy right away. The truly hooked leave their TVs tuned all day long, snatching up their phone on a regular basis to buy merchandise they will likely never use.

Men are more likely to be sports addicts, and the program providers are counting on their being willing to shell out real dollars for pay-per-view.[4] The added draw will arrive with online betting, which will expand to enable people to spend real money punching in their bets on the results of the next football play while the players are in the huddle. The big corporations in America will not originate electronic casinos; foreign countries will jump in first, via the Internet, Visa and Mastercard accepted. The U.S. government's attempt to stop it will drive gambling underground rather than eliminate it. As tax and lottery revenues fall, the government may be forced to capitulate, allowing the major U.S. corporations free rein.

People will make money with video on demand, with 500 or 1,000 narrow-cast channels, with home shopping, sports, and gambling. However, the real use of the webs of cyberspace will be connecting people with people. Prodigy, like other online providers, was envisioned as a money-capturing machine. People would pay for information services. People would do home banking online, paying a surcharge for their trouble. They would order airline tickets, look through catalogs for new TVs, and wander the aisles of a cyberspace grocery store, ordering up food that would arrive a few hours later. All of these services are in use today, but they are not why people are connected to the net.

People want to talk to other people. The smash-hit application of the information providers has been e-mail. They did everything they could to discourage it, but the people kept coming. The providers have discovered they are spending a lot more time wiring together more network and storage capability than counting money from all the soup they've sold.

Chat rooms are filled 24 hours a day with people typing frantically at each other, desperately trying to fill their need for human contact over a plodding modem. When fiber reaches our homes, Oprah and America Online will converge. People will no longer need a mass media

....

4 The failure of pay-per-view during the last Olympics put a little fear in people in the industry, but the sight of Americans flooding back to the arenas and stadiums at the end of sports strikes, ready and willing to shell out even more money at the box office, have cheered them up considerably.

moderator to visit the lives of other real people vicariously. They will be able to meet with them face to face, safely and anonymously, in cyberspace. The ratings of today's tabloid TV shows illustrate that the more down and dirty the story, the more people are interested in it. Just as cyberspace allows people to publish freely, without the filter of the establishment press, cyberspace will enable people to talk—confess—freely, without any moderation, whether to a single person or a vast audience. A night flitting through the wilds of cyberspace may prove interesting indeed.

Today many chats are public affairs. In the future, people will want to join more intimate, private clubs, places where members only can meet of an evening to sit around and talk. My wife and I have a group of around 20 friends scattered across the country who meet with us each January at a different Club Med. We spend the week stuck to each other like magnets, then go our separate ways for another year. How pleasant it would be to arrange a cybersocial every few weeks, where we could get together, perhaps over a meal in front of the monitor, and share with each other what has been going on.[5] We will see battles in the next decade as more and more people try to split off into private clubs, with those left out crying foul.

Meanwhile, traditional communities may be making something of an electronic comeback. Blacksburg, Virginia, now exists equally in real space and in cyberspace. The Blacksburg Electronic Village is lined with the same shops, libraries, museums, and houses as its physical counterpart. Its citizens spend their evenings humming away happily at their keyboards, keeping up with family and friends and taking advantage of the latest values down at the variety store.

Chance Encounters

A century ago, people often first met their lovemates at church. During the heyday of the sixties and seventies, people hung out in bars on Saturday nights looking for action. Today certain supermarkets, such as the Marina Safeway in San Francisco, have taken over that role. On weekend evenings, hopeful lovers prowl the aisles, surreptitiously

....
5 Delphi already offers private club rooms, although today they are decorated only with text.

inventorying the contents of potential soulmates' carts. People visit libraries and museums not only in search of interesting books and art, but to find new friends and love interests.

Cyberspace has lots of adult-oriented chat rooms, places where people get together in hopes of getting together. Many other people first touch psyches in chat rooms or public messaging areas devoted to discussing other subjects. In the future, people will also find birds of a feather while wandering the electronic halls of the history museum, or flitting across the expanses of a virtual sculpture garden. As with such encounters today, people will begin their friendship in certain knowledge of a common interest.

Michael Crichton set a scene in the depths of cyberspace in his novel *Disclosure*. Equipped with advanced virtual reality, his users were able to see strangers passing in the night. His technology will not see widespread use until long in the future, but we do have the opportunity to make (voluntary) telepresence, discussed in the next chapter, a more central and pervasive feature of our cyberspace now.

Love Online

> *Cybersex is a solitary sexual self-stimulation on some levels, but there is a very important difference. The interaction is more than just reading a magazine with erotic words and images. The words on your screen are from a live, breathing (make that heavy breathing) human at the other end of the connection. It's even more compelling than phone sex, because with cybersex, your partner has got you by the brains!*
>
> Phyllis Phlegar (1995)

Thirty-five to 40 percent of the revenues of online services today can be traced directly to sex. Chat rooms, private "conversations," and e-mail are all conduits for people who want to get really, if virtually, close together. The online services would not even be in business were it not for sex. VCRs and neighborhood video rental stores wouldn't be either. They had their first and largest success in X-rated videos. In the United States, 900 numbers were established so corporations could offer people service and advice in return for anywhere from $120 to $1,000 per hour in phone charges. What has been the overwhelming success story? Sex recordings. Sex chat lines. Sex "with a beautiful woman who is waiting breathlessly for you to call."[6]

Cybersex in the future will feature live video, live audio, and digital sensory attachments. Those who today might wander out to a bar of a Saturday night will find it safer and even less commitive to tryst with each other on the net. The inevitable imbalance between males and females will mean that the 900 numbers of today will move directly over to the cybercommunity[7]. Because of live video, that move will cause the same kind of exodus that occurred at the end of the radio era. And the "beautiful women" will, for the first time, actually have to be beautiful.

Cybersex will also be packaged. A short film a few years ago told the story of a young man's renting, assembling, and attaching a quite elaborate virtual reality system to various parts of himself on a Friday evening, setting the shut-off timer for early Monday morning. As the programmed virtual reality experience began, a gorgeous blond-haired creature stepped dripping from the sea and advanced across the sand toward his prostrate body. Just as she dipped her head to kiss him, flash! she was back in the sea, and the experience started over again. And again. And again. And again. (They claimed the problem would be fixed in the next release.)

Cybersex has a strange agglomeration of advocates, drawn by its twin advantages of being procreation free and inherently safe sex in an overpopulated world awash with news of date rape, where a single evening of uninhibited passion can result in a viral attack ending in death. Attacks against sex on the net will be blunted as children are restricted from access and the seamier clubs go private and encrypted.

Online Addiction

The digitally savvy have long whispered about the mesmerizing capacity of life on line. They are predominantly male, and their wives have become computer widows. One addiction specialist dubbed the on-line habit "computerism."

Molly O'Neill (1995)

....
6 These services are aimed exclusively at men, and for good reason. Women have no time for such nonsense. They are too busy chatting with their "psychic friend."

7 As we go to press, the first of these has just appeared on the World Wide Web.

For many, it began so innocently, with just a few hours each week over a 1,200-baud modem. Now they find themselves spending the only part of their lives that seems to matter glued to their computer screens. Some people, writes Howard Rheingold (1993), "such as the most addicted players of Minitel in France or Multi-User Dungeons (MUDs) on the international networks, spend eighty hours a week or more pretending they are someone else, living a life that does not exist outside a computer." Rheingold goes onto suggest that MUDs are "susceptible to pathologically obsessive use." They also suck up a lot of computer time, so much that they have been banned from Australia.

Computer addiction can spill over into criminal behavior. Kevin Mitnick was captured by the FBI in February 1995 after a long run that netted him thousands of credit card numbers and millions of dollars worth of software. He made little or no use of his ill-gotten gain, however; he was driven by obsession (Hale 1995). Mitnick's arrest was not his first. In 1989, he was convicted of computer fraud and formally declared a "computer addict." He was sent to a rehabilitation program, but it didn't work out. Now he faces a $500,000 fine and 35 years in prison.

Mitnick is not the first to fall. In 1977, an early computer and phone hacker, "Captain Crunch," was arrested after using his computer, "Charlie," to place 20 percent of the long-distance calls in the San Francisco Bay Area, all at no charge. He spent six months in stony lonesome, during which time he wrote Easy Writer, the first commercially successful word processor on the Apple II. He emerged a millionaire. Blair Newman was not so lucky. One of the prime movers in making laptop computers successful, he ended up committing suicide after being banished from northern California's the Well (Whole Earth 'Lectronic Link) for nonpayment of a huge connect-charge bill.

So far most identified computer addicts have hailed from two groups: hackers, who are brilliant but socially inept, and net surfers, whose obsessive-compulsive personalities have previously found outlet in gambling, drugs, and drink. It remains unclear at what point computer interaction will become so compelling that normal people find themselves being lured past the point of no return into addiction's web. "I'm hooked" said "Miriam," as quoted by O'Neill (1995). "If you hear of a twelve-step program for on-line abusers let me know. One in my area, not on the net."

Around the House

Most of us already have dozens of microprocessors scattered around our houses, controlling everything from microwave ovens to toothbrushes to wall switches. The only thing they don't do is talk to each other. That will change dramatically in the next ten years. When you pick up the phone, the sound will drop on your TV or stereo. When your thermostat notices the temperature dropping, it will suggest vocally that you close a few windows instead of turning on the furnace and attempting to heat the world. Before your sprinkler timer waters your lawn, it will make a call to the weather service. Why water if rain is expected tomorrow? When someone approaches your front door, his or her picture will appear in an inset on your TV. If the TV where you are in the house is off, it will pop on. (Optionally, your twin machine guns will whirl themselves around and train themselves on the intruder.)

All this processing will be distributed. People will have no central computer. If you want to change which wall switch affects which light, you will not bring up a map of the house and start moving things around. Instead, you will aim an infrared beam at the light, telling it to listen up, then walk to the switch and flip it.

The added complexity will probably result in a few reports of people plugging in a new clock-radio upstairs and having their refrigerator downstairs suddenly decide to defrost itself to death. Most people, however, will experience an improved quality of life and lower resource costs.

Information at Home

In the olden days before TV, people stayed current by reading their morning newspapers, subscribing to specialized magazines, and collecting books, including reference works like encyclopedias and dictionaries. Today we veg out in front of a television, listening to CNN news. Tomorrow every home will have access to vast libraries of knowledge. Who cares? We'll all still be lying on the couch watching TV. Or will we?

Two things motivate adult learning: need and curiosity. Curiosity is a powerful motivator, so powerful that it has required a minimum of

12 years of education to drive it out of our minds. Computers have the power to bring it back.

The Brown family is at the dinner table when sister Sue says, "I wonder if Abner Doubleday really invented baseball." Dad and brother Billy get into quite an argument, with Billy insisting that story was all made up by the sports equipment manufacturers. It ends when Dad tells Billy to shut up. The rest of the meal is eaten in silence.

If this sounds familiar, you probably didn't grow up with an encyclopedia. In households with encyclopedias, when a question arises, someone—usually the smallest member of the family—is assigned to look it up. Arguments get settled not based on who's bigger, but who's right (Billy, in this case). Sister Sue, while paging through the open book, is then likely to notice something else of interest, and the conversation turns.

When we live in a condition where questions can't be answered, we usually have sense enough to stop asking. When those conditions change, we do, too. The first few months people own encyclopedias, they may not refer to them at all. Then the pattern changes.

People who own bad encyclopedias—those that contain everything except anything you might be interested in—get turned off. Nothing can be more frustrating than to spend 15 minutes trying to glean a simple fact, only to discover it just isn't there.

Tomorrow's encyclopedia will encompass all of the world's knowledge. What we consider an encyclopedia today will be just a jumping-off point—a well-structured index into the world beyond. The people now publishing reference books will come to understand that their strength is not in providing information but in organizing it. They will index the world for us in ways not possible with automated browsers or agents in the foreseeable future. When curiosity strikes, the answers will be just a touch away.

HyperTV

The coming revolution opens up the possibility of passive viewing augmented by curiosity relief: HyperTV. Today, if something interesting comes up on television news, we make a mental note to look for it in the morning paper, then instantly forget we ever saw it. With HyperTV, viewers will be able to remain in a passive slouch for as long as desired.

However, should a watcher become interested in a 30-second segment on the NBC Nightly News entitled, "Catfish Grabbing: Divers Hook Giant Prey with Bare Hands" (Booth 1993), they can press a button on the remote to dive into unshown raw footage and collateral materials on the bizarre hobby, such as contemporaneous newspaper articles. When the viewers are through exploring, they can return to the news exactly where they left off.

Today's news shows are little more than headlines. With HyperTV, they really become headlines, with their attendant "articles" at arms' reach.

Life is complicated enough at work and school. The thought of returning home to a set-top box with 12 layers of menus and a 200-button remote gives me the willies. Developers will need to keep their designs simple. Let people warm up to their own level of activity, explore at will, and lie on the couch when they need to.

The People's Right to Know

People with satellite dishes are blocked from watching regional sports in their old home town by network contracts, in place because the networks are afraid people might be watching their home town instead of some relatively uninteresting network game. The home-town game is up there on the satellite, but the commercial interests are powerful enough to jam it.

America's publishers are sitting on rich libraries of useful information. They dole it out with an eyedropper, attempting to maximize profits on each tiny piece. The economics of the mass net market will bring the price of information down but may not stop the hoarding. Should this keep up, people will rebel at some point. Today's cries of an inalienable right to privacy may soon be joined by cries of an inalienable right to information.

Nomadic Computing

We live in a society that has been warped and twisted out of shape by the needs of the industrial revolution economy. The industrial revolution is a brand-new phenomenon, just over 200 years old. Humankind has been around for hundreds of thousands of years. We did not evolve during the Industrial Revolution; we evolved during the hunter-gatherer era. The Industrial Revolution was about conforming human beings to the needs of machines. The third wave is about conforming machines to the needs of human beings.[1]

We grow up assuming that people all over the world live just as we do and that they have forever done so. I grew up assuming that radio had always existed; my kids are growing up believing that television always existed. When I tell them of those ancient days that preceded TV, they listen politely, but I can tell it doesn't really sink in. The information society has only now begun to question the assumptions that we grew up with—those natural laws that seemed so immutable.

Assumption: People should go to work.

The reality is that people have been going to work for only the past 200 years. Before that, almost everybody worked at home. Farmers lived on the land. Manufacturing was often broken up into a cottage industry. A shoe cobbler, who lived over his store, would cut the various leather parts of shoes in town, then distribute the parts to many country families who would assemble the shoes in their homes, returning the completed shoes to the cobbler for eventual sale.

---

1 "Third wave" is a term coined by Alvin Toffler (1980) to refer to the post–Industrial Revolution age through which we are passing right now.

Until recently, only farm workers and heads of state continued to work at home, while the rest of us commuted, costing our society billions of dollars in road construction and maintenance, fuel, and vehicle wear and tear. More devastating are the human costs: people spending one, two, sometimes three or more hours a day fighting their way through traffic, producing nothing in the process except excess gastric juices and the occasional fatal accident.

Solution: Telecommuting.

Pacific Bell likes to quote a study that found that allowing people to telecommute increases productivity by approximately 20 percent, a big leap. I've been telecommuting for the last 16 years, and I love it. It saves me time, energy, and the cost of commuting. As I'm writing this book, I'm not sitting in my drab, gray office above a parking lot. I'm in my living room at home, in the redwood forest, looking out on the koi pond in my small Zen garden. I can concentrate on writing without interruption. The costs of telecommuting can be minimal. In my case, it has been the price of a computer and a modem. I would have bought them both anyway.

Telecommuting is taking hold even in large corporations. Pacific Bell, admittedly with a vested interest in the subject, held a corporate-wide work-at-home day last year. Bell regularly has several thousand employees working from home, including 10 percent of management, telecommuting one or two days each week (Hetzner 1994).

The recent "State of the Commute" report from southern California's Commuter Transportation Services found that 12.5 percent of the employees in the area are allowed to telecommute, and 85 percent of those eligible do so. They average four working days per month, or close to 20 percent of their time, away from the office (Moskowitz 1994). As of 1992, 26 million Americans were already working at home either part time or full time—a whopping one-quarter of our entire work force—and 16 million of these work for corporations (Popcorn 1992). Video viewports, casual and inexpensive conferencing, and fully integrated collaboration-support systems will enable them to work a higher percentage of hours at home and encourage many more millions to join them.

Business has been slow to embrace telecommuting. Industrial Revolution managers like to control their people, and having people work at home destroys some of their illusion of control. People might be going to the bathroom at the wrong time. They might make a personal phone call or two. They might even wander outside for a breath of fresh air. The few studies done on telecommuting find that all these incidents and more take place, but they also show that telecommuters get their work done on time and with quality equal to or greater than their desk-bound counterparts.

The Industrial Revolution management model is changing. Managers are judging people on their performance, not punctuality. As we provide business with greater communication services, companies with far-flung work forces will be able to maintain a sense of connection and community.

The United States has reached the end of the era of constant road construction and unbreathable air. Many businesses are being forced to introduce expensive intracompany bus systems, with extensions to the local mass transit stations. Businesses built away from mass transit facilities are facing higher taxes as communities come to realize the costs of workers' driving over their roads. As these costs escalate, telecommuting will begin to make ever greater economic sense.

Halfway measures, however, result in few cost savings. I work at home one or two days per week on average, but my company maintains the same complete office at work that it would if I were to be there every day. Telecommuting works at Chiat/Day because the company has embraced the fully decentralized workplace. With employees checking out cubicles only as needed, Chiat/Day has reduced office facility costs by 50 percent.

Many companies, such as telemarketers, will reduce their office overhead close to 100 percent, with workers coming in only for occasional meetings and training sessions. With fully implemented telecommuting, we will return to the comfort of cottage industry. Workers will benefit, the environment will benefit, taxpayers will benefit, and businesses will benefit, big time. It will be a win-win-win-win situation.

The biggest threat from blurring the line between home and office is not that workers will not work long and hard enough but that they will work too long and too hard. Today many people are finding themselves enslaved to the cellular phones they thought would liberate them. Telecommuting pioneers are finding themselves drawn into their home offices on weeknights and weekends, time that they should be spending with their families and are instead spending on "just that one little thing" they need to get done (Wright 1994).

Assumption: People stay at work.

Desktop computers were designed under the assumption that people remain glued to their office chairs from morning to night. Nothing could be further from the truth. Some tiny fraction of workers out there do make their entire living carrying out some repetitive task on a keyboard, but what about the vast majority of us who travel for meetings halfway around our corporate campuses or halfway around the world?

We have to stop assuming that personal workspace should exist only on a desktop at work. I am as much in need of my calendar at home on Sunday when I want to plan Monday as I am in the office on Monday when I want to plan Tuesday. I need my calendar even more on Wednesday, when I'm on an airplane winging my way to Toledo and find I would do well to stay over for an extra day. Can I stay over, or has someone entered an appointment on my machine at work I cannot afford to ignore?

Whether I am using my home computer, office workstation, portable, or a coworker's workstation half the world away, I need to be working in my personal cyberspace. The documents need to be the same, and they need to be equally up to date. Certain physical limitations to this exist: I may be linked by fiber, coax, twisted pair, cellular phone, infrared, or nothing at all. The systems cannot work magic. Today, however, they do not work at all. When I draw my portable near my office workstation, nothing happens.

Another important component of nomadic computing is remote log-on. Some of the most sophisticated systems, including Sun's, allow the most sophisticated users to log on remotely, but common folk are excluded by an impenetrable interface, remaining in the same isolation they would if the feature did not exist at all. A few portable manufacturers also offer some form of utility for doing file transfers and updates. Car manufacturers used to offer kits for adjusting the spark gap, too. Users don't want utilities. They want their computers to update each other on their own. No technical barrier lies in the way.

At a recent Usenix conference, I asked during my address if everyone would please hold up their portable computers. Perhaps 100 of the 950 did so. I then asked if all who do not maintain their calendars on said computer would return their computers to their laps. Around 25 remained in the air. I then asked them to keep holding if, were they to add an appointment for next Thursday at 3:00, their office computers would be automatically notified. The remaining computers went down. We have a ways to go.

Solution: Telepresence.

Whether traveling or telecommuting, people need to keep in touch. As much as I like to get off by myself to write and think, I need equally to interact with others. Telepresence, in the form of casual video conferencing and collaboration, can eliminate barriers to intimacy. Within a year or two I expect to be able to glance into the offices—home or business—of perhaps 60 people with whom I normally inter-act—the same number of people who might have made up my wandering tribe in hunter-gatherer days. Right now, I see many of these people only once every couple of weeks. In some cases, they are across the country. In other cases, they are just down the hall, but behind closed doors.

So far, most video conferencing has been used for remote meetings with many people in attendance. This made sense initially given the high costs of carrying out such meetings, as well as the supreme incon-venience of everyone's trekking to a teleconferencing center. In the last few years, several companies have jury-rigged "inexpensive" teleconfer-encing systems, so corporations might have centers in many or most of their buildings. Employees save time getting to the center, but the equipment is usually so primitive that half the meeting is spent getting everything working, sort of, and the other half of the meeting is spent trying to figure out which of those floating phantom images is the person actually talking. With the advent of wide-band digital networks, ease of use and quality are going up, and the telecommunications center is moving into our personal computer or workstation. As the technology becomes more widespread, most meetings will consist of two people collaborating under casual circumstances.

Telepresence will go beyond the blurred floating images of today's teleconference. It will let us connect with each other with our eyes, our ears, our hands, and our minds.

Some of the workers who will gain the most from telepresence are the field workers, the nomads of today—be they salespeople, field engi-neers, journalists, or FBI agents—who are currently cut off from the mainstream activities of their organizations. They go to the occasional meeting or convention but spend the rest of their time in splendid isolation. Telepresence will offer these people the benefits of corporate society: a sense of the group, connection with the day-to-day events of the organization, and the ability to mentor and be mentored.

The filtered information streams that emanate from corporate headquarters often do more to isolate than connect. They are no substitute for seeing the face of a carefree coworker live in the home office. In the telepresence organization, the most far-afield worker will be as inherently capable of capturing the ear of the CEO as the worker two doors down the hall. Access to people will be based on policy and need, not geographic accident.

On the Road: A Scenario

Faith Popcorn calls our hermetically sealed cars, bristling with high technology, "wandering cocoons." People listen to books, talk on the phone, send faxes, eat meals—essentially carry on with their lives at 55 miles per hour.[2] The biggest shift in our road life in the next decade will be radio-networked navigational computers. In the scenario that follows, we explored how such navigational aids can help civilize the afternoon commute. We then went on to explore the preparations for a longer jaunt: the family vacation.

Jerome and Alicia are a working couple living in greater Los Angelopolis. This afternoon, Jerome, ready to drive home from work, gets into his car and immediately opens his computer. The computer wakes up in the Commute user context, since it knows it is in a car.

Jerome checks his traffic overview. Through a subscription traffic service, his computer has been able to create summary video images of the last 5 minutes from live traffic cameras located at select points in the city. He notices a slowdown along his favorite route, so he decides to take an alternate route.

He closes his computer, then selects customized audio news for the drive home. On the road, he first hears a brief generic news roundup, followed by

....
2 In residential districts. Freeway speeds may vary.

stories that are filtered and ordered according to his interest. Just after Jerome hears a specially chosen commercial announcing the season-end sale of ski equipment at his favorite sports equipment store, the news is paused as the car notifies Jerome that there's a slowdown along his current commute route. It offers a suggested alternate route, vocally delivering instructions as he approaches each required turn.[3]

After Jerome gets home, he starts working on vacation plans. He first charts how much discretionary income he and Alicia will have during the next three months, adding a small amount from their savings to the beginning total. After fixing a budget, he pastes it into a document he labels "vacation planner." He has the system browse his home and work calendar as well as his wife's calendars to identify possible open weeks. He explores their proposed destination by using his customized news service to get some local news (text/graphic and video) and a calendar of upcoming events (tailored to their interests).

Jerome looks at a custom catalog of hotels, based on his family's stored travel profile. For each entry, he's presented with a video advertisement created by the hotel, coupled with independent consumer ratings and travel reviews. When he selects a final candidate, the Harbor Villa, he explores it and its environs with a 3D video model showing buildings, tennis courts, pools, scuba access habitats, and beaches. Rooms available at various rates are displayed by using

color coding. He swoops down on a few and checks them out. Recognizing that he'll want to consult with Alicia about the resort and room choice, he stores a couple fly-throughs and makes some tentative reservations.

Jerome is drawn to an ad for a play at their destination. The show is selling out fast, but he doesn't want to shell out $50 to $100 for theater tickets

....

3 Perhaps not. Perhaps your attention instead will be directed to an on-board display showing your route, so you can figure it out for yourself. Of course, while you are staring at the screen, you will be plowing into a concrete pylon.

The only communications channel that makes sense for on-board navigation in a moving vehicle is voice, the system that will soon be available in Europe. Negroponte (1995) points out that America's love affair with litigation is forcing American companies to offer only visual maps, which have a known limit of liability. The law, ever the friend of the status quo, will do its best to block every twist and turn of the coming revolution. It will be up to our courts and legislators to provide some common sense and change the rules before a lot of people get killed.

without discussing it with Alicia first. He double-clicks on her electronic representation, an object resembling a business card.

Alicia's system receives the page on the subway and quickly connects them. Jerome smiles as he spots Alicia's eye scan jump right to the advertisement for the play; he figured she'd be excited about that. With the audio link opened, he pulls up the layout of the theater on their screens and suggests they buy some inexpensive seats over toward the side. She touches a likely pair of seats to pull up a view of the play from that angle. It's rather obvious they will be missing quite

a bit of the action. They try a pair of the $80 seats toward the edge of the orchestra section and buy them, figuring that it is, after all, a vacation and you only live once. Besides, when he drops the purchase onto his chart, they are still well within budget.

Jerome and Alicia break their connection, and Jerome gets up to start cooking dinner. Some things still aren't fully automated.

Nomadic computing is not about portables; it is about people. It's about a return to the cottage, a return to the freedom (and profitability) of wandering to where the work is, a return to a natural, and thus productive, style. Nomadic computing is about letting people communicate with ease no matter where they might be. To see through virtual reality and simulation beyond their physical horizon. Nomadic computing is not free of structure but dependent on structure, the infrastructure we have begun to build.

PART 2

Future Computing

The fundamental shifts in the organization of society in the next ten years will be largely supported and facilitated by the changes we make to our computing systems. The needs of the future dictate systems that are agile, reliable, facile, and connected. Dividing lines between today's electronic systems—TV, telephone, computers—must disappear. The powerful modality represented by documents within applications must disappear. The screen clutter brought about by today's limited human-to-computer communication must disappear. The future will be defined by two words: *integration* and *simplicity*.

What will this brave new world of computing and communication look like? How will people act, react, and interact in this fast-approaching future? In 1992, SunSoft launched Starfire, a project to develop an advanced integrated computing-communication interface. It can offer us a glimpse into the software design of the future. You have already read several of the scenarios that resulted.

Moving from this first phase, we proceeded to design a real interface for our projected world. We constructed a single, complex scenario that embodied most of the problems we had identified in forming the earlier stories. We then set about solving those problems by applying new hardware, software, and human interaction approaches.

We envisioned two end results: a phased-in implementation plan for Sun and a video prototype that would enable the rest of the industry to absorb what we had learned. (You can read about video prototype production in Appendix B.)

Our industry is being hamstrung by our very success. Projects like Lisa, Star, and Macintosh worked because there was no legacy software to hold them back, and the small teams had free rein to design and build the hardware they needed. Today companies, and the industry as a whole, are so big that designers work in isolation, free only to work on their own tiny piece of the puzzle. This has led to inordinate amounts of energy being expended— for example, by software designers attempting to fix the significant limitations of the hardware mouse by twiddling images on the screen.

Starfire freed us to explore where the industry can be if we all work together on a common goal. You will find an offer to buy a copy of "Starfire, the Directors' Cut," at the back of the book. It is our aim to make it available for as long as possible at as low a price as possible. Seeing it will increase your enjoyment and understanding of much of the material that follows. Please get the tape. End of sales pitch. In the meantime, you will be able to enjoy the full cognitive, if not emotional, experience by reading the annotated script that follows.

Starfire

We set the Starfire story at a Fortune 100 automobile manufacturing company primarily because such companies are the bread and butter of Sun Microsystems, which underwrote the film; however, we made the story and the software design it drove as universal as possible. The tale involves Julie Moran, first-time product manager of a new sports car, in her battle against an older, more experienced, and generally slimy opponent, Mike O'Connor, as he attempts to knock her car off track so he can advance his own.

Much of the discipline of the project arose from our building extremely tight time deadlines into the story. Any user can do anything on a computer, given sufficient time. We wanted to make sure that our new designs would result in nimble, responsive software that would let people hit tight deadlines. We don't all have a Michael O'Connor breathing down our necks, but we all could use responsive computers that spend more time facilitating our work instead of getting in the way.

The purpose of Starfire was not to predict where the world might be in 100 years, or 30 years, or even 20 years. It was to predict where it might be on November 16, 2004. As a result, we based it on technologies that we can either build today or that are well launched in laboratories around the world.

Annotated Starfire Script

Cyberspace came into being in 1837, with the invention of the telegraph. Boys who became trained in Morse's esoteric coding scheme could communicate with their peers hundreds of miles away. The pure abstraction of the keyed communication offered little sensation of a cyberspace experience, but the thing worked on electricity, and the boys were quite excited.

That all changed in 1876 with Bell's invention of the telephone. Regular people were suddenly able to directly sense other people in and through cyberspace using their ears. By the early 1960s, video conferencing was born, and, although limited to businesspeople with deep pockets, it began a new era of even greater sensory connection.

Finally came the Internet, a throwback to all the emotional connection of the telegraph, using ASCII code instead of Morse.

Even today, so-called electronic chats consist of nothing more than two or more people typing at each other. The paucity of the link was exposed a few years ago when someone studied the evening romantic encounters taking place over the French Minitel teletext system. It appears that close to 50 percent of the participants were claiming to be of a gender other than their own. Only telegraphy could sustain such an illusion without any effort on the part of the perpetrators.

If cyberspace is to truly tie people together, it must have certain properties:

- People must be able to communicate visually, vocally, and verbally.[1]

- People must be able to connect emotionally as well as intellectually.

- People must collaborate—work in concert—not just communicate.

....
1 Visual communication starts with body language. "Vocal" refers to the sound of the voice, whereas "verbal" is its abstract content. Telephone communicates both vocal and verbal information; the Internet, until now, has communicated only the verbal message, which, as the French researchers discovered, can often be the least informative. To read further about the relative importance of these three channels, please see Chapter 16, "Information Theory," in the fascinating Addison-Wesley book, *Tog on Interface.*

Cast of Characters

ADRIAN ST. JOHN
Adrian, a proper Englishman in his 50s, is chief engineer on a new sports car project, as well as mentor to the project lead, Julie Moran, below.

JULIE MORAN
Julie is heading up the sports car project. This is the first time she has been project lead on a car, and she is scared but, as it turns out, well prepared to overcome adversity.

MOLLY
Molly, though young, is talented enough to have become lead designer on the project. She has been involved in a relationship with Fred that has, for some time, been going nowhere.

A.J.
A.J. produces corporate videos and also provides raw shots for executives assembling their own presentations.

NATALIE
Natalie is Julie's best friend and confidante.

FRED
Fred, Molly's boyfriend, works in the construction industry. Last night, he and Molly had a fight. It seems he has had a wee bit of trouble making a commitment. Most unusual.

BILL
Bill is Julie's husband. He can do a fair imitation of HAL, the computer in 2001. He has a sense of humor and is quite capable of being both a mature, almost father-figure to Julie and in the next moment become one of her kids.

SAM & BETSY
Julie's kids.

MIKE O'CONNOR
The bad guy. He wants to knock Julie's car off schedule so he can bring his car out first.

REG, THE CEO
Nonpolitical, even-handed, fair, and impartial, Reg is a fictional character.

Exterior: The Skies Above London's Stanstead Airport—Day

PILOT [VOICE-OVER] Good afternoon, and I would like to thank you for flying Air Ukrainia's Flight 554, providing service from Kiev to London.

Interior Airport Concourse: Day

Adrian St. John bursts from the jetway, clearly in a hurry. He strides through the Stanstead concourse, passing beneath a banner that reads, "Welcome to London, InterCHI '04!" He continues walking.

PA SYSTEM [VOICE-OVER] Princess Di has been reappointed to the House of Lords. For additional information, please pick up a copy of the *Evening Sun* from the newsstand or your personal information space.

   Your personal desktop is just a few steps away at a Sun Video Collaboration Booth.

   For the high-speed train to Paris, please proceed to Terminal D.

Adrian approaches an electronic sign suggesting, "Your office is just around the corner." He pauses to read the sign, glances at his watch, then veers off in search of the SunBooth.

❖ ❖ ❖ ❖ ❖

When Adrian enters the Sun collaboration/conferencing booth (SunBooth) and holds his watch (chronometer, memory, and authentication device) close to a reader, that booth becomes his office. His workspace is just as he left it. When he looks at the screen, he sees a picture of Julie, his coworker, representing his direct connection to her, no matter where she might be (if she wants to be found).

   He need only touch her picture to place a collaboration call halfway around the world. When she answers, they will see each other, hear each other, and be able to touch any and all documents they want to share. With an advanced sensitive surface, they might even be able to touch and feel each other's hands as they work.

   Cyberspace must have one other property if it is to fulfill its real promise: it must be continuous—with you everywhere and at all times.

   Adrian can access his cyberspace wherever he is through a variety of means. On the airplane, he can jack into the seat back in front of him. In his car, his watch authorizes his connection, via radio. Even on a desert island, his solar-powered

laptop or pocket computer-phone can connect him to the world via low-orbit satellites. Adrian has chosen the SunBooth over his pocket computer only because of its large screen and greater communication facility.

❖ ❖ ❖ ❖ ❖

Interior of Julie's Office: Day

The visual centerpiece is Julie's workstation, where she is seated. It is an extended surface, curved in three dimensions. Adrian's corporate PR photo occupies the first viewport. From the viewports of Molly and Natalie, two coworkers, we see them at work from behind.

Julie seated at wrap-around computer desk

On the left side of the viewport we see:

- *What appears to be a picture of Julie's husband and kids. This is actually a private viewport to her family.*

- *Julie's calendar and a notepad, where friends and coworkers can leave her notes.*

- *Her mailbox. As the day progresses, we see the contents change as she reads what's there and new letters arrive.*

In the center of the viewport is her information space, represented as a highly detailed 3D image. If Julie wants information on medicine, she can "visit" the hospital. If she wants to research religious history, she can "drop" by the church. The local car dealership is her entranceway into a vast database on cars.

In the viewport area on the right side, we see:

- *A Geochron clock, showing world time, displayed as a map. (See "Envisioning Information," page 116.)*

- *A "photo" of Adrian with a brightly lit garden scene outside his London office window.*

- *Natalie, soon replaced by a sign in her viewport saying, "Away from my desk."*

- *Molly working in her office.*

Before Julie are two documents: a report she will be working with throughout the film and the dreaded memo from Mike O'Connor, which turned this from a peaceful day into a nightmare.

❖ ❖ ❖ ❖ ❖

It is not by accident that Julie has a hardwood floor and shelves filled with books.[2] This film is only ten years in the future. We will not be living in Plexiglas pods and heating our houses with the contents of our public libraries, or at least not all the contents.

You probably noticed immediately that her computer is large. I chose to make it so to get the attention of the many who think that screens will only grow smaller. In fact, they will grow in both directions.

Starfire envisions a world where people can assemble all sorts of objects for their computers, with all fitting nicely together. When the Chiat/Day employees lost their private offices, they also lost their bulletin board for family photos and that little shelf that held their teddy bear or a trophy. Personal items in the future will exist in cyberspace, so they are with you wherever you go.

People want to display memorabilia, and they will want to add personal touches to their cyberspace environment. Natalie was able to go out to her favorite card store and pick up a packet of electronic Jetsons cards that show up in her viewport when she is out or busy. She could have as easily picked up Snoopy cards or pretty scenes of New England.

❖ ❖ ❖ ❖ ❖

....
2 The "hardwood" floor is really a clever paint job. We knew we had pulled it off when one of the film editors tried to buy the lumber from us.

We hear Julie's "phone" begin to ring. Julie says, "Close information space." Then we see Julie flick her hand, and a memo from Mike O'Connor smoothly slides up the vertical wall of the workspace and sticks.

❖ ❖ ❖ ❖ ❖

Most of the clutter of our screens and much of the complexity of our designs are there because the communication from users to their machines is so limited. In Starfire, we made use of a wide range of input techniques so that we could get rid of the galloping clutter of today's displays. One technique is gesture. For example, when we first enter Julie's office, we see her slide a memo up to the top of her display. She accomplishes this by splaying her fingertips across the document and sweeping upward. The computer recognizes the configuration and direction of the movement and sends the document on its way.

(We made an error in the filming by directing the actress to sweep her hand too far up the screen. An artifact of the special effects process ended up causing the document to appear to flutter in response, as though her hand were a magnet. Although some research in interpreting exactly these kinds of "free-floating" gestures is underway, we do not expect fruition by 2004. Julie "threw" the document with enough intensity that it would travel to the top on its own.)

❖ ❖ ❖ ❖ ❖

JULIE Answer.

Julie's eyes follow the viewport as it moves toward center screen.

ADRIAN [CONTINUING] Good morning, Julie. I've been trying to reach you. How are things in Detroit?

❖ ❖ ❖ ❖ ❖

Today's postage-stamp images can create the strong impression that someone in the next office is actually on the moon. Adrian's picture is not some tiny black-and-white image being updated five or ten times a second. It is a full-motion, full-color, life-size, high-resolution image. It helps fuel the illusion that he is there in the office with Julie, not half a world away. Is all this bandwidth necessary for them just to communicate? Probably not, but it is vital for building and maintaining the emotional bonds necessary for effective teamwork.

❖ ❖ ❖ ❖ ❖

Julie Oh, Adrian, we've got trouble.

Adrian Oh? What's wrong?

Julie O'Connor. He sent a memo to the executive committee saying that our car is going to be late, so his should ship first.

Adrian Getting a bit anxious for his bonus, I see.

Julie . . . and Reg called a special meeting this afternoon!

Adrian What?! I thought he was in L.A.

Julie He is. So you'll get to whisper in his ear why you've slipped our production schedule three weeks.

❖ ❖ ❖ ❖ ❖

More than a few people have found this line confusing. Adrian is in London; Reg is in Los Angeles. So why does Julie say that Adrian will "get to whisper in his ear why you've slipped our production schedule three weeks"? Because Julie knows they will be seated next to each other in cyberspace during the big meeting that will follow. Because of the design of the conference system, they can lean toward each other's images and whisper, just as they could if they were in physical proximity.

❖ ❖ ❖ ❖ ❖

Adrian Look, Julie. I didn't slip anything. Kiev had to enlarge the fuel cell.

Julie I'm sorry. I'm just so . . .

Adrian And anyway, the production problem is solved!

Julie What? [SNEEZES]

Adrian Bless you!

Julie No, bless you, Adrian. That's great news!

We hear pages turning on Adrian's and Julie's desks.

Adrian I've pasted in the solution on page 26 of your report . . . but, you know, now that I come to look at it, you may want it over here instead.

Adrian's fingerprint appears on Julie's screen as he slides the chart onto opposite page. Construction lines guide him to an alternate position.

Adrian releases his finger and the illustration slides into place

❖ ❖ ❖ ❖ ❖

Most collaboration systems offer some symbolic feedback, such as an arrow, to show where your partners are working or pointing. We wanted to make the feedback more direct. Displaying Adrian's fingertip where it touches their screens carries an emotional connection that even the most finely formed arrow cannot. We had originally intended that the fingerprint would be a reproduction of the user's (something within the proposed capability of the workspace surface to capture). We changed our minds after someone pointed out that routinely transmitting high-definition reproductions of people's fingerprints just might be a sight security risk. The fingerprint whorls are simulated, but the actual contact area is faithfully transmitted.

❖ ❖ ❖ ❖ ❖

JULIE Good. I'll tear off a new control panel.

Even as Adrian finishes the drag, Julie touches the control panel beside a simulation on the opposite page and drags out a copy of the panel.

❖ ❖ ❖ ❖ ❖

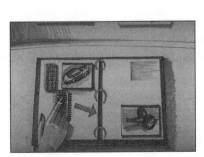

Julie doesn't make a copy by clicking on the old control panel object, then selecting Copy from a menu, then Paste to make a duplicate, followed by her dragging the new copy into place. She places her thumb and forefinger on the original and then slides her forefinger away. Had she used only her forefinger, the computer would have known to move the existing control panel. The thumb as anchor said, "Hold it where it is and also move it away." The only way the computer could logically comply was to make a copy. This kind of gesturing is fast and efficient, and all the screen clutter devoted to making copies goes away.

❖ ❖ ❖ ❖ ❖

Adrian's fingerprint appears on the edge of the new control panel, and he swiftly moves it down the page, touches the new simulation with it, and pulls it away. Wire tags, momentarily glowing red, show the connection between the panel and the simulation. Then they fade away. Adrian's finger presses the Play button, and the simulation runs.

❖ ❖ ❖ ❖ ❖

The screen layout agent that lives in computers and offers them aesthetic guidance as they move elements around their documents we adopted from Vellum, the wonderfully inventive computer-aided design (CAD) system from Ashlar. Such agents ease the job of masters, help educate apprentices, and save the rest of us from having to become masterful at all. I have tested Vellum and have found that 8-year-old children, with no training, using Vellum can outperform professionals who have used the leading CAD system for years.

❖ ❖ ❖ ❖ ❖

ADRIAN [OFF-SCREEN] You see, Austin can drop the new fuel cell right into place.

JULIE This is wonderful, Adrian!

Julie's eyes flick slightly to the left, where A.J.'s viewport appears on her screen.

JULIE Here's A.J.!

We hear Adrian's viewport swoosh to the left as Julie's eyes follow.

JULIE I got the poor guy up at the crack of dawn.

An image of A.J. has appeared on the left side of Julie's screen. He's looking around as though he can't see her. Julie touches A.J.'s image, and suddenly he sees.

JULIE Hi, A.J.

She connects the two images, of A.J. and Adrian, by sweeping her hand between them, creating a conference.

❖ ❖ ❖ ❖ ❖

The 3D keystone view helps make it appear to Julie as if the other two participants really can see each other, providing feedback that the conference connection was made.

❖ ❖ ❖ ❖ ❖

A.J. Oh, hi, Julie. Adrian.

ADRIAN Hi, A.J. Do you have our new retro roadster?

A.J. Sure do, and it's running smooth as silk.

Julie sneezes again.

A.J. Gesundheit!

ADRIAN Bless you. Okay I'll let you two go. And Julie, take care of that cold.

A.J. Bye!

JULIE See you.

Julie watches Adrian's image slide off-screen right. A.J.'s image is enlarged as it slides to the center of her workspace, where Julie returns her gaze.

A.J. [OFF-SCREEN] Here's the uphill shot for the chart.

We see the "Chart Clip" appear over A.J.'s image.

JULIE Hmmm . . . The car's a bit far away.

The clip continues to emerge, revealing the shape of the hillside.

JULIE But I can take care of that with an auto-pan. That should work.

❖ ❖ ❖ ❖ ❖

People somehow feel the role of software design is to simplify computers to such a degree that anyone can use them without learning anything. This is not realistic. The best that software design can do is to enable the user to concentrate on learning the task instead of the tool. Julie does desktop video just as comfortably as we do word processing today. We know all about fonts and formatting; she knows about auto-panning. (You will too, later on in the film.)

JULIE Now I'll need an ending shot... Maybe we could...
Ah, will you link the camera to me?

A.J. Sure.

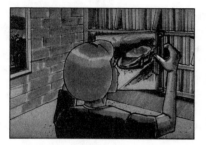

A.J.'s hand reaches out to touch his screen. Julie snatches up her electronic SunPad, a device that allows her to view and control remote cameras, both real and virtual. She stands, holds the SunPad out in front of her face, and looks at the SunPad display, which now has the camera controls slaved to it. It's as if the SunPad were a large camera viewfinder. She presses the button that turns on the pad, then zooms out using the Zoom button as she begins to move the pad.

❖ ❖ ❖ ❖ ❖

Everything connects to everything. Julie doesn't have to close her eyes, dream up a possible shot, then try to talk the solution through a phone line. Instead, she can take control of A.J.'s camera rig out in San Francisco, using the same familiar tool, her SunPad, that she uses many times each day for a wide variety of activities.

❖ ❖ ❖ ❖ ❖

Julie moves the SunPad downward until the camera is centered just above the roof of the car and appears around 10 feet in front.

JULIE [VOICE-OVER] Let's have the car sweep into view...
[BOOM CAMERA SWOOPS DOWN TO THE WHEELS]... and as it comes to a rest... push in on the wheel.

The camera moves in toward the hubcap. Finished with her task, Julie releases the SunPad activation button and returns to her desk.

A.J. Can do!

JULIE Bye, A.J.

After A.J.'s image fades away, Julie looks down at the report on her workspace. As we look at the viewport into Molly's office, just below Natalie's "At Lunch" sign, we see a gentleman from McNealy Floral delivering a dozen red roses.

JULIE [TO HERSELF] Hmmm. Molly got flowers?

Molly, after assuming they must be for someone else, accepts them.

It's now about 2:30 P.M. in Detroit as Julie enters carrying a sandwich on a plate and a cold drink. She reaches her workstation, and in the viewport area we see:

- *The Geochron clock, with the sunlight now having moved westward.*

- *The same "photo" of Adrian as in the beginning, but now the garden is not so bright: it is evening in London, and Adrian's office computer has corrected the electronic photo to match the outside twilight.*

- *Natalie, as she touches her screen to get a close-up view of Julie, then grabs a newspaper and strides out of her office.*

- *Molly, her office now nearly overflowing with flowers as two more flower deliveries are made.*

JULIE [TO HERSELF] Look at all those flowers! Can't be Fred.

❖ ❖ ❖ ❖ ❖

If all this peering into Molly's office is making you just a little uncomfortable, we want you to be. Privacy will be a major issue in the next few years. We need to start talking about it now.

❖ ❖ ❖ ❖ ❖

As the scene in the viewport catches Julie's eye, Natalie bursts into her office and starts speaking immediately.

NATALIE Honey, have you seen McCormick's column?

She thrusts the latest edition of the afternoon news at Julie. Julie takes the paper and reads to herself as Natalie sits down.

JULIE This is great! Let me scan it.

She lays the paper on the workspace and quickly rubs the area of interest. When she lifts the newspaper away, we see just McCormick's column, perfectly justified and properly reversed on her workspace.

 ❖ ❖ ❖ ❖ ❖

Julie's extracting a brief quotation from McCormick's column is likely legal under U.S. intellectual property law—the fair use doctrine. (You never really know until the trial is over.) When we showed the Starfire film in Australia, however, the lawyers in the audience almost had a coronary.

In the absence of a fair use doctrine, this scene could still work. Instead of the computer's actually taking in the contents of the document, it could be scanning it for keywords, then going out on the network to find a match. Since the paper has its name and date just above McCormick's column, making a match would be simple. The electronic version, bought and paid for, could pop up in place on her workspace, just as we see in the film.

❖ ❖ ❖ ❖ ❖

She turns to her report, flicks a few pages to the PR section, which contains the 3D car image with call-outs, and indicates an insertion point with the stylus.

JULIE [TO COMPUTER]

Open report. Insert. "As Mike McCormick wrote in his column today . . . " End insert.

Her hand slides across the workspace as she drags the quotation, "The finest PR campaign I've seen come out of this town in a long time," out of the clipping and into her report.

❖ ❖ ❖ ❖ ❖

Julie's speech recognizer is aware of context. The system knows whether she is on the phone or has a visitor in her office. In these cases, it will not attempt speech recognition unless it detects specific command words, surrounded by pauses, command words such as *open* and *insert*. In this instance, when the computer detected, "Open report," it opened the report that has been taking up all of Julie's time today—another example of context awareness. When she touched a point on the report and said, "Insert," it knew to accept dictation and place her words at her chosen insertion point. When she then dragged the quotation into place, it knew to surround it with quotation marks and to footnote the source. These are the kinds of tasks that computer agents will soon be able to accomplish, freeing us from much of the drudgery we face today.

❖ ❖ ❖ ❖ ❖

Julie leans back to look Natalie in the eye.

JULIE You know, I'm still struggling with this 3D model.

NATALIE What's the problem?

JULIE It just looks like . . . like . . . [BEAT] It looks like an engineer did it!

NATALIE Well, darlin', let's dress it up a little! Move it up where we can work on it. I came across an old TV ad in the corporate library . . . Where is he? There he is!

Both women look down. Julie flicks the 3D sports car model to her vertical display area, while the car commercial clip opens just to its right.

JULIE Hide callouts. Vellum: Mannequin.

Various engineering labels—callouts—disappear. Her 3D modelling toolset, Vellum, has placed a female mannequin next to the sports car. (Vellum, discussed in Chapter 25, "Ease of Use," is a cool CAD package. By 2004, it will be really cool.) Julie and Natalie glance at one another, exclaiming in unison:

JULIE AND NATALIE Male!

The mannequin becomes male.

❖ ❖ ❖ ❖ ❖

In this scene, the two women select the moving image of a man out of an old TV ad and "pour" it over a preassembled 3D mannequin, ending up with a fully articulated man they can move into place. It is again based on integration: two different commercial applications (called "tool sets" in the Starfire world), from different vendors, work together with the system to enable the women to carry out tasks that today would be extremely difficult for even professionals to accomplish.

❖ ❖ ❖ ❖ ❖

JULIE 5'11" . . .

NATALIE 6'2"!

JULIE [TO COMPUTER] Texture map.

Vellum types: "Source?"

JULIE [TO COMPUTER] Adobe: Wand.

Julie selects the male model from the old TV ad using her video editing toolset from Adobe Systems.

❖ ❖ ❖ ❖ ❖

When you see the film, you will immediately notice a difference in the selection process. The selection is made not by color and shape on a still image but by jogging the film back and forth, so that the computer can find the moving object against its background.

The way of representing the selection is different too. The familiar "crawling ants" surround the selected object, but the man is also full color, while the background has turned into shades of gray. The color-against-monochrome representation is for Julie; the crawling ants are for the film's audience. When I tested the original animation, lacking the crawling ants, people didn't connect the color change with selection. Once they knew, they loved it, but I still had to add the ants for the film.

❖ ❖ ❖ ❖ ❖

JULIE [TO COMPUTER] Source.

Man is "poured" onto model.

JULIE OK. Let me move him over . . . ahhh, there.

Julie moves the model into position.

NATALIE Link me to the model, will you?

Julie hands Natalie the SunPad.

NATALIE I want to nudge the viewpoint just a little.

Natalie presses the button and begins to move the SunPad around. Julie stares intently at the same image on her screen as we see the "camera" move around the car to a new angle.

❖ ❖ ❖ ❖ ❖

This is the same SunPad that Julie used earlier to move A.J.'s camera rig out in San Francisco. Now Natalie is using it to move a virtual camera in cyberspace—same tool, same activity, just an alternate reality.

❖ ❖ ❖ ❖ ❖

JULIE That's perfect!

NATALIE Yes!

❖ ❖ ❖ ❖ ❖

If you've seen the film already, you know that here (in the interest of making a film shorter than *Heaven's Gate*), we ended the scene. It's too bad, because what Julie and Natalie did next would have been pretty interesting. Here is the material from the original script not used in the film.

As Molly continues to argue, Fred, looking somewhat abashed, reaches into his jacket pocket, extracting a ring box. He opens the box, revealing a diamond engagement ring.

JULIE [TO HERSELF] Oh, wow! He finally proposed!

Molly smiles, a tear runs down her cheek, and she embraces Fred. As they wheel around, she suddenly realizes that the camera outside her door is transmitting their tender moment to all the members of her extended work group. She reaches for the door and closes it. At first we see the backside of her door. Then the door is replaced by a sign announcing, "In a Meeting."

❖ ❖ ❖ ❖ ❖

We wanted to raise the privacy issue forcefully in this film. Our error was in adding too much sugar-coating. Many viewers have assumed we did not take privacy seriously. We do.

The "In a Meeting" sign was triggered by a multibutton switch on the wall beside Molly's door. She could have chosen "Out to Lunch" or some other notice. She did not have to return to her desk, boot her computer, start a special application, then plug in her modem. Molly's cyberspace is always up and running, distributed not only around the world but around the interior of her office.

❖ ❖ ❖ ❖ ❖

Julie lifts up the remnant of the sandwich to put it aside so she can use her mouse. We see a perfect reproduction of the remnant where it lay. She brushes the reproduction away, like crumbs.

❖ ❖ ❖ ❖ ❖

Who would believe Starfire was a real computer if didn't have at least one bug? And anyway, we're going to fix the bug in the next release.

❖ ❖ ❖ ❖ ❖

Grabbing her mouse, she moves toward the chart clip A.J. gave her earlier.

JULIE [OFF-SCREEN] Auto-pan target.

❖ ❖ ❖ ❖ ❖

Ah, the legendary auto-pan mentioned in the first act. Here's the theory: Julie is going to end up creating an object consisting of her sales chart superimposed on the film clip A.J. sent her earlier of the car going up the hill. When the car first starts up the hill, there will be no sales line on the chart. Instead, the car will progressively reveal the sales line as it climbs the hill.

Julie first points out the car as the object she will want the computer to use by selecting the car, then saying, "Auto-pan target."

A.J. shot the car going up the hill in high resolution using a wide-angle, unmoving-depth camera that not only records a visual image but also records a model of the scene in true 3D. Once Julie has called out the target for the auto-pan, the computer blows up A.J.'s clip to poster size—much larger than the window that will look onto it. The car now appears much larger, and the computer can pan and scan around the poster to place the car anywhere it wants in the window without hitting any edges.

At the end of this scene, Julie will ask the computer to combine the chart and film, then synchronize the chart line and the car, finally tying the line of the sales chart to the rear end of the moving car.

Some might think this process impossible. They are wrong. I know, because I followed it in creating the animation in the film. The final animation, which Julie shows in the boardroom, took me just over 150 hours to produce and lasts just over 3-1/2 seconds on screen.[3] That's what I meant earlier about anybody being able to do anything on a computer given enough time. The next generation of software must reverse today's trend toward slower and slower response. Julie doesn't have 150 hours; she doesn't have 150 seconds. With good design, she should need hardly any time at all.

❖ ❖ ❖ ❖ ❖

Julie sneezes once again, but this time her computer apparently responds in a HAL-like (from 2001) voice.

"HAL" Bless you, Julie. It's 3:30. Have you taken your cold medicine?

JULIE Cut it out.

3 I didn't use a depth camera, because they are still a couple of years away. Instead I had to separate out the layers by hand, but that only took a couple of hours. Oh, and I also had to animate the car, since there was no road up the hill. You can see the original 35-mm still and the still of the car at the far end of the Directors' Cut tape.

"HAL" I'm sorry Julie, I can't do that.

Julie turns to address the family photo and, through it, her husband, the source of the mysterious HAL voice.

❖ ❖ ❖ ❖ ❖

This was our little way of poking fun at some other video prototypes that have featured anthropomorphic agents that were so perfect that you would have sworn they were some actor dressed up in funny clothes; actually, they *were* some actor dressed up in funny clothes. Agents are currently as dumb as posts and likely to remain so for a long, long time.

❖ ❖ ❖ ❖ ❖

We hear a giggling sound.

The family photo sparkles into a real image of Julie's husband, Bill, with their kids. They are calling from a soda fountain.

❖ ❖ ❖ ❖ ❖

What appeared to be a simple family photo actually turns out to be a specialized viewport that connects Julie with her husband or kids wherever they are. I took my inspiration from the old "George Burns and Gracie Allen Show." George had a TV set in his den that would show him Gracie, no matter where she was and no matter what she was up to. I always liked the idea.

❖ ❖ ❖ ❖ ❖

JULIE [ANNOYED] Bill . . .

BILL Oh, I'm sorry, Hon. Betsy put me up to it.

BETSY What? No way, Mom. It was Sam!

SAM It was not!

❖ ❖ ❖ ❖ ❖

The actors are my kids. Very talented. They actually make you believe they like burgers, shakes, and fries.

❖ ❖ ❖ ❖ ❖

BILL [TALKING OVER KIDS] Oh, listen, Hon, the bank just sent these papers. The loan was approved, but they need your signature on the truth-in-lending form . . . right there.

❖ ❖ ❖ ❖ ❖

Most of us have gone through a scene like, this, except when we did it, we had to take a couple hours off work and rendezvous at the bank or title company. Electronic signatures and employers' willingness to allow us to overlap our personal and professional lives will result in everybody's coming out a winner.

❖ ❖ ❖ ❖ ❖

Julie leafs through the papers, then applies her digital signature.

JULIE There you go.

BILL Thank you. Bye, bye.

BETSY Bye, Mom.

As Betsy leans into the camera, Sam shoves her away, causing her to retaliate by throwing french fries at him.

❖ ❖ ❖ ❖ ❖

Did you see the way she hurled that fry? That girl's got an arm on her.

❖ ❖ ❖ ❖ ❖

BILL [FADING] Oh, hey, guys, calm down now, all right?

Julie gazes at the photo briefly, then turns her attention back to the sales chart.

JULIE [TO COMPUTER] Combine chart and film. Sync... and ... posterize.

Picture in the background of the chart is "posterized," giving it an arty look.

JULIE [OFF-SCREEN STARTING HESITANTLY] Mmm, ah, we are... in conclusion, we are poised to offer...

A message shows up on her display, stating: "Verbal Command Not Recognized." It fades.

❖ ❖ ❖ ❖ ❖

Julie's speech recognizer knows she is alone so attempts to recognize her speech. In this case, there is no open text field to which she is dictating, so it scans for known command words. When it fails to come up with a match, it lets her know by placing a message right where she is looking on the screen.

Because of eye tracking, the computer can place the message in her field of view, eliminating the need for warning bells or sirens. The computer, knowing she is looking, doesn't have to require her to acknowledge receipt by pressing an OK button. It simply displays the message and removes it. In real life, the message would be a good deal smaller; we had to ensure that film viewers could see it too.

❖ ❖ ❖ ❖ ❖

JULIE The first ... zero-emission, high-performance sports car in history. The last hydr ... the last hydrogen, the ... plant ....

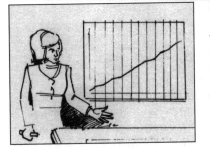

INTERIOR: Boardroom. Day.

Julie is standing in front of a projector screen, wielding a laser pointer. She is giving her presentation to the executive committee.

JULIE [OFF-SCREEN] ... the last solar-powered fuel plant went on-stream this week, the delivery infrastructure is in place, and, as our Austin/Kiev simulation shows ...

Near the back of the conference table, a man, who turns out to be O'Connor, is scribbling on the top page of a thick sheaf of paper. Behind the table is a tinted transparent plastic screen, with the images of Adrian, Reg (the CEO), and the vice president of production in South Korea. Adrian, as Julie predicted, is now sitting next to Reg and is quite able to whisper in his ear. He only need lean toward the image of Reg, as it appears on his screen in his home office to ensure that no one else can hear what he is saying.

JULIE [CONTINUING] ... we have passed our last production hurdle. Our first cars hit the showrooms March 26 ...

Julie clicks her pointer and the sports car takes off, tearing up the hillside, revealing the chart line.

JULIE [CONTINUING] ... and we project shipment of more than 5,000 cars per month by the end of spring.

We see O'Connor listening to the sales figures. He smiles and makes a note.

JULIE [CONTINUING OFF-SCREEN] Our numbers suggest that total domestic sales volume for the first full model year will exceed 80,000 automobiles.

Julie shows A.J.'s second clip of the sports car rolling gently toward the camera. This is the clip A.J. shot after Julie had shown him what she wanted during the SunPad scene back in her office.

JULIE In short, we are ready to build a car that will make this company a lot of money . . .

The car slides to a stop.

JULIE . . . now!

The CEO turns to O'Connor. In the foreground, one of the physical attendees slides on a pair of virtual reality "shutter glasses" and scopes out the car.

❖ ❖ ❖ ❖ ❖

Real, immersive virtual reality is going to be a big thing no doubt, but there will still be lots of situations where immersion will be just plain inappropriate. A boardroom meeting will be one of them. The attendee putting on the sunglasses is using what some call second-person VR. The virtual reality lies in the hand-held screen, not in a pair of wraparound goggles. The shutter glasses let the hand-held pad know where the user's eyes are and act like the old 3D movie glasses, directing the correct image to the correct eye. As the virtual attendee moves the screen around, he or she is able to look around the sides of the 3D image. The SunPad is also a second-person VR device, albeit not projecting a 3D image.

The following script is from the original; it is not in the film.

❖ ❖ ❖ ❖ ❖

CEO Hiroshi, how do Julie's numbers jibe with yours?

HIROSHI They're using our old model. **[TO JULIE]** Didn't Molly update you this afternoon?

JULIE I'm afraid Molly's been . . . mmm . . . otherwise engaged. But if you have the new numbers, I'll drop them in.

Hiroshi pops up the display on his notebook and pinches his workspace, shrinking it by 20 percent to reveal an abstract map of the room with an icon for each system in it. He slides the icon representing the new data onto Julie's computer.

Meanwhile, Julie, who has just reached her portable, watches the document icon pixilate onto her workspace, then slides it onto the chart, which automatically redraws itself. Its slope becomes even steeper. Julie moves back to the front of the room.

❖ ❖ ❖ ❖ ❖

Today, materials presented at meetings, and therefore meetings themselves, have become static. We wanted to explore software designs that would result in a flexible system that could increase the immediacy of a meeting.

❖ ❖ ❖ ❖ ❖

JULIE Even better.

❖ ❖ ❖ ❖ ❖

And now back to the film . . . .

❖ ❖ ❖ ❖ ❖

CEO What do you say now, Mike?

O'Connor stands, slapping the Auto Week *copy against his thigh.*

O'CONNOR Very impressive presentation, Julie. However, I have to seriously question these sales figures, Reg.

O'Connor strides to the front of the room. Julie steps away from him. O'Connor holds up the Auto Week *headline: DX9: SPRING LAUNCH FALLS FLAT!*

O'CONNOR Just look at the DX9 launch in April '99. It was an unmitigated disaster! And why? [TRIUMPHANTLY] Because you cannot launch a sports car in spring!

Julie is stricken. She returns to her place at the corner of the conference table. O'Connor glances at Julie, as if lecturing her, as she begins typing on her portable.

❖ ❖ ❖ ❖ ❖

Actually, she is "chording." Her keyboard has only eight keys, but by pressing two or more in combination, she can generate all characters. Chording keyboards have never gained much favor. It's likely that in 2004, Julie will still be using a familiar QWERTY keyboard, but Alison Armstrong's design was so light and airy, it seemed criminal to weigh it down with 90-plus keys.

❖ ❖ ❖ ❖ ❖

O'CONNOR All you have to do is look at the percentage of exotic cars that end up in California. [LOOKS TOWARD JULIE] We've all seen the figures. Californians buy 85 percent of the exotic cars in this country!

REG What's that got to do with...

O'CONNOR No, Reg, just a minute. Let me run with this.

Julie types in the following query:

```
? Show Auto Week DX9 sales 99 spring
```

Meanwhile, O'Connor is continuing in the background.

O'CONNOR Now, by the time their marketing ramps up, it'll be fall. And that's a best-case scenario! It rains in California in the fall, and when it rains, you can't sell sports cars!

The relevant article appears on Julie's screen, the most important areas highlighted.

❖ ❖ ❖ ❖ ❖

This highlighting is not magic. To read how it might be done, see the section "Organizers" in Chapter 9.

❖ ❖ ❖ ❖ ❖

We see the following sequence of messages on Julie's screen:

❖ ❖ ❖ ❖ ❖

Following is the original sequence, which you can see in *"The Making of Starfire"* segment of the accompanying video. For the film, we had to shorten it; I didn't have O'Connor speak long enough.

❖ ❖ ❖ ❖ ❖

```
Searching Further..."
Follow-up Found!
```

Later issue of Auto Week *appears.*

```
Finding key reference
```

❖ ❖ ❖ ❖ ❖

Agent has found highlighted reference in follow-up article and is looking for the original.

❖ ❖ ❖ ❖ ❖

```
Linking to Chicago
```

❖ ❖ ❖ ❖ ❖

Agent has left the company and gone onto the Internet (or its successor).

❖ ❖ ❖ ❖ ❖

```
Linking to Los Angeles
L.A. Chronicle News Service
```

❖ ❖ ❖ ❖ ❖

Agent has tracked down the original article and is agreeing to pay for it.

❖ ❖ ❖ ❖ ❖

```
Reference Found!
```

❖ ❖ ❖ ❖ ❖

Agent has recovered the headline that will enable Julie to defeat O'Connor.

❖ ❖ ❖ ❖ ❖

O'CONNOR [CONTINUING OFF-SCREEN] My luxury car, on the other hand, is a year-round car, and we are ready to start production and promotion.

A column of icons materializes on the projection screen behind O'Connor as he speaks.

❖ ❖ ❖ ❖ ❖

Julie is now finalizing her presentation. Total elapsed time? Less than 40 seconds in the film. In real life? Maybe a slight bit longer, but that time would not be spent waiting for the documents to arrive, which would be almost instantaneous. (I stretched out the film so viewers could watch the sequence.) Julie would need a certain amount of time to understand what her agents have found for her and prepare her plan of attack.

Today, people can, given sufficient time, prepare beautiful presentations, but once those presentation are finished, so are the speakers. Any questions and answers instantly revert to palaver and gesticulation.

In Japan, business is not conducted at meetings. Instead, people make formal presentations and new proposals. Then everyone goes off to think about it. American meetings have been more productive because people actually thrash things out. Color slides and multimedia have been adding to a meeting's formality and inflexibility, often lowering productivity.

The ability to continue research and present relevant documents in real time during a meeting represents a real departure from this trend. Coupled with the ability of anyone at the table to throw up graphics on the big board, it will result in a lot less standing at the projection board reciting, and a lot more rough and tumble give and take, restoring real fire and interaction, while at the same time cutting down on false claims and wild speculation.

❖ ❖ ❖ ❖ ❖

O'CONNOR I want to launch now! We can bring out Julie's car in the fall when she's had time to reassess . . .

Julie bursts out of her seat and strides up to the front of the room.

JULIE [TO CEO] Reg! May I interrupt?! **[TO O'CONNOR]** First, our PR is in full swing, all over the world.

She slaps the first icon, and the photo of the magazines appears.

JULIE Mike McCormick, who is not exactly loose with the compliments, just today . . .

She slaps the second icon, showing the Detroit newspaper quote: "The finest PR campaign I've seen come out of this town in a long time," which she had scanned in earlier from the newspaper Natalie brought her.

JULIE [CONTINUING] . . . called it "one of the finest PR campaigns to come out of this town in a long time." As for the DX9 launch: it was hurt, not by season but by . . .

Slapping the third icon, she splashes this headline from the Los Angeles Chronicle *onto the screen—and right across O'Connor's forehead.*

JULIE [CONTINUING] . . . earthquake!

Remember: she didn't even know about this car's connection with the California earthquake 1 minute ago. In a business situation today, O'Connor would have won this round, and everyone would have had to assemble for another $10,000 meeting after Julie had discovered the truth.

❖ ❖ ❖ ❖ ❖

JULIE [CONTINUING] The "Big One of '99'" was the real cause of Mr. O'Connor's sluggish sales . . .

Julie touches the fourth and final icon. The headline disappears and is replaced with her sales chart, and the page from Auto Week *with the chart of the DX9's postquake sales appears, just slightly overlapping it.*

JULIE But when the people calmed down and the highways were reopened, sales soared. In fact, if I slide their line onto our chart . . .

Adrian, having anticipated Julie's need, slides the DX9 sales line onto Julie's chart. The DX9 chart pops into the back as its numbers are incorporated.

JULIE [ASIDE] Thank you, Adrian.

❖ ❖ ❖ ❖ ❖

Adrian's sliding the DX9 sales line onto Julie's chart is actually one of the most important statements of the film. This is a far more complex act than Hiroshi's, earlier. Consider what is necessary for this to be able to happen:

• Adrian has to be able to collaborate with Julie's computer (with her prior assent, of course), so he can be in a position to move the line in the first place. This implies not only the hardware and software to support such collaboration, but security and privacy systems that will make Julie feel comfortable in allowing it.

• The chart in this online magazine cannot just be an image, as it would be in today's CD-ROM products. The computer has to be able to access the underlying math.

• The industry has to develop a set of uniform standards for how information is stored and transferred. In today's "babelized" world, when Julie's computer tried to make sense of the chart, it would have found the chart was in Excel for the Macintosh format, while the computer only understood 1-2-3.

The kind of cooperation and coordination that must occur in the industry to make this seemingly simple shot come true will be unprecedented, but it must occur if we are ever to enjoy the real promise of next-generation computing.

❖ ❖ ❖ ❖ ❖

JULIE [TO GROUP] You can see that their run rate at year-end is identical to ours. So unless Mr. O'Connor has some early notice of another earthquake . . .

O'Connor slinks back to his seat.

JULIE [CONTINUING] . . . I think we can safely look for sales to explode!

Most board members are grinning and nodding their heads in agreement.

CEO Thanks, Julie, I think we've heard enough. You and your team [NODS TOWARD ADRIAN] have done a superlative job. Let's build it!

Julie gathers up her portable and begins walking toward the door, exchanging angry glares with O'Connor.

CEO [OFF-SCREEN] Now [SIGH] . . . Mike's car.

O'Connor's head whips around to the CEO.

CEO We'll go back to the original production schedule, although Hiroshi, I believe you had some concerns about Mike's projections of cost setting up the production line . . .

The CEO's voice trails off as Julie exits the conference room and Adrian fades from the screen.

INTERIOR. Boardroom Corridor: Day

Julie approaches the camera with still-serious steps. She stops, sniffs, and breaks into a huge smile as she hugs the computer, exclaiming "Yes!" in a stage whisper.

ANNOUNCER Sun Microsystems. The Power of the Future.

Julie sneezes as we fade to black.

Beyond the Mouse

*T*oday's computers are already pretty good at communicating to the user. They can talk, generate sound effects and music, and display information in 16 million colors on large screens. Meanwhile, input hardware has stagnated. Users can type words and commands on a keyboard with a layout that has remained essentially unchanged since the 1870s. They can gesture using a mouse invented in the 1960s. Up, down, left, right, and click. Not much of a transmission channel for use by a creature with as many communication skills and nuances as a human being.

Many people are bent on eliminating even these devices. Northwest Airlines launched an in-flight digital entertainment system in 1994 that used a game paddle to let people navigate a labyrinthine menu structure. Changing TV channels required navigating menus three levels deep. A year later, they dropped the system. Proponents of the set-top box intend to have people navigate information spaces of upwards of 100 million documents using a TV-like remote control.

Most of the clutter of screens and much of the complexity of designs are there because communication from users to their machines is so limited. Now is the time to expand that communications link, not contract it. If you watched the Starfire film, you undoubtedly noticed how clean the screens were. Gone were the myriad of icons, buttons, dials, and switches. Their absence can be largely traced to input methods that enable expressive communication in lieu of today's simple point-and-click.

The mouse is not the ideal pointing device. It is just the best that we've had until now. The complexity of our tasks is hitting the wall. We are swimming in menus and icons. Microsoft Word 6.0 for the Macintosh, when run on a standard Apple monitor with all icons displayed in their full-size glory, leaves only 23 percent of the screen available for the contents of the document.

In the next ten years, we must expand the capabilities of today's pointing methods and devices, as well as perfecting and adding new ones. This will be a challenge, for until a new device is included with the computer "in the box," no one will write software to support it, and without software, hardware manufacturers will be loath to lay out hardware dollars.

The few lucky companies still supplying hardware and software have a natural advantage over firms that operate in only a single sphere. Hardware and software integration is clearly the reason that mouse software came into being on the Macintosh, not the PC. It may be that these integrated companies will again prove the vanguard of the kinds of changes needed in the coming years, if only their expanded size does not prevent their hardware and software people from talking to each other.

Mice

Mice can be improved. They should have pressure sensitivity. The mouse button should register pressure, so that information can be used, for example, in a drawing program to alter the density or spread of ink. The mouse itself should be pressure sensitive, so we can "push under" things by applying slight downward pressure. By adding a "squeeze" sensor, we could let people fly upward in their object spaces by squeezing gently on the side of their mouse.

The side walls of the screen have an extreme advantage in mouse interfaces. Fitts's Law dictates that mice can acquire targets arrayed along an edge much faster than those wandering about in unbounded space ("Fitts's Law: Why Pull-Down Menus Work Best," Tognazzini 1992). As screens grow larger, the natural edges draw farther and farther away. One use for pressure sensitivity would be to enable us to lock people within windows or zones, giving them hard edges to bounce off—edges that could be lined with menus and tools. To escape, people would squeeze the mouse on their way out, sliding deftly over the wall.

We also need to get rid of mouse cords. In cramped quarters, people discover their cords are sometimes propelling their mice in unintended directions. Mice need to be made featherweight, with light touch switches, to reduce the potential for repetitive strain injury.

We are also far from fully exploring the software possibilities of mouse drivers. It may be that mice should respond to an object's "local gravity" or "friction," slowing down when over a clickable device.

None of these approaches is enough. No matter what we do to the mouse, it will still be a genuflective input, limited to up, down, left, and right. The human body is capable of 200 degrees of freedom.[1] The mouse reduces that to 2 degrees.

Gestures

We showed the power of gesture early in Starfire, when Julie made a duplicate of the control panel device within her document. Most of the reduction in screen clutter seen in the film is a direct result of the addition of gesture. Gesture enables users to communicate directly with their computers without using a mouse, tablet, or any other pointing device. It is natural, powerful, and effective.

The more expressive the code is, the fewer instructions that must be sent. Our hands are capable of communicating in a rich language of movement. Gestures can greatly reduce the overall amount of movement needed to perform tasks. As important, gestures vary the movement of the hands. Repetitive stress injury, by definition, is caused by repetition. Having the hand carry out the same movement or even remain in the same position for long times can cause damage.[2] The far more dynamic activity of gesturing will reduce both of these effects.

Gesture is not inherently difficult. It is not nearly as intractable a problem as handwriting, which is, after all, a form of advanced gesture. We have ignored gesture because, up until now, the mouse has worked. It isn't working any more. The industry needs to invest heavily in gesture if users are to progress.

....
1 A "degree of freedom" is fancy engineering talk for the ability to move back and forth in a single direction. A single human fingertip is capable of 3 degrees of freedom, in that it can be waved up and down, left and right, and also be extended and retracted. Some people have proposed as a means of low-bandwidth video conferencing that we send single, articulated 3D models of the callers, then send only updated body positions, based on changes to each person's 200 degrees of freedom. The data compression would dwarf current video compression schemes.

2 Many of the tortures of the Middle Ages were based on this second effect: people were placed in hanging cages or otherwise constrained so they could not move. The result was agonizing. (Later, the hanging cage technology was applied to elementary school furniture.)

Handwriting

Today we create whole computers around the concept of handwriting, but they have yet to sell in large quantities. A really effective handwriting system would be good for making brief notes, particularly in a meeting room, where it is impolite to type while others are speaking. But handwriting has significant limitations.

Handwriting is not the best way to write a book, or even a report, using Western languages or even Katakana. People can type Western languages much faster than they can write. They can speak them even faster, although one cannot always politely talk out loud. Handwriting is an important tool, but it is not the only tool, and until we accept that, I think handwriting computers will continue to find little market acceptance.

This situation is similar to the introduction of microwave ovens. Early ovens came with elaborate cookbooks, hundreds of pages long, giving all kinds of recipes for everything from breads to French soufflé desserts to huge roasts of beef. Microwave ovens, by their very nature, ruin wheat breads. They make very puffy soufflés that, tragically, instantly collapse, and they turn tender beef into shoe leather.

Microwaves are no good for bread, soufflés, or beef, but they are good for heating water, reheating leftover food, even for softening ice cream (as long as you don't leave the oven on for more than 15 seconds). Microwave ovens are an important kitchen tool, but they are no good if you try to make them the only kitchen tool. In the same way, handwriting, regardless of its bad reputation, will become a very important tool as soon as the developers of handwriting stop trying to make it the only tool.

In the meantime, Palm Computing, a Silicon Valley company, has invented Graffiti, a very low-cost, accurate character recognition system. It requires a writing space only 1 inch square, and people can achieve speeds of 20 words per minute with 90 to 95 percent accuracy within about a week. Graffiti requires a small amount of learning. Most character are entered exactly as they appear in English. A few of the more difficult ones, such as *E* and *K*, have been simplified to allow their entry with a single stroke. Numbers and uppercase characters need to be preceded by special strokes.

Graffiti is a good example of designers accepting the limitations of current technology, then making the minimum compromises necessary to build a useful tool. Users have to put in a little effort in learning some new gestural strokes, but the payoff is a handwriting system that works.

Voice

Voice can be used three ways: to command the computer, enter information, and communicate with other people. We are today at the point where voice is a reasonable way to command a computer. Because of the limited vocabulary required, several voice systems offer enough sophistication to be able to handle the task. Most of them, however, require the user to wear a microphone headset. Today this is still unfashionable. The users I have studied tend to use voice for a few weeks and then give it up because they tire of having to put on a headset every time they want to give a command.

This will change. With the integration of communication and computing, people will need that same headset for talking to other people. They will grow used to putting on their radio headsets early in the morning and not taking them off until they arrive home.

We will experience a major change in the acceptance of voice technology when the error rate of continuous speech recognition moves to perhaps one tenth of 1 percent. Carpal tunnel syndrome may well become a quaint medical malady of the past as people spend their time pointing to positions with their hands, while entering dictation with their voice. An unfortunate, but probably unavoidable, side effect will be a new onslaught of verbal overload, as people commit to paper their every thought and flesh out a single idea into ten chapters.

Eye Tracking

Eye tracking is another form of input that works well in combination with others. Speakers sometimes do indicate objects by looking at them, but more often they point them out with their hands. However, listeners make use of eye-tracking information constantly as a way of checking the accuracy of messages being sent through voice or expression. Eye tracking helps them build a contextual framework.

Computers could make use of eye-tracking information in a number of ways. In Starfire, Julie's computer delivered messages where she was looking instead of in some fixed location that might have been far from her gaze. Knowing the message has been seen, the computer was then able to whisk it away without waiting for confirmation.

During a video conference with three people, a user might look at one person and lean closer. The communication agent can use that information to enhance the drop in the user's voice level as delivered to the other conference participants. Users could also use eye tracking in a more direct way. They could stare at a window and say, "Close," instead of having to grapple with a pointing device first.

An eye tracker could cut down the cost of maintaining a high-resolution display. The only spot on a screen that needs to be updated in high resolution is the part we are seeing with the center part of the retina, the fovea. Areas outside the fovea can be updated in low resolution, and areas outside peripheral vision need not be updated at all. The same techniques could be used to protect the privacy of portable users in public spaces by adding a little twist: instead of failing to update areas outside the fovea, they could be updated with gibberish. Those peering over the user's shoulders would see nothing understandable unless they tracked the user's eye movements exactly.

India Starker and Richard Bolt (1990) of MIT's Media Lab used eye tracking to guide the narration in a children's story. They constructed a 3D model of a planet rotating against a background of twinkling stars. On the planet are several objects (e.g., eight-sided cones and staircases). If the user's eyes sweep the planet as a whole, the narrator will say something about it—for example, "This is where I live. It's not very large, maybe about 200 feet across, but I call it home." If instead the user's eyes dart among the staircases, the narrator will describe his recently adopted hobby of staircase collecting. If the eyes dwell on only a single staircase, the narrator will zero in.

Today sophisticated eye tracking requires bulky and expensive equipment. Soon most of the equipment will be replaced by a low-cost, mass-produced chip. Simple eye tracking has already made it to the chip, appearing in Canon's A2E 35-mm camera. The camera focuses on the same thing the user is focusing on. If you want the people in focus, look at the people. If you'd rather have the tree in focus, look at the tree. Simple. Effective.

Keyboards

Keyboards are likely to stay pretty much as they are. The Dvorak keyboard layout, which results in around a 10 percent increase in typing speed and efficiency, has never made any inroad on the familiar Sholes QWERTY layout. Chording keyboards have been around almost as long as the Dvorak. The darling of the court reporter set, they have had no impact on the home or business market.

We have had two significant advances in keyboard design in the past 15 years. One is Jef Raskin's information appliance keyboard, which featured special jump keys that made searches more than 50 times faster than they are on a Macintosh or Windows machine today. The other advance, more recent, is Ted Selker's Trackpoint device. This little red pencil-eraser object appears in the middle of IBM portable keyboards, available to the index fingers. It enables people to move their pointer around their screens without lifting their hands from the keys, lowering the search time typically suffered when using other devices.

Several keyboards on the market are long overdue for improvement. The Macintosh, alleged to have a one-button mouse, actually has a four-button mouse: one atop the mouse and the other three on the keyboard. The Command, Option, and Shift keys are used routinely to modify the meaning of the simple click. I enjoy this system far more than the two- and three-button mice that I have used (which only confuse me), but the Macintosh's modifier keys are in the wrong position. The situation is made worse by having the command key directly under *Z, X, C,* and *V*—the shortcut keys most often used in conjunction with mouse movement. This arrangement leaves the left thumb curled up in an awkward position.

Other manufacturers' keyboards are awash with extra keys for special functions. The resulting oversized keyboards cause the mouse or other pointing devices to be moved too far away from the user, slowing pointing operations and increasing the odds and severity of repetitive strain injury. Nor has any evidence been presented demonstrating that people would not be better off with a good pointing device interface and a lot fewer "shortcut" keys. People can be fooled into believing that shortcuts are faster, but it ain't necessarily so. (I went into exhaustive detail on this subject in *Tog on Interface*. Refer to that discussion for further information.)

When we finally achieve continuous speech recognition with extremely high accuracy rates, we will begin to see keyboards disappear from computers.

Tablets

Graphics tablets continue to be held back by the presence of keyboards. Compared to a mouse, tablet styli are far more difficult to acquire when one needs to bounce back and forth between keyboard and pointing device. Remove the need to bounce by getting rid of the keyboard, and this natural disadvantage will disappear. Tablets also need to be in front of you, not off to the side, where mice can live comfortably.

In the meantime, tablets are firmly ensconced in graphic design, CAD-CAM, and other areas where drawing is prized over ability to enter text.

I keep waiting for someone to make a small graphics tablet that will double as an ordinary mouse pad. Use the mouse when using the keyboard; switch to the tablet when it becomes time to draw.[3]

Tablets now come in the new junior size, too. Users stroke the pads, in effect entering gestures.

Touch Screens

Touch screens have found their niche in public kiosks, where people need an interface that can be instantly learned and used. They are limited in desktop use because of the weight of the hand and arm. Requiring people to hold their hand in the air perhaps several hundred times per day would result in great injury.

Once we get rid of keyboards in favor of voice input, touch screens will probably become the input device of choice on portable systems, enabling the display surface to cover the entire front surface of the device. These displays would then be used in a horizontal or near-horizontal position. When I did a research study on pointing devices at Apple several years ago, I found only one device that outperformed the

....
3 I have seen a few that try, but their "mouse" devices have a long latency, giving the mouse a squishy feeling that is disconcerting.

mouse: a pencil applied to paper. When performing the same tests using pencil and paper, test subjects were able to complete the tests approximately 50 percent faster.

In studying the differences in media, I reached two conclusions. First, users are more accurate with a pencil than other devices because of the density of paper "pixels." Because 72-dpi pixels are relatively large, mouse users may believe they are whipping right along toward their target when in fact their true position is drifting ever so slightly up or down.

In Figure 7.1, the user's actual track is represented by the fine brushed line. The gray blocks represent the path as seen on the user's 72-dpi display. Because of the limitations of the display resolution, the user is led to believe that the pen is tracking directly toward target B, when in fact the user is drifting slightly downward. Just at the point of intersection, the pen has dipped below the target, the next lower pixel lights, and the user neatly zips right by. Users experiencing this effect tend to slow down to try to compensate, but slowing does not improve accuracy, since, slow or fast, the feedback is simply not there. Slowing only reduces their productivity further.

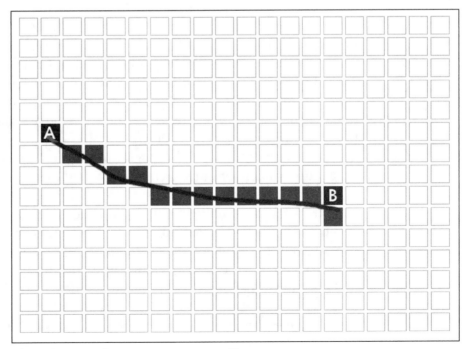

Figure 7.1 *Actual versus apparent pen tracking*

The second effect I noted was parallax. Touch screen users may think their pen is directly over a target when, because of the thickness of the display and their angle to it, the pen is too low. High-resolution displays with zero-parallax fiberoptic faces would neatly solve both problems.

Force Feedback

Input and output devices flow together as one in force-feedback devices. These devices not only track as you push on the input device, they push back. One early force-feedback project resulted in Atari's Hard Drivin' arcade game, a race car simulator in which the user could feel the road through the steering wheel and brakes. Large stepper motors provided the tension. PHANToM, (Personal Haptic Interface Mechanism), developed by Thomas H. Massie and Kenneth Salisbury at MIT, is a more subtle device, allowing a single finger to delicately trace the surface of an object. (Two PHANToMs can be used to enable the user to grasp objects using thumb and forefinger.)

At the CHI'95 Computer Human Interaction Conference, I had the opportunity to try out the device, at first just discovering invisible objects lying on the bottom of a visible space. The effect of bumping into a half-sphere and literally having to lift my finger to slide over it to the other side was disconcerting, but the next task they gave me was downright macabre. They displayed an MRI scan of a human brain, complete with a brain tumor. My task was to use a thin needle to puncture the outer skull, penetrate the brain, and remove a sample of the tumor. I found myself bearing down hard, trying to fight my way into the skull. Then I shot past the outer skull, only to have my probe caught up in a kind of slimy friction as I passed through the brain. When I reached the tumor, I was surprised to find a layer of resistance around it—far more subtle than the skull, but there nonetheless. I was told this was a layer of calcification. Pushing on with great reluctance, I penetrated into the interior of the tumor.

I've played around with lots of medical imaging applications, but this was truly unnerving. The force feedback delivered a level of reality that was primitively powerful in its ability to make me believe. I still shudder when I think about the experience. Today's virtual realities have a soft, cotton-candy sense to them. Adding force would not only advance their realism, but go far toward solving today's problem of users becoming confused and disoriented.

Advanced Input

Users manipulating 3D images need more advanced pointing devices—perhaps a stylus with 6 degrees of freedom plus pressure sensitivity or a lump of moldable high-tech "clay" that can transmit its current form into the virtual world.

Users will also need lightweight stereo glasses and equally lightweight appliances for sound: telephone headsets capable of projecting a 3D, binaural sound field in space. Multiple microphones and radar, blending into the environment, will join cameras in producing spatial data for projecting convincing telepresence.

Most of these devices exist today, at least in the laboratory; within a few years, they will, with luck, be available at popular prices.

The Shape of Tomorrow's Computers

Requiem for a Heavyweight

ATLANTA. May 23, 2003—Today the last desktop computer rolled down the production line and into history. Even those of us who long anticipated their demise were unprepared for how quickly the unwieldy behemoths actually went. It was as if, on a single day, people woke up no longer seeing any need for the glass monsters. While a few hold-outs continued buying them—people isolated geographically, financially, or chronologically—for most of us, the desktop computer suddenly became a thing of the past. Still, this reporter experienced a twinge of sadness watching the last worker on the last line experience a twinge of pain as he lowered the heavy monitor into a waiting box.

We visited the hangout favored by many of the former assembly workers at the plant. The Ferguson Chiropractic Institute stands on a bluff overlooking Silicon Valley, long its primary source of patients—and revenue. We spoke with Clara Tydewaller, a rising assembler until the fateful day she toppled attempting to lift a 435-pound, 26-inch color monitor by herself. "I always told them that big screens were going to disappear. Why I remember the time...."

*H*old everything. That's not quite what is going to happen. True, the desktop computer is going to disappear, but not because of portables. In fact, I expect portables, as we know them today, will also disappear, and the sooner, the better. People cannot reasonably be expected to haul around everywhere a 6-pound portable that requires a battery change every 3½ minutes.

In the next decade, portables will shrink in weight, power consumption, and thickness. The need for back lighting will be eliminated. In many cases, the need for even a screen will be eliminated as powerful computers shrink down to the size of wristwatches, with all interaction being done through voice.

Reduction in size will not be the whole answer, however. Screens will also be getting bigger.

Big Needs, Big Screens

For many years, I have invited readers of my columns and articles to write to me with their questions and comments. Brad Schrick has been one of my more consistent correspondents:

> Tog,
> I wonder if you saw the series of articles by P. J. Plauger in *Computer Language* about human sensory limits as they relate to computers? Plauger points out that the ideal working surface for a technical person is the size of a large drafting table, and for an office worker it is the size of a desk. This has evolved because you must have your work at hand, which is not necessarily true of a computer. But it still is a good gauge, I think.
>
> Then he points out that if you want 300 dots per inch in true color over this surface, you need a VERY fast processor and VERY good display technology. Then extend this need to video, and the processor requirements go through the roof. And he makes the case that this is indeed what people want. That is why he can't understand why so many computer pundits ask what we are going to do with a little more processing power; his point is that grandma wants 100 times more than we can give her, and Larry Livermore wants more than that.[1]

....

[1] Lawrence Livermore Labs in California, where various devices for killing large numbers of people have been developed over the years, was named in honor of the brother of the man who invented the Sony Trinitron picture tube. In this case, writer Schrick is using "Larry Livermore" as a synecdoche for "power user." (Okay, okay, *synecdoche* is a figure of speech where the part stands for the whole, or vice versa. "John Law" as a stand-in for "police" is a similar instance.)

I liked that argument, and it helped explain why I feel so frustrated in front of such a wonderful machine. Its screen is the equivalent of a postage stamp, relative to a human eye, even though that is a great improvement over the last generation.

Brad Schrick, Engineering Software Concepts, Inc.

Brad has captured well one of the chief reasons stationary computers will be with us for a long, long time. Just as theaters gained a competitive advantage by supplying their spectators with wide-screen color and high-definition pictures, so too will desktop hardware manufacturers. As I write this, I'm using a system with three contiguous 21-inch displays, filled with letters, articles, illustrations, and various viewports onto information systems, all directly related to the task at hand. Being able to see them all at once offers me a clear advantage over people who must view their cyberspace through a keyhole ranging from 9 to 16 inches.[2]

In the not-too-distant future, stationary computer systems with displays as tiny as 20-inch glass monitors may well be the stuff of history museums, not homes and offices. Today such a prediction may seem fanciful, but only because of a limitation of the moment. Yield problems (high manufacturing failure rates) are currently plaguing flat panel production, keeping sizes small and prices high. Several lines of research promise to raise yield effectively to 100 percent in the not-too-distant future. (One approach is to use perhaps four "lights" per pixel, so that should a single pixel prove defective, it would suffer a 25 percent drop in intensity, not a 100 percent drop.) Once yield is no longer a problem, panels will grow in size, increase in density, and drop in price. Plauger's vision will come true sooner rather than later.[3]

The Really, Really Big Display

Both Plauger and Mark Weiser of Xerox PARC have been crying out against the mad rush to miniaturization (Weiser 1991). During the Starfire project, I became interested in carrying their work one step

....
2 Moving to a large display area is as much a one-way street as moving from floppy to hard disk. You'll never go back.

3 Conventional wisdom dictates that Japan will not enjoy this size revolution, due to the petite size of their offices. The offices I have visited there are small, but not so small that a 25- or 30-inch wide monitor would not fit were it only 1 inch thick.

further by revisiting the assumptions that have led to our current planar designs.

Today's real-world desktop surfaces are invariably flat and level. Why? Certainly not to make it easier for us to access every inch of their surface. When we sit at our desks, we typically have a prime area within the sweep of our arms, with diminishing real estate values toward the back and sides of our desks. Items shoved into the far corners are likely to remain in residence, unread for days, if not decades.

Desks are level because gravity tends to make paper slide downhill. Drafting tables are not level; they're tilted, and thus they require users to tape, clamp, or hook their paper and tools. The payoff for this decrease in document mobility is a large increase in draftsperson mobility. Draftspersons typically trade off between pacing the length of their drafting tables and wheeling back and forth on mobile high stools. In either case, they fluidly command the entire surface of their table, even if they must still reach for the extremities.

Cyberspace has no inherent gravity. Therefore, cyberspace displays can be set at the most convenient angle for the user. Today's angle is most often vertical (the face of a CRT or flat panel display), with users indirectly interacting via keyboard, mouse, or trackball. The increasingly popular alternative is a horizontal or hand-held display with which a user interacts by use of touch or a stylus directly applied to the display surface.

In designing an easy-access large surface display, I wanted to make use of both horizontal and vertical display areas. Horizontal displays enable comfortable direct interaction and can also double as a conventional desktop, where people can continue to open terrestrial mail and sign the occasional letter.

Vertical surfaces have their own payoffs. Work done by Abigail Sellen and William Buxton at Xerox EuroPARC, confirmed by the Solaris Live project at Sun, has shown the need for vertical surfaces for desktop video communication. The EuroPARC experiments have used small "towers," topped with 3- or 4-inch monitors, elevated to the user's eye level. For conference calls, several of these towers can be set apart in a rough circle on a standard desktop to simulate the normal separation between speakers. This enables people to assess at whom you are looking at any given moment by the angular difference in eye gaze. It also allows you to whisper to a single member of the conference by leaning toward his or her tower. The other participants can no longer hear you, although they can see what you are up to, just as in real life.

In our experiments at Sun that led to the Starfire film, Frank Ludolph used a wide-screen vertical display with images of other callers that, rather than being straight on, were "keystoned," or angled somewhat away from the viewer and toward each other. The result was a heightened sense of eye gaze (Figure 8.1).

Having horizontal and vertical display areas also enables users to move their work between orientations, allowing them to shift their body and neck positions, relieving physical stress and discomfort. Perhaps the biggest reason for building a large display incorporating both orientations is accessibility. If you swing your arms around your body, you will find that they describe the inside of two large, overlapping spheres, each having its center at the joint of your shoulder and arm. The greatest surface area you can access without moving your entire body fits within these contours.

We built Julie's Starfire display inside the limits of the spheres. The result was a semicircular workspace that surrounds the user, curving side to side, like a personal Cinerama screen, as well as vertically, beginning as a flat, horizontal surface in the center, where the user sits, but

Figure 8.1
Teleconferencers can "look at" each other

sweeping gently upward until, near arm's length, the wall becomes vertical (Figure 8.2). Even with its large area—equivalent to the square footage of a normal desktop—test subjects were able to touch any spot on its surface without undue stretching.

Different areas of the screen will call for different pointing devices. The human arm weighs a good 5 or 10 pounds. A user accessing a mouse twice per minute during the course of a 6-hour typical workday touches the mouse more than 14,400 times per month. Imagine having to lift your arms all the way up in the air 14,400 times per month. This would bring about repetitive stress injuries on a scale undreamed of today.

Our conjecture was that people would tend to do their more intensive work on the level part of Julie's workspace, saving the vertical surface for communication, reference, and viewing. When people did want to move to their vertical surface, they could, as they do today, use an indirect pointing device such as a mouse, so that their hands could remain horizontal and supported.

Figure 8.2 *Long view of Julie's office showing curved desk*

The display was based on 300 dot per inch (dpi) resolution, working today in the laboratory. We will eventually reach densities of 1,200 or 2,400 dpi, which will allow scaling the desk back in size without reduction in information. With a smaller overall desk, a user could look out over the top without obstruction while still seeing the same level of detail. Having 1,200 to 2,400 dpi also begins to enable good 3D graphic display. On today's low-resolution monitors, all but the foreground appears out of focus, not because it really is out of focus but because there are not sufficient pixels to define it.

Sensitive Surface Displays

We have grown up in this industry with the reality that we can never have enough memory or enough processing power. We tend to let that spill over into a belief that we can never have enough of anything. Not so. Human perceptual parameters have true upper limits. The 16,777,216 colors we can display with 24 bits per pixel is greater than the number of colors a human being can perceive; 24-bit color solves the problem.[4] Likewise, we will reach an upper limit on display density. It may prove to be 2,400 dpi or even 4,800 dpi, but it will stop. A 30 frames per second rate does not solve the flicker problem, but probably 120 frames per second will.

With 120 frames per second, 1,200 to 2,400 dpi resolution, zero parallax, and 24-bit color, display problems will be solved. Then we can turn attention to weaving in other sensory and motor devices, producing a sensitive surface—an amalgam capable of being simultaneously a high-definition display, scanner, pressure sensor, and tactile feedback generator. Add to it an array of cameras—or even an array of lenses within the surface matrix—and you have the makings of a first-class workspace.

What would it be like to sit at tomorrow's Starfire display, experiencing a sensitive surface display? You saw one obvious advantage in the film. When Julie wanted to scan in the newspaper, it instantly became part of her cyberspace when she flipped it over and rubbed it, so the

....
4 Actually our phosphors are not really quite up to the task of displaying all that we are sending, but glass tube technology is already way ahead of print, and improvements will continue.

intelligent surface knew to "read" it, converting it into an optical-character-recognized and optical-graphic-recognized cyberdocument.

Scanning will probably be the first added capability. It requires only the addition of a fourth element to the current red-blue-green triad: a photocell. Scanning today requires a special piece of equipment, with its own special drivers and its own special software. Starfire is about simplicity. By adding scanning capability to the display, a major source of physical and mental clutter is removed forever.

What if you want to reach for a cyberdocument that is to the side of the desk? If it were real paper, you would probably glance over long enough to see that your fingers were somewhere near the document. Then you would bring your eyes back to begin lining up where you want the document to end up, leaving to your fingers the task of finding the edge of the document so you can slide it to the new position. The same process could work with a sensitive surface display: once you have touched the paper with your hand, the surface deforms into "goosebumps" above the paper. You can then slide your hand, without looking, until you find the edge of the goose bumps. A quick flick will send the paper on its way, where your other hand can "catch" it, indicated by the arrival of the goose bumps beneath your fingers. If you want to "straighten" the paper, give it a twist with your fingers. The agent in the system will show you when you have reached a position where the paper is tangential to your body. Through working with it? Flick it away from you, as Julie did, and it will slide up the vertical wall of the display until it pins at the top.

Have you asked your computer agent to present you with a viewport onto Financial News Network? It will find a spot on your intelligent surface other than where your coffee cup happens to be resting.

Want to use your mouse? Then use it. Would you rather use voice, or gestures, or paint with an electronic brush? Do so. The interfaces of tomorrow will allow you to work the way you feel most comfortable at the moment. They will also allow those with limitations to do the same. Today, enabling technology often means building special devices for people with disabilities, but the same flexibility that will allow most people to shift rapidly among methods will bring the disabled fully into the fold. Enabling technology can and should be approached as a technique for helping everyone.

Physical Infrastructure

The revolution of the computer has outstripped the ability of the infrastructure to keep up. During the next decade, we will bring computer and infrastructure back into closer balance.

A primary function for computers today is presentation preparation. The resulting presentation is then often converted into slides[5] and projected using late-nineteenth-century technology. This limits the power of users in several ways, not the least of which is that presentations must often be completely planned in advance, particularly when slides, rather than overheads, are used.

Tomorrow, we'll plug our portable computer into a readily available high-definition interactive video projector—and the combination will work. A projector won't be a available? We'll take one with us. They will weigh only 5 or 10 pounds. The presentation software of tomorrow will allow changes on the fly, so that presenters will no longer be forced to fall back on hand waving upon the first change in direction dictated by the needs or desires of the audience.

Few conference rooms are equipped with video projectors, and even when such a room is found, connecting equipment to it usually becomes a nightmare. We will need to work toward standards, so that the infrastructure can begin to fill in.

Another aspect of infrastructure will be public networks. Our scenarios play around with such ideas as low-power radio networks on transportation systems, public terminals in airports, and fiberoptic home and hotel networks. These kinds of networks will become available in the next ten years. The computer industry needs to see that this infrastructure is being designed to fit our needs as well as those of our customers. We must guard against any more instances like the upside-down keypads on our nation's phones or rectangular TV pixels, seriously limiting their compatibility with computers.

Tomorrow's machines will also become "aware" of activities just beyond the confines of the screen. Armed with an array of input

....
5 People with their own printers have little problem with this step. Those of us using community printers soon discover that as soon as we switch to transparency stock, someone else, unaware of what we are up to, will invariably come online and start printing an unexpectedly transparent, 500-page report.

sensors, like built-in "awareness" devices in bookcases, desk drawers, cars, and refrigerators, your personal agents will be able to extend their domain well beyond the edges of your sensitive surface. This increasing power will generate even more need for privacy and security.

CHAPTER 9

Information

*T*he first 30 years of the personal computer revolution concentrated on providing people with a tool for the generation of information. Over the next 30 years, we will face the task of focusing the same level of intensity on delivering information. After some 4,000 years, we have little better access to the teachings of our elders than did the Babylonians in 2000 B.C.E. They trekked to the library. We trek to the library.[1] Computers hold the promise of bringing the power of the U.S. Library of Congress, in all the grandeur of its 100 million documents, into every office, home, briefcase, sailboat, off-road vehicle, and wristwatch.

We could accomplish this aim from a technological point of view by either putting the Library of Congress online or capturing it in ROM, if the publishing community were to sit still for it.[2] This, however, is not nearly enough. Knowing a needle lies in the haystack is all well and good, but only if you have a very large magnet with which to search. Agents will be those magnets, and while they will gain in power over the next half-century, for now we are probably better off placing our needles in constructs more easily examined.

Prolific Publication

The power of the Internet is that anyone, anywhere, can produce and publish anything. Unfortunately, they are. By mid-1995, 20,000 "home pages" were dotting the World Wide Web, with hundreds more appearing

....

1 More accurately, they did everything possible to avoid trekking to the library, and most of us do too. Ain't a whole lotta trekking going on.

2 Nanotechnology, that science of making things really, really small, holds the promise of fitting 30 million volumes on a single chip. A four-chip computer could hold the Library of Congress, with room left over for every episode of "I Love Lucy."

every week—most of them of low information value. Commercial home pages acted as surrogate reception rooms, lined with corporate propaganda and armed with an electronic receptionist that might or might not help you find your way. Private home pages were, for the most part, little better, acting as an entrance hall in which, in the preelectronic age, we might have displayed our most prized physical possessions. Bowling trophies spring to mind.[3]

Most of the creative use of the Web occurred early on at the world's colleges and universities, but these quality sites became progressively harder to find as the sheer volume of pages climbed. As the HTML (hypertext mark-up language) tools for creating home pages become simpler and more "user friendly," home page propagation will accelerate. It is conceivable that by the turn of the century, they will number in the tens of millions.

Many people expect that the publishing empires we know today will crumble in the face of individual home pages, as the need for physical production and distribution falls away. They are depending on the power of agents to help people seek out and somehow concentrate these private ramblings no matter where in the world they might be found. Don't write off publishers just yet.

Home pages will continue as sources of narrowly defined information. Want to know where your nearest Gap store is? Instead of using the Yellow Pages, check out the Gap home page. Need the school soccer schedule for next week? You might today pick up the phone and call the coach. In a few years, you will be confident you can surf to her home page and, with suitable authentication, look at the schedule for yourself.

As commercial and nonprofit information providers join the net, home pages will be joined by new objects, acting as entryways into the organized information spaces of tomorrow. All the players in today's information world will be standing at the door to greet us.

Publishers

Publishers traditionally have been the manufacturers and distributors of books, films, recordings, and other tangible information

....
3 In March 1995, one individual protested the dearth of Web content by devoting his own home page to a photograph of his toilet. Within hours, it became one of the most frequently visited locations on the net.

objects.[4] As owners of the press, they have exercised considerable control over available content. The anarchists of the net have been joyous over the prospect of breaking what they see as this yoke of oppression, but before we release the oxen, we need to consider the value that publishers have traditionally added.

Publishers do more than print and ship. They select, edit, and concentrate information. Publishers are our first line of defense against mediocrity of effort and result. Their looming presence provides a discipline to budding artists and writers, causing them to focus on their audience and take the time to develop their ideas before committing them to paper or film.

We are not lacking in informational output in this country. American print publishers ship tens of thousands of new books every year. We still have scores of newspapers, and the number of magazines is growing by leaps and bounds. To date, much of the information on the net, to be found in the various news groups, has been dilute, filled with half-truths and innuendo, and accompanied by emotional torrents and personal attack.

Least I raise the ire of net purists, I am firmly committed to news groups and chats and all other anarchic forums continuing unabated. (Not that my opinion matters; they will continue anyway.) However, they must and will be joined by other more stable information platforms.

We will not just see the usual lineup of mass media publishers. They are already being joined by legions of "zine" publishers—individuals whose personalities, openly expressed, reflect clearly and concisely their biases and criteria. The democratizing effect of a truly free press will be felt. Mediocrity will be what falls before the onslaught of the publishers, not breadth of viewpoint and experience.

Publishers on the net will engage in retail and wholesale operations. If you know you want the hypermedia edition of *Tog on Software Design,* you will be able to travel directly to Addison-Wesley and download it from the publisher's "stores." If you only know you want something on software design, even though it be from a different author (not generally recommended), you could instead visit your favorite media store or library.

....

4 In the movie and TV industry, publishers are called "studios," but their role has been essentially the same.

Media Stores and Libraries

The differentiation between bookstores and libraries will soon disappear. As Negroponte (1995) has pointed out, when bits replace atoms, selling and lending become the same thing. Public-supported libraries would have a natural advantage over bookstores were they able to open up their stacks, but intellectual property lawyers are seeing that they cannot.[5]

When the dust settles, today's public libraries joining the net may well offer cyberspace views onto our publishers' works, but we will pay for the privilege of browsing. With a proper financial model in place, however, the cost for our wanderings will be pennies, not dollars.

The quality independent bookstores of today may well become the online specialty media shops of tomorrow, offering up-to-date selections that might be laborious to uncover in a more mammoth setting.

Bookstores and libraries are not the only distributors of today's information. We now have an extensive infrastructure for distributing entertainment, sports, and television news. (I talked about some of the changes we can expect in their distribution in Chapter 4.)

Organizers

Organizers will offer indexing, linking, and annotation services.

Indexing services are already appearing in nascent form on the World Wide Web. By having the address of a single home page index, the Web surfer can choose from a filtered selection of interesting places to jump. Today these indexes tend to be assembled for fun and for free at major universities. Soon commercial services will join them.

Organizers will not stop at simply getting people to a document. They will also give them a hand once they are there. People will subscribe to annotation services that will yellow-highlight key points within documents and form reference links to related material. These highlights and links will be used by both humans and their software agents as they traverse the material.

....

[5] Under the fair use doctrine, our nation's schoolchildren are now gaining free run of the electronic libraries. Their parents are not.

Organizers will not act to exclude information but rather to make more sense of it. As an example, newspapers are organized temporally: everything that happened today is there today. If you want to find out something that just happened, a newspaper, with its temporal organization, is structured perfectly. If you want to go back and explore the course of an event that unfolded over weeks or months, the original organization of a newspaper is of little use.

Periodicals, paper or microfilmed, also fail to update themselves as new information comes in. For example, on May 18, 1993, President Clinton had his hair cut inside *Air Force One*, which was parked at the time on a runway at Los Angeles International Airport. It was widely reported over the next several days that hundreds, perhaps thousands, of passengers had been left stranded, cluttering lounges or circling the airport, with no way to land. The cost estimates for the haircut fiasco ranged into the hundreds of thousands of dollars.

More than one month later, when an intrepid reporter from *Newsday* explored the airline, airport, and FAA records by then filed about all the aircraft involved, a different picture emerged: one single unscheduled air taxi flight was delayed for exactly 2 minutes. No other take-off or landing was in any way delayed (*Newsday* 1993).

If you go to your library today and look back at the newspapers for May 19 and 20, 1993, you will still read about the terrible crisis Clinton caused at the airport, as you should: the original text of record should remain, errors included. What should be added, however, is a note with a link to the follow-up article. The note should read, "Never mind."

Similarly, information and theories presented in scientific articles are often superseded, but if you look back at the original, you will usually fail to find a note reading, "It turned out the dude was wrong." In the legal literature, perhaps the best organized today, organizers do form forward links in a process called "shepardizing." In the future, independent annotation services (and the periodicals themselves) will be shepardizing, adding notes, and attaching more substantial sidebar articles.

In Starfire, the magazine articles that Julie pulled up in the boardroom were yellow-highlighted. At some point five years previously, someone had laid the groundwork that allowed Julie to ask for a single article and be presented with the entire arsenal she needed. Someone noticed the follow-up article. Someone formed a link to the *Los Angeles Chronicle*. It might have been Julie herself, it might have been her friend Natalie, it might have been a professional annotator. It made what would otherwise have been an impossible job for a computer agent simple.

Criticism and Review

Traditionally, critics and reviewers whom we are likely to hear have worked for large publishers and organizations. Now we are hearing more independent voices as the cost of publishing and distribution plummet. Regardless of who was the reviewer, they can offer little beyond their opinion except a generalized pointer toward our nearest bookstore, theater, or video rental counter, where we may or may not find the work in question.

On the net, when you reach the end of a review, you may soon click on a link to download the product reviewed. The line between reviewer and specialized media store could thus blur—with the potentially unfortunate effect of making reviews suspect, as good reviews will be more likely than bad to result in sales and revenue. Certain network television reviewers, whose stations make huge profits off movie advertising, are notorious for finding redeeming value in the worst of offerings. On the other hand, most newspaper reviewers maintain high marks for playing it straight, regardless of advertising revenues. Time will tell how corrosive revenue tie-ins will prove.

With direct access to documents through reviewers, many people may choose to do their shopping through a trusted reviewer instead of visiting either media stores or publishers. The downside is that this may tend to fragment cybersociety in the same manner that viewpoint-driven news sources do today. The upside is that people will not face the prospect of 100 million documents. They will be able to pick and choose among a small, prereviewed subset of material that, at least in the eyes of the reviewer, represents the best there is.

Notes and Votes

Individuals should have absolute freedom to mark up any document that crosses their work surfaces. (These markups are not incorporated into the author's work. They are equivalent to the kinds of handwritten markups students apply to textbooks today.) Small groups of people will often want to share these markups, secure in their knowledge of who did the markups and what level of trust that person's work deserves.

Larger groups, such as corporations or universities, may also want to share markups, but they may begin to want to apply some controls. With 10,000 people all chattering away, such annotations could begin to take on some of the aspects of chaos.

We will need mechanisms on the net to enable people to make notes and yet not overwhelm the original material. People should be able to challenge others' notes, and mechanisms should be provided to repeal notes that are proved to be inaccurate. Other mechanisms must prevent the removal of notes simply because the opinions expressed are unpopular. The notation environment should be rich, allowing notes to grow greater in prominence when more people quote from them and to fade toward oblivion when they are ignored.

As important as notes will be votes. Several services on the net are already asking that people judge both the services and the individual contributions. Hill and associates (1995) collected data from 291 people as to their opinions of 1,750 different films and amassed a database with more than 55,000 ratings. They then performed statistical analyses to be able to group people of similar taste and used the system to predict whether people would like films they had not yet seen. Jakob Nielsen (1995) found the system to be "fairly successful . . . with a correlation of 0.62 between the system's prediction of how well people would like a film and the actual rating given by users. In comparison, the correlation between ratings from nationally-known movie critics and the users' own ratings was only 0.22." It is unclear whether the low correlation with movie reviewers reflects the true state of affairs. People often use the opinions of reviewers conservatively, after noticing where they and a given reviewer's taste differs. Nevertheless, statistical analysis opens the way for effective machine criticism and review, offering capabilities that will make agents look clever and alert.[6]

Commercial Speech

People in America are now hit with 1,500 advertising impressions per day, according to low industry estimates. (Some estimates are more than double that figure.) Advertising is not about truth; it is about

----

6 They also raise significant privacy issues. See Chapter 36.

selling a product or service. Open access to information will overcome some of its more obvious abuses. When you see an ad quoting a movie review that says, for example:

"I . . . love it! . . . See it now!" —*Los Angeles Examiner*

you will be able to access the original text instantly:

"*I hated this film. In fact, only a fool could* love it! *Don't* See It Now *or Ever!*"

Advertising does not stop where content leaves off. We already have information spaces that are not quite as they appear. For example, the big airlines reservation systems are designed to sell seats on their sponsors' airplanes, not to see that you get to your destination on the most reasonable route, at the best time, and at the lowest fare. *Consumer Reports Travel Letter* notes that airline "reservation computers are sales tools, not information utilities. Even when the system itself isn't biased, it can carry biased information. Finding an attractive price in the computer is no guarantee that it's the best deal" (Perkins 1993). Soon every airline may have a reservation portal. Your personal electronic travel agent may do the necessary comparison shopping, removing the bias of today's systems, owned and operated by a few major carriers.[7]

Reduced cost of distribution may mean more advertisement-free sources. *Consumer Reports* may soon be joined by legions of specialty testing and reporting services, beholden to no one and able to spend their revenues on experiments and explorations instead of ink, paper, and stamps.

Most of today's computer and technical magazines could not publish and distribute without advertising revenues from the very companies they review. This has led to the strange sight of magazine columnists' condemning a recent software release as junk while the

....

7 In the spring of 1995, the airlines began to put the squeeze on travel agencies, significantly reducing their potential revenues. Travel agencies came into being when selecting and placing reservations was a daunting task. It may be the airlines now realize that, with simple telephone and cyberspace reservation systems firmly in place, the need for human travel agents may be drawing to an end.

"official" reviews find much to recommend it. As these magazines leave the real world in favor of cyberspace, some may discover they can drop manufacturer advertising, remove bias from their reports, and make more money at the same time.

If you flicked on your TV 20 years ago, you were likely to be greeted by an obnoxious parent surrogate yelling in your ear, "You have bad breath, baaaaad breath!" Or a friendly coworker chanting, "Ring around the collar, RING AROUND THE COLLAR!" Now many people collect Coca-Cola commercials the way people collected limited edition prints in an earlier era. What drove the change? Artistic integrity? Human decency? No. Remote control.

Time-dependent advertising (TV-type commercials) will make little inroad into cyberspace. Few people will put up with a 30-second jingle as the price of admission into a chat room. Ads appearing now are in the form of static visuals, similar to what might be found in a magazine or newspaper.

Many new ads will likely be hypermedia links to further content. Advertising will thus take on a greater role in offering people straight information rather than acting simply as psychological motivators. Cyberspace will also offer the opportunity for conditional advertising: magazines such as *HotWired* will be able to offer a low subscription price with advertising, a higher one without.

Advertising will likely become one of the most powerful economic forces driving increased bandwidth and capabilities in our information infrastructure. Newspapers turned to color in the past decade not to please readers but to keep the support of advertisers who were hearing the TV siren song of sound, color, and animation. Even the *New York Times,* the venerable "gray lady" of the publishing world, was not immune to the sight of falling advertising revenues.

Advertisers have to tread very softly now, as they pump their images over the wire. People will not accept their screens' locking up for long intervals as unsolicited advertising images slowly materialize. They would be even less receptive to moving images whose transfer might lock up their systems for minutes at a time, but these are just the sorts of images that advertisers would dearly love to place. Advertisers will make it clear that the money will flow when our network capabilities grow.

Envisioning Information

Making huge amounts of information accessible and comprehensible to regular people may prove to be the biggest challenge of human–computer interaction over the next century.

Data can be highly compressed with good information design. Consider the clock. If we want to know the local time, looking at a simple digital or analog clock or watch will solve our problem admirably (Figure 9.1).

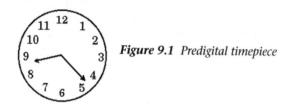

Figure 9.1 *Predigital timepiece*

Problems arise, however, when we need to contact someone outside our own time zone. People have come up with one workable solution for that problem, involving a multiplicity of clocks, each with a representative city as a label (Figure 9.2). This solution works admirably if, for example, you want to call London. But if you want to call Barcelona, you had better be up on your geography and knowledge of time zone borders, so you'll know what reference city to pick (London).

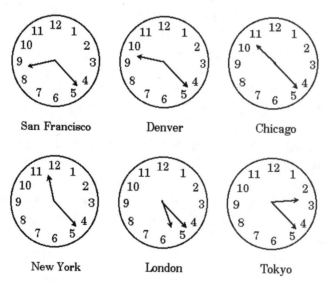

Figure 9.2 *Wall o' Time*

Figure 9.3 *The Geochron clock*

Geochron on March 21/September 21.

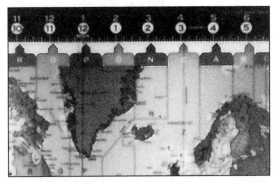

Close-up of Geochron showing time zone letters and corresponding local times. Standard time is in white circles.

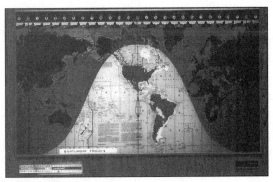

Geochron on December 21.

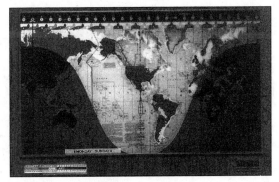

Geochron on June 21.

The disjointed data in this scheme tend to keep people slavishly dependent on the array of clocks. Because of the isolated nature of the data points (individual clock readings), most people do not form an internalized picture of the time relationships among the cities presented.

The Geochron clock,[8] invented by James Kilburg, gives people a way of not only ascertaining what time it is in isolated communities, but what the relationship is between time and geography (Figure 9.3). The Geochron aids several dimensions of visualization. First, each time zone, displayed on a familiar continuous surface (a map of the world), points toward its own local time. Rather than highlighting a few representative cities, the Geochron shows hundreds of them, like any other world map. It goes further: by heightened illumination, the clock lets

....
8 Geochron Enterprises Inc. in Redwood City, California.

the user instantly see where the sun is shining. The shape of the illumination changes over the seasons of the year.[9]

Making the annual sun cycle visible helps people build a model of the effects of the passing seasons. However, even if the clock never cycled from its spring display, it would still enable people to tell at a glance, from 10 or 20 feet away, whether the person they want to call could be expected to be up and around. It does all this and more in a fraction of the space of the array of wall clocks it replaces.

The Challenger: *An Information Disaster*

Why did the space shuttle *Challenger* explode? Many people assume it was because of poorly functioning O rings on the booster rocket. However, those O rings didn't send that ship up on a cold winter's morn. People did, and those people drew their most critical information from two simple charts, screened by an overhead projector (Figure 9.4). The graphs displayed tiny pictures of each shuttle booster, lined up in chronological order, showing launch temperatures and any O ring damage. They looked like so many crayons in a box, and when the engineers and managers finished looking at them, they didn't know any more than they had before. The launch was made, and seven people died.

Figure 9.5 contains the information the *Challenger* engineers looked at but could not see, reorganized by one of the world's foremost experts on envisioning information, Edward Tufte.

Poorly constructed overhead slides don't normally kill people, but they do often leave people in the dark. Tufte, author of the seminal works *The Visual Design of Quantitative Information* and *Envisioning Information,* demonstrates time and time again how careful design of information can communicate in a single glance information that might take hours or weeks of effort to ferret out in its raw form. Just as important as new, clean software design in the coming decade will be designs that result in equally clear information.

....

9 One inch equals 1 hour. To figure out how long it will be from now until sunset, for example, you need only lay a ruler on the map and read the distance from your location to the trailing edge of the sun's position. If the distance is 3½ inches, sunset will occur in 3½ hours. This is a bit eerie until you get used to it.

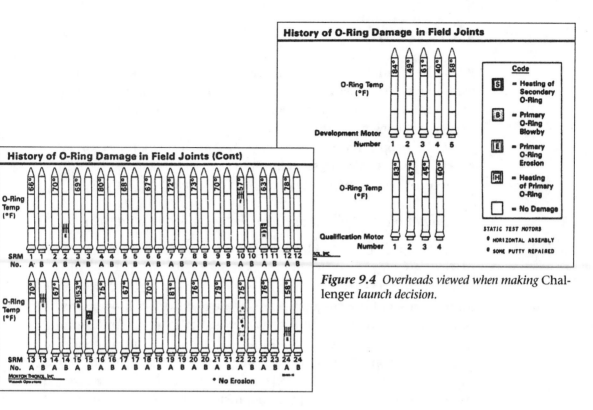

Figure 9.4 *Overheads viewed when making* Challenger *launch decision.*

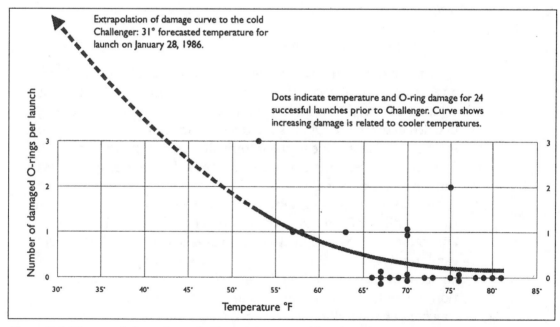

Figure 9.5 *The same information as in Figure 9.4, presented in a form that even a child could understand. (Tufte, Edward R.* Visual Explanations. *Cheshire, CT: Graphics Press, 1996. Reprinted with permission.)*

Retrieval

People have at least two motivations for seeking information: they want to retrieve a specific piece of information they know exists, or they want to explore a given region of the information space in search of new and relevant information.

When people already know what they are looking for, we should give it to them in the most rapid, straightforward way possible. This is no time for pretty visual interfaces or easy-to-learn type-in boxes.

Do not place "helpful barriers" between people and their work.

Today's artificially intelligent front ends to databases have been a grave disappointment. Usually the designers have set about to allow "natural language input," when in reality they support only a severely limited subset of the language. Even those few words supported usually have sharply restricted definitions. Users suffer extreme confusion as they struggle to travel up an invisible learning curve, trying combination after combination of normal, everyday words, secretly converted into a cryptic code. The learning curve is many times more severe than were the words completely made up, instead of pretending to be normal and familiar.

Make agents' jobs simple.

For the short term, we need to place the burden for information annotation and interpretation on people, reducing the challenge of creating an effective agent to a manageable level. With a sufficiently detailed description, agents should be able to fetch a document within seconds from anywhere in the information space. Should the user have failed to provide enough detail, agents should be offered questions they can ask to narrow the field.

Agents will be successful not because they are capable of inferring the "meaning" of a given piece of material but because the author or annotator will have supplied the raw material from which the agent can form its queries. Users will experience the illusion that they have an agent of great discernment. They will really only have an information system that is well constructed, well organized, and a snap to traverse—at 500 million instructions per second.

Construct metaphorical views onto the information space.

No one can "see" 100,000,000 documents. The very thought can make a body's head spin. Fortunately, most of us will never need access to more than a thin fraction of that total information. Metaphorical views can offer us a custom look into this vast world, one that will enlighten rather than overwhelm.

A first approximation of such a view might be drawn from the famous *New Yorker* cover showing a map of the world as seen through the eyes of a typical New Yorker. Manhattan island looms large, while Los Angeles and Japan appear as tiny dots, and Indianapolis appears not at all. To a great extent, this is the way most of us maintain our information spaces now. Those items of most interest to us line our bookshelves and stuff our file cabinets. We subscribe to information services that most directly affect us. We learn to cull from the Sunday paper all those sections that hold so little promise they are not worth pursuing.

Our information spaces, through design and evolution, could take on such a metaphorical view: subject areas in which we have expressed interest can begin to take on greater prominence and proximity. Areas in which we have shown no inclination to explore can fade further and further into the background—never disappearing, only receding.

Over the next decade people will be trying out dozens, perhaps hundreds, of new metaphors and ideas. If we are to have a rich information space, we will want many of these ideas to survive. Diversity, not uniformity, should be our cause.

Principles for Content Providers

Content enrichment will be the task of tomorrow's information suppliers: writers, artists, producers, directors. Here should be their first principle:

Make information easy to understand and absorb.

Implementing this principle will be different depending on the medium involved. Let us explore this principle from the writer's point of view.

Write clearly. Use the active voice, and avoid obscure vocabulary.

The largest barrier to understanding literature, particularly scientific literature, is bad writing. Amateur writers have learned to obfuscate at every turn. They have been taught by equally bad writers to avoid active voice ("we discovered that") in favor of passive voice ("it was found that") to ensure the appearance of objectivity. Unfortunately, they too often achieve only incomprehensibility.

Writers adopt jargon and obscure vocabulary as a secret code to demonstrate that they are members in good standing of the in-crowd. This practice is a catastrophe to the free flow of information and should be avoided at all costs. Every profession needs specialized vocabulary to cover objects and concepts that do not exist outside the profession, but most go far beyond necessity. Clear writing does not mean writing everything at a third-grade level. It means writing for peers with differing backgrounds who have no time to stumble through purposeful obscurities.

Chaos theory was first hit upon by a meteorologist in 1961, but it didn't begin to gain recognition throughout the scientific community until the 1970s (Gleick 1987). Why? The first guy, Edward Lorenz, wrote it up in a meteorological publication. Weatherpeople didn't grasp its importance, and no one else read it for a lot of years.

A single, universal information space promises to launch a strong attack on the problems of access and distribution that have prevented scientists and engineers from peeking beyond their own limited bailiwicks. It would be tragic if people could at last find the works they needed, only to discover they couldn't understand them.

Write to structure.

Information embodied in the clearest writing in the world is of no use if people cannot find it. Future content providers must bear the responsibility of making their material not only far more accessible to their human users but also to computer agents.

Unlike most other writing, scientific papers are already written to a structure. Unfortunately, once one transcends the boundaries of a single paper, chaos reigns supreme. In the field of medicine alone, close to 20 feet of medical research is refereed and published each year, none of it structurally interrelated. Papers referring to each other are rarely to be found together in their original sources. A simple search soon turns into a nightmare.

The content-provider community needs to develop far more communicative structures for all writing, structures that will make the task of organization simpler for our human agents and enable our first-generation agents to locate and extract the information they need. We could approach the problem by requiring that people write in such a rigid structure that the agent could, for example, look at the last sentence of paragraph 5 in any document to find out how many, if any, experiments were run. Rather than a structure that represses expression, we need to explore structures that might result in far more expressiveness than scientific papers now allow. Meanwhile, software designers must ensure that the needs of agents do not supersede the needs of their human masters.

PART 3

Managing the Future

The past 10 years have produced great change in the power of personal computers. Ten years ago, most of us were lucky to have 128 kilobytes of memory. Today many people enjoy 1,000 times that much. Today's computers are much faster—as much as 200 times faster than the computer of 1985—and speeds are increasing every day.

Ten years ago, the average PC had a black and white (or black and green) display. A few lucky individuals sported perhaps 16 fixed colors. Today most displays feature 256 colors drawn from a rich palette; soon the industry will move to 16,777,216 colors as standard equipment.

In the face of all these changes, software design has remained stable. The interface of today is barely changed from that of a decade ago. Applications are bigger (and slower), people have larger monitors with more windows and a whole bunch more icons, but other than that, everything has stayed pretty much the same.

Change is in the wind. The next hardware revolution is already upon us; the next software revolution has begun. It will be our job as managers, as developers, as designers, and as users to increase the pace. It took almost 30 years for the software revolution, in the form of the World Wide Web and Mosaic, to catch up with the Internet of the sixties.[1] To retain its role as world

....
1 The name Internet officially came into being in 1981, but the network itself began with the ARPAnet, first put online by the Defense Department's Advanced Research Projects Agency in 1969. (The Internet's packet store-and-forward architecture was originally designed to enable the system to keep functioning even though parts of the net had been destroyed during a nuclear war. This architecture resulted in a remarkably reliable, resilient system, but also made the system impervious to efforts at central government control.)

leader in software technology, America won't have another 30 years to catch up with today.

Staying ahead of users in the next ten years will be a tall order. The designs of the late 1970s we are hobbled with today fall far short of the mark. Quick fixes to software systems will not suffice; we are going to have to rethink the fundamentals of both hardware and software if we are to compete in the world market.

The industry is not lacking in either design talent or fresh ideas. We have only lacked a willingness to implement. This section will offer managers at all levels, from line to CEO, guidance in changing direction, in building teams that can generate competitive differences in appearance, usability, and quality of design. The competition is building. None of us wants to be left behind.

Nehru Jacket Computers

More than ten years since the Macintosh took form, people continue to copy the original faithfully.[1] Oh, sure, the windows have a different appearance and the menus pop up, in, out, and around instead of just pulling down, but for all practical purposes, we've made little change. The reason seems traceable to a firmly held belief that somehow the folks at Apple hit upon the ideal interface in the early eighties and that the best anyone can do now is to duplicate it.

Apple ran a multipage magazine ad in the early eighties extolling the virtues of word processing over typing. The ad displayed a series of drafts of a business letter revealing the story of a knock-off clothing manufacturer in Los Angeles that decided to duplicate a designer-original Nehru jacket. The LA folks had sent a sample of the jacket to their Far East supplier and received back ten thousand copies. They were now writing to the supplier to complain about the accuracy of the supplier's duplication effort. It seems the boys in the Far East had not only duplicated collar, cuffs, lapels, and buttons but had painstakingly reproduced a cigarette burn that showed rather glaringly on the left sleeve. The first draft of the letter was addressed, "Dear Cloth-brained Fools" and went downhill from there. The final draft began, "Dear Sirs or Madams."[2]

....

[1] A portion of this chapter was originally published in A. B. Farrand et al., "Common Elements in Today's Graphical User Interfaces: The Good, the Bad, and the Ugly," proceedings of INTERCHI, 1993 (Amsterdam, The Netherlands, April 24-29, 1993). ACM, New York, 1993, pp. 472-473.

[2] The campaign was designed by Chiat/Day, the agency described in Chapter 1.

Burning Clones

The copiers of the Macintosh have also been carefully reproducing a series of "cigarette burns" associated with the Macintosh's original design, flaws that seriously detract from the functionality of the resulting systems. The Macintosh people never wanted to include these drawbacks; they were dictated by the limitations of the original hardware.

The Macintosh started out with 128 kilobytes of memory, a 9-inch black-and-white computer with a single, single-sided, floppy disk drive and no hard disk. This design led inexorably toward a number of critical decisions from which not only today's Macintosh suffers but also all the other visual interfaces that are such faithful copies.

What follow are a few examples of the decisions forced by the original Macintosh design and the alternatives that await the fleet of foot.

Documents Inside of Tools

We have come to accept that the way to create or edit a document is to open that document inside an application, or tool. This is equivalent to having to slide your entire house inside a hammer before you can hang a picture on the wall or having to put your teeth inside your toothbrush before you can brush them.

The alternative is Starfire's document-centered design. Tear off a piece of fresh stationery, and do with it what you will. Place a picture here, work out a spreadsheet there, lay some text in behind it. Tools—any tools—are brought to bear on a single, final compound document.

Why don't we have the compound document model in use today? Because the Macintosh was a 128-kilobyte machine with a single disk drive. A user couldn't possibly have more than one tool in the computer at any one time because there wasn't room. Since only one tool could be used with a document, then the tool might as well handle the opening and closing of that document.

The Apple Lisa and Xerox Star computers that preceded the Macintosh were both document-centered machines. They weren't copied because the Macintosh was the first commercially successful windowing system. It was the computer all the copiers saw, and they never revisited the decision.

Today, through OLE and OpenDoc, the industry is finally building a semblance of a document-centered machine. It's a start but falls short of what we will need for the real thing. (See Chapter 19.) The coming object-oriented operating systems and Sun's Java "applets" will support tool sets and other independent objects. Objects and applets will be the mammals of the future, as the overgrown, overblown application dinosaurs of today finally rumble to the ground. More on this later.

Explicit Save

In most applications on the Macintosh—and all at its introduction—users had to save their work, explicitly, or it would be lost. This approach has resulted in a six-month cycle of doom that begins the day the power goes out when we haven't saved for the last 2 hours. After exhausting our store of epithets, we all swear we will never, ever forget to save every 2.3 minutes again. And for the first night we don't. By the end of the first week, we are up to 15 minutes between saves. Then 20. Then 30, and by the time 6 months rolls around, we are back up to 2 hours, primed for the next power failure.

We are the lucky ones. Not so lucky are our new users who have no inkling of just how hostile a monster they really have. Take the case of the poor fool who spent 8 hours typing in his theories on some of the deeper questions of the universe. When he finally attempted to quit the application, the program inquired, "Save changes?" He had never saved anything during the 8 hours, so he wasn't quite sure how to interpret "changes," but he eventually came to the conclusion the computer wanted to know whether he wanted to save the last few changes he'd made during the last few minutes. Since he really wasn't too thrilled with them, he clicked on the No button. In less than 14 microseconds, his 8 hours of work disappeared forever.

Why don't our so-called friendly computers better protect our work? Because on a 128-kilobyte machine with a tiny, single disk drive, it was impossible to have both the program disk and the data disk in the computer at the same time. And the program disk had to be there most of the time, because there wasn't enough room in memory for all of the program, so program segments had to be swapped in off the disk all the time. Hence, there was normally no disk in the computer to which the computer could save. Another faithfully reproduced cigarette burn in windowing systems designed for multi-megabyte computers with resident hard disks. Continuous save, discussed in some detail in Chapter 24, is the cure.

Trash Can Subject to Indigestion

Among the longest-running claims of the Apple–Microsoft–Hewlett-Packard lawsuit was Apple's contention that Hewlett-Packard wrongfully adopted the idea of the bulging trash can to indicate that someone had dropped something in it (Samuelson 1993). Never mind the legal niceties of the copyright law; these lawyers were arguing over company B's reproducing company A's mistake. The trash can shouldn't bulge to begin with.

On the original Macintosh, the trash would fill up disks, without notice, leaving no room for new documents. Rather than fixing the problem—which we eventually did in System 7—an engineer invented an icon that made the trash can appear to be in great gastric distress if the tiniest file were slid into it. The result was that new users, fearing for the health and safety of the can, developed the habit of emptying the trash each and every time they dropped anything in. This completely eliminated the principle that drove the design of the trash can in the first place: forgiveness. With the trash can empty within 2 or 3 seconds of a document's entering it, its intrinsic undo was undone.

Second-Generation Visual Interfaces

The Macintosh interface is almost a decade old. The computers of today don't sport 128-kilobytes of memory; they sport 128 megabytes of memory. Gigabyte hard disks are all around us, and terabyte storage is waiting in the wings. The assumptions that drove the design of the Macintosh have not been valid for at least ten years, and they will not be valid tomorrow. It is time to get on with the task of developing the interfaces that will leave the doddering old Macintosh interface in the dust, even as the Macintosh left the command line interface of old in the dust behind it.

The interfaces to be built in the coming decade will break down the barriers that plague us today. Tool sets will be brought to bear on any document the user wishes. Documents will be protected from loss at all times. Things like spurious menus and objects that work under some conditions and not others will be swept aside in favor of a tightly integrated visual environment that is far more in tune with the exploding task needs of users.

The Macintosh is not the perfect interface that will live forever. People are no longer doing text editing; they are doing page layout and document processing. People are no longer doing black-and-white doodles; they are manipulating true-color images, editing video, and building 3D rotational models. They are no longer trying to search out the memo they wrote last week; they are wandering the Internet, looking for a half-remembered quotation in Livy's *The History of Rome* or a video clip from last Sunday's "Meet the Press." These new tasks require a new level of power and simplicity.

It is impossible today for anyone but the richest of corporations to bring out a new word processor application, instantly supplying the breadth and depth of current offerings. With tool sets on top of a document-centered, object-oriented, applet-enhanced operating system, individuals (or corporate information systems departments) will assemble their own word processors, using a well-designed text processor bought from one company, coupled with a spell checker from another. They will then select their graphics tool set, their outlining function, and a myriad of other possible add-ons, many of these potentially the product of small 1- to 10-person shops. Their dictionary and thesaurus will be bought directly from the information provider or accessed throught the net.

Users will benefit by being able to put together flexible systems that meet their needs without a lot of useless features.[3] The independent developer community, with its attendant creativity and energy, will be revitalized. About the only possible losers will be those large application software developers today enjoying their seemingly unassailable positions. Is it just coincidence that some of these are also the operating system suppliers that ensure the continuation of these monopolies?

....

3 Studies of word processors and spreadsheets typically find that most people use only a small percentage of features. The problem developers face today is that different people are using different subsets.

Several companies are hard at work today on object-oriented systems. Any one of these, armed with an architecture supporting document-centricity, tightly integrating with the coming revolution in network applets, could be the foundation of the software breakthrough so long overdue. If done right, the software design world will come alive as it has not been for years. The first company to really go back to the drawing board, eliminate all the obsolete assumptions of the past, and build a new interface responsive to needs and abilities of today's sophisticated users can expect as great a win as Apple experienced with the original Macintosh.[4]

....

[4] Don't feel bad for the copiers out there when it happens: they're desperate for a new interface to come along so they can begin knocking off the next generation.

Managing Software Designers

*T*he only way to ensure your product design will offer high productivity and low training costs is to hire experienced, competent software designers, either full time or as consultants. Software designers can be recruited at the annual conventions of ACM/CHI, Human Factors Society, ACM/CSCW, or ACM/UIST.[1] They also respond to newspaper ads placed in papers close to the technology centers: Boston; Silicon Valley; Raleigh, North Carolina; and Seattle.

Fifteen years ago, microcomputer software products were typically conceived of, designed, coded, and often even documented by programmers working in isolation. These efforts tended to produce software that only other programmers could love, filled with cryptic codes, blank screens with blinking cursors, all based on the popular "black cave" wander-around-until-you-hit-a-wall metaphor.

Times have changed. Today's market leaders depend on teams of specialists: architects, programmers, behavioral designers, graphic designers, usability testers, writers, video directors, even marketers. The change has not been an easy one for the engineers. The same move toward specialization that took our wildly accelerated industry 15 years took over 150 years in the medical profession and more than 1,500 years in the building trades.

....
1 The Association for Computing Machinery/Computer–Human Interaction; Computer-Supported Cooperative Work; UserInterface Systems Technology.

Medicine

One hundred and fifty years ago, most doctors were either general practitioners or barber-surgeons. Surgeons spent the majority of their time cutting hair, occasionally taking a break to hack off a human limb or two. General practitioners split their time between holding people's hands while they died quietly in their sleep and holding people's hands while the surgeons sawed them off. (My wife, the Doctor, also points out they spent a fair amount of time wrangling leeches.) Then there was an explosion of technology, fed by the twin inventions of germs and anesthesia. All of a sudden, doctors could begin to prevent *and* treat infectious disease. All of a sudden, people could lie still for extensive surgical procedures, and surgeons were able to lay their hacksaws aside and pick up scalpels.

The explosion of technology resulted in an equal and continuing explosion of specialization. Can you imagine today going to either a general practitioner or, God help us all, a barber to get a triple bypass operation?

Building Trades

Originally folks designed and built their own dwellings. Later some of them might have worked for what today we would call general contractors, who would handle the business end of a retail operation, while the builders concentrated on masonry and wood.

With the advent of community buildings, the architect was born. These people, rather than concentrating on assembling stones or tying together bits of trees, thought in terms of people and the spaces they would occupy. Through their good offices, buildings moved beyond pure functionality. Religious and political architecture was born, designed to induce powerful emotions of awe and majesty in the visitor.

Earlier buildings had induced powerful emotions in visitors, but they were usually generated when the buildings fell on the visitors, which brings me to structural engineers. These worthy individuals, with the science they have developed, have freed architects to soar. The finer examples of modern architecture have all been achieved through a powerful fusion of structural engineering and contemporary architecture. This fusion is the same partnership shared by today's computer programmers and designers. The fusion of hard science, psychology, and art will build the information machines of the future.

How Software Designers Earn Their Keep

Good software designers, trained in human interaction and working in conjunction with usability testers, lower customer product training and support costs. They also reduce developer engineering costs. Everyone wins. Speculation? No. It's been proven at company after company (Bias and Mayhew 1994). We'll focus on just two areas where using software designers pays off big.

Reducing Technological Complexity

Many engineers panic at the sight of software designers, knowing these misguided do-gooders will not stop until every bit of power and performance is stripped from the product. Not true.

Let's look at a classic example of user-centered design for the most macho engineers in the world: astronauts. The time: December 1985. The project: Space station. The various pods that make up the space station are to be attached to a framework, built in 9-foot sections, that will ultimately stretch over the area of two football fields. As originally engineered, a team of two astronauts would emerge from the space shuttle to assemble each 9-foot section, fastening together the section's struts by tightening bolts, using various optional tools slung from rubber cords on each astronaut's arm. When tested in the underwater facility, it took more than 50 minutes to assemble a single 9-foot section. At $250,000 per hour, the costs of putting up two football fields worth of these things in space was prohibitive.

Enter Robert Glass, trained as a perceptual psychologist, acting as a human factors engineer. He watched the tapes of these astronauts clumsily trying to use earthbound tools in the simulated outer space. The astronauts, their gloves pressurized to 15 pounds per square inch, could barely grip the tools they were using, suffering fatigue and cramping. Meanwhile, the rest of the tools would float away from the astronauts' bodies, becoming tangled in the struts. In attempting a cranking motion, the astronauts ended up tangling their own bodies in the struts. It was Laurel and Hardy at a quarter million dollars per hour.

Dr. Glass started by studying what the astronauts could do when in a pressurized space suit. He measured the natural spread of their grip, the range of their arm movement, the effect of various types of movement on their body's stability. Then he worked in partnership with the engineers to build a whole new strut system requiring no tools. The struts themselves were the same diameter as an astronaut's resting grip. The ends of the struts would slide freely into waiting holes, after which the astronaut would make a single, low-effort downward movement to slide a sleeve toward the hole, locking the strut firmly into place.

When the astronauts hit the simulation tank again, it took them just over 3 minutes to assemble the new section. These ultimate power users performed their task more than *15 times faster,* and they were happy about it.

The cost per minute of orbital time is astronomical. This simple change will make America's future space station endeavors cost-effective.

Preventing "Human Error"

In the good old days, the nuclear industry paid little attention to human factors. Control room design was done with emphasis on efficient engineering layout and little thought for the people who would be using the rooms. What little layout planning did occur was typically performed by people with no training in human interaction design. They would apply principles that "just seemed like a good idea." (See Chapter 27.)

The nuclear industry didn't feel the need for human factors types. Their control rooms were working out just fine—right up until Three Mile Island. After so-called human error almost caused a disastrous meltdown, the nuclear industry went after human factors specialists in volume, resulting in a major advance in power station safety.

Our society likes to identify users who have made predictable errors and brand them as culprits. Around ten years ago in San Francisco, an armored car driver was making his rounds when the back door he'd forgotten to fasten opened up and a sack of cash, holding around $100,000, fell out of the back. The good citizen who found it apparently just couldn't locate a police station as hard as he must have tried, for the money was never turned in. The newspapers announced the verdict was human error on the part of the driver, but the real reason the money was lost was a lousy human interface design.

People do make mistakes—lots of them. One study cited by Abi Sellen in her doctoral dissertation (Sellen 1990) found that trained medication nurses gave one in seven doses in error (Barker et al. 1966). One critical job for human interface designers is predicting and preparing for error. Even the most novice human interface designer, faced with the back door on an armored car, would have fitted a one-dollar switch on the door lock, wired it to a doorbell by the driver, and connected them both to the ignition switch, so that starting the car without the door fastened would make the doorbell ring: 100,000-to-1 return on investment. Not bad.

It may be true that some customers will find a way to screw up even the clearest of processes—but this is not useful information. The attitude of development teams that produce minimal-error software is that the "customer is always right." Software designers are trained and talented in flagging errors before the product ships. Eliminating errors at the source saves users a lot of frustration, saves information resources departments from having to train people how to walk across the minefields, and saves developers a lot of money in 200-pound manuals and technical support.

Making the Best Use of Software Design Resources

Use designers as designers, programmers as programmers.

Many managers still expect programmers to design the human interface; the new software designer's main official function is to teach the programmers, usually through a series of three hour-long in-depth seminars, everything anyone ever needed to know about psychology and design. These approaches don't work.

As a designer who has had the honor of working with some of the best programmers in the world, I cannot express the depths of my respect for the wizards of this craft. However, coding has no more to do with human interface design than movie set construction has to do with directing live actors. Programming requires looking inward, toward the machine. Software design involves looking outward, toward the person. A few gifted individuals in this world can straddle both worlds and be highly competent in both. Most of us have made a choice to live in one world or the other. Managers who insist on trying to force people into the opposite camp are doing everyone involved a severe disservice.

Use software designers for quick reviews.

Project teams, no matter how careful or disciplined, will lose sight of how difficult both the syntax of an interface and the underlying concepts on which the interface is built have become. After all, the project team has months or years to learn a product that end users will be expected to master in a few hours or days. When a human interface designer walks in cold to review a project, he or she is wearing a new pair of glasses that can see right through glaring problems even the best designers and engineers who have lived with the project will fail to see. When I have done this kind of consulting, I have limited my time to a maximum of four days. Any more than that and I, too, will have joined the team and will likely begin failing to see the obvious.

Jeffries, Miller, Wharton, and Uyeda (1991) presented a study in which they tested four groups using different approaches to user-interface evaluation. Their first group, experienced human interaction specialists, formed their evaluations based on experience and an understanding of human factors. The second group consisted of a trained usability tester with six test subjects. The third group, three experienced software engineers, applied a preformulated set of guidelines. The fourth group, also engineers, used the intellectual testing process called cognitive walk-through. When the smoke cleared, the human interaction experts were the clear winners (Figure 11.1). They had found almost four times as many problems as the next closest group, and they found more than three times as many serious core problems. They did so at a significantly lower cost and in a matter of days.

Use software designers for the long haul.

If I'm expected to go beyond the kinds of surface changes I can accomplish in a fast review, I have to drown myself in the project. I have to explore existing applications and their interfaces. I have to

	Problems Found		Person-	Benefit-
	Total	Core	Hours	Cost
Human interface experts	152	105	20	12:1
Usability testing	38	31	199	1:1
Engineers with guidelines	38	35	17	6:1
Engineers with cognitive walk-through	40	35	27	3:1

Figure 11.1 *Results of different approaches to user-interface evaluation (Jeffries et al. 1991)*

meet with a range of the people who will use the product and internalize the way they look at their work and at their life. I want to absorb their very essence, so when I sit down to selfishly design an interface that will work for me (which is the only way I can work), I am designing an interface that will work for them as well.

Some companies try to spread a very small resource way too thin, and designers may be assigned to so many projects that they end up doing none well. From 2 days to 2 weeks into a project, I'm pretty much useless. I'm beyond the new user-observer phase but have not had the time to dive far enough into the problem domain to internalize the wants and needs of the users. (If my involvement is kept really low, this blackout period can be extended indefinitely.)

If you are a manager, prioritize your projects (or pieces of a large project) with your human interface experts to identify where they can do the most good if they become heavily involved and where they can add value by doing simple reviews.

If you are a team leader, make a decision to find a designer and make him or her a core member of the team, or hold this person at bay except for brief periodic reviews. Designers who are expected to be part of the team should be getting their hands dirty. If you string them along with how much you love them while keeping them out of the day-to-day hallway discussions and decisions that are the real heart of any project, you will not only be doing them a disservice, you will be setting everyone up for a fall when the eventual interface pleases no one. Being able to point a finger at the hapless designer may get people off the hook in the short run, but the products will still be less than successful.

   If you are a designer being spread so thin that people are mistaking you for an oil slick, wave this article under your boss's nose and beg this person to reprioritize. He or she will thank you for it. Eventually.

A Word to Information Services

Several years ago, a company that chose microcomputers rather than workstations (silly they) started up a flexible benefits program, enabling employees to choose how and where their pretax benefit dollars would be spent. Employees would make their selections from an elaborate menu, spending so much for their choice of health plan, taking or refusing dental insurance, perhaps electing to sign up for day care. To collect the information from the employees, each was sent a self-explanatory questionnaire disk that the employee would "fill out" and return via intracompany mail.

The collection program seemed quite efficient. Disks were mass-produced, slid into a computer-addressed mailer, and sent off. The returned disks were popped into a disk drive, where custom software read the data and added them to the growing database. The department was able to bring in the information on time and under budget.

Or so it seemed.

Actually, the program was costing the company a lot of money, all of it hidden. Every employee received the same disk—full of questionnaire, empty of information. Every employee had to type in his or her name, home and work addresses, employee number, various phone numbers, e-mail numbers, etc., etc., etc. This company employed around 12,000 workers. Let's say, to be generous, that half the employees did this typing at home, on their own time. That leaves 6,000 people typing in, on company time, information already on file with the benefits department. Let's say it takes 20 minutes to read through the instructions, enter, and check all this redundant information. That's 1,000 person-hours of work at (conservatively) $75 per hour, including overhead burden, or $150,000 of lost productivity, unaccounted for anywhere.

At the same time, the folks at Sun set up a phone-in system, where employees listened to instructions (also covered in a hand-out) and pressed touch-tone buttons. The central system already knew the employee's personal information, so having entered the employee number, people were able to begin gliding through the various options immediately. This system was probably cheaper for the information systems department—after all, it didn't have to reproduce all those floppies—but the bulk of the savings went to the company as a whole.

Any proposal to the information services department for a new methodology or system should include data on the expected effect on end-user efficiency, productivity, and morale. Current systems should face periodic user testing, surveying, and review to measure the real effect on employee performance.

Most of the corporate costs of inefficient systems today are hidden only because we are not looking for them. Usability professionals and software designers are trained to carry out studies to reveal them. These people should be able to provide hard numbers to management on the real costs of current systems and the expected savings of proposed systems.

Given the explosive growth of the industry, it is reasonable to assume that systems offering new efficiency and effectiveness will appear with fair regularity. Only by giving the executive staff solid figures on the real costs of an obsolete system to the entire corporation, not just the information services department, can the executive staff be expected to grant the kind of funds necessary for substantive change.

Be Proactive

Every day this country experiences millions of dollars in lost productivity because of e-mail. What percentage of the mail you receive do you ever need to see? The information services department is the only agency that can act to stem the tide.

Some electronic communication systems have structures in place that allow people to do other than mailings. For example, some companies place all their press releases and general employee announcements in a bulletin board system. Job postings and vacation schedules are handled as exactly what they are: periodically updated documents. Anytime an employee wants to look at the latest version of the document, he or she calls it up. Otherwise, it remains in a central document library. Contrast this with mail systems that send out everything to everybody every time anything changes. Information systems departments take a hit, as literally millions of redundant copies of unwanted materials are generated and stored. But the real cost is to the users.

First, users don't have the information they want when they want it. Unless they maintain a sophisticated file system on their computer, they will usually have thrown away anything other than the most time-dependent material long before they find they need it. Second, users are wasting hours per day reading through and eliminating unwanted mail. Hours per day. Multiply that by a large number of employees, and individual companies may find they are wasting tens of millions of dollars per year in lost time and productivity.

Little of this loss will be found within the information services department itself. Most will be absorbed by every little department in the corporation. Employees will periodically complain, but unless the information services department takes a leading role in tracking the real costs of such inefficiency, these kinds of systems may hang on for years, draining enormous resources without ever being an identifiable expense against the bottom line.

Be diligent in reviewing alternative systems and methodologies.

Because a system has been in use for 20 years doesn't make it good. In fact, it probably makes it bad. One of the fundamentals of high-quality systems is continuous improvement. Unless every single system has been growing and changing, almost certainly you can do better.

Supply Information, Not Data

Millions of employees are today being given instant access to extremely low-yield information sources, such as the Internet. An employee can wile away hours of company time reviewing the terabytes of opinionated gibberish on subjects having nothing to do with the business of the corporation. Meanwhile, most corporations make employees jump through the most elaborate of hoops to gain the simplest information that might actually improve the quality of their work. An employee in need of articles on specific subject matter may be required to fill out a company form, mail it to a central library location, then wait several days to receive either inappropriate articles or a form letter explaining that the request resulted in 11,386 possible matches.

Employees soon learn through experience to use their direct, if low-yield, sources because those are the ones that work. That can cost a business big money. It may take an employee 2 hours to find something a commercial service could have delivered in 5 minutes. Even if the source of that material is absolutely free, those 2 hours represent $150 of wasted employee time, minimum. And that is assuming that the "free" information was actually correct.

> *Concentrate on quality of information, not quantity. Give employees fast access to concentrated, high-yield sources.*

We are long overdue for the era of low-cost, high-volume commercial information. The technology for bringing information to the screen is well understood; the libraries are built. High expenses today can be directly traced to the costs of running a low-volume business. Information services departments have the clout to change all that. Bring information into your employees' workspaces. Insist on simple, effective end-user interfaces. Pump up the volume, and expect a pricing structure consistent with such volume.

Represent All Your Company's Users

Information services departments care deeply about their own primary classes of users: programmers and system administrators. They do a bang-up job of representing their wants and needs to their suppliers. They do less of a sterling job in representing the primary users in the rest of the company: end users.

> *If the wants and needs of end users are to be met, information services must take an active role in being their advocates.*

I recently heard a well-known management consultant speaking at a conference announce that information services departments care only about on-time delivery and low programming and maintenance costs and that time and money spent on improving the lot of the end user is time and money wasted. He's never heard a word from an information services department manager that led him to believe differently.

Improving the efficiency and productivity of end users will have a deeper effect on the corporate bottom line than fixing up the information services receiving dock. End users need a strong advocate if we are to see our current interfaces and system designs improve. The corporate information services group must be that advocate.

Software design stagnated not because pushing the technology forward would be expensive and not because the result would be anything less than a spectacular increase in efficiency and productivity. It stalled purely from lack of demand. Buyers can change that. Tell your suppliers what you want, and support the ones that respond. The feedback loop between end user and supplier is broken. Fix it.

PART 4

From Quality to *Kansei*

Storm clouds roiled in growing anger across the dark night sky. Beneath the trees, the family huddled hard by the few glowing embers of their dying campfire. Mom suggested it was time for the kids to snuggle into their sleeping bags, but the oldest girl played for time. Braver than the rest, she asked her father to tell them a scary story. He thought for a moment, then reached into his knapsack, slowly unfolding a scrap of paper, cracked and yellowed with age.

As he began to read, the children's eyes opened up in fright. They began to whimper and their bodies shook in terror. Before Dad was halfway through, the kids, as one, leaped to their feet and raced for the safety of their tent and the warmth of their sleeping bags within. Watching them scamper, Dad, his face wreathed in a knowing smile, turned to give Mom a squeeze. The paper slipped from his hand and fluttered close to the campfire, where it was bathed in amber light:

> THIS COMPUTER PRODUCT IS PROVIDED AS-IS WITHOUT WARRANTY OF ANY KIND EITHER EXPRESSED OR IMPLIED. IN NO EVENT WILL THE COMPANY BE LIABLE FOR ANY SPECIAL, INCIDENTAL, OR CONSEQUENTIAL DAMAGES, WHETHER BASED ON CONTRACT, TORT, WARRANTEE, OR OTHER LEGAL GROUNDS, EVEN IF WE HAVE BEEN ADVISED OF THE POSSIBILITY OF SUCH DAMAGE. YOU, AND YOU ALONE, ARE FULLY RESPONSIBLE FOR ANY LOSS OF DATA, PROFITS, OR HUMAN LIFE.

I understand that in a country where you can be successfully sued for serving a hot beverage hot, we can hardly be too careful, but do these warranties reflect the high regard in which we hold our efforts? Our users think so, and our products have offered them good reason.

The most striking conclusion we drew from the Starfire project is that no hardware or software in the industry is up to the task of supporting activities like Julie's. Can you imagine whipping out any portable computer today when you have 45 seconds to come up with an effective counterargument? We know that the batteries would be dead, or the system would have crashed, or the first application we touched would blow everything to smithereens.

Workstation manufacturers live and breathe reliability. They have to. At many sites, when a workstation system goes down, everyone goes home. Workstation manufacturers have been able to achieve reliability by building capabilities such as memory protection in from the start. They have also taken natural advantage of the nature of mission-critical computing: companies typically run only one or, at most, a few stable applications. Bombproofing such a system is far easier than doing the same for a general-purpose machine. Even when something does go wrong, the workstation user picks up the phone, and a system administrator appears, casts powders and types strange incantations, and soon the user is back up and running.

Personal computer users are not so lucky. Their computers die at the drop of a hat. The more applications, the more extensions they add, the worse the problem becomes, and usually there is no one to help them. People making critical electronic presentations sometimes bring two or three backup systems with them to avoid potential embarrassment. Computers quickly train people to save their work constantly, and even this strategy can fail when systems die in the middle of save operations.

The world of workstations and personal computers is merging. Workstations will take on the burden of many more applications. Computers will be more intimately tied to the net. Most of us will be using a range of intelligent devices to help us get through the day. Any one of them that fails to work may bring us to a halt. Low-reliability computing worked when computers were an adjunct to our life. As they become more and more central, the challenges we face in semicompatible hardware and untried software will become intolerable.

When Quality Is Job 1.1

*I*n the 1940s and 1950s, America was the world's largest manufacturer of automobiles, with people snapping up cars just as fast as they could be shoved out the factory door. In 1948, 54 percent of American families owned cars. That figure had jumped to 73 percent by 1956, just eight years later (Diggins 1988). By this time, however, just about everyone with money for a car had bought one, and sales began to slump. In the rush toward quantity manufacturing, quality had gone out the window. Nonetheless, with market saturation staring it in the face, Detroit felt that its owners needed an additional nudge to force new car purchases. Detroit's solution was what General Motors car designer Harley Earl dubbed "dynamic obsolescence": changing the style of each year's car so completely that last year's model seemed almost instantly dated. Ford designer George Walker: "We design a car to make a man unhappy with his 1957 Ford along about the end of 1958."

Of course, everyone has critics. A Methodist bishop of the day inquired, "Who are the madmen who built cars so long they cannot be parked and are hard to turn at corners, vehicles with hideous tail fins, full of gadgets and covered with chrome, so low that an average human being has to crawl in the doors and so powerful that no man dare use the horsepower available?" Harley Earl responded to such criticism, "Listen, I'd put smokestacks right in the middle of the sons of bitches if I thought I could sell more cars" (Mingo 1994).

The whole system seemed ideal. New cars required their owners to spend the first 90 days dragging their cars back and forth to the dealers to correct initial problems. Then the cars would work pretty well for perhaps a year or two. About the time the third year rolled around, when everything would begin to deteriorate seriously, owners would trade their cars in for even snazzier models.

Things could have gone along this way forever, except Americans began getting a choice. The first real alternative to Detroit's low quality and "featuritis" was the Volkswagen Beetle. This car was marketed as being opposite to American cars in every way. Instead of buyers spending hundreds of dollars of their purchase price on this year's new styling, VW "bugs" rolled off the assembly line year after year virtually unchanged.[1] The car was so devoid of gadgets, it didn't even offer a gas gauge. Instead, when the engine began to sputter, drivers would fiddle underneath the dashboard with a mechanical valve that would give access to another couple of gallons of fuel, enough for another 60 miles.[2] The car was extremely reliable because it was mechanically simple, leaving few things to go wrong, and because its manufacturer took quality very seriously. (The doors fit so tightly that the car could float.) The car sold well among a counterculture who prided themselves on owning the ugliest, most primitive car on the road, but the mainstream of America was too much in love with their jet stream buggies.

When the Japanese imports began to arrive in the 1960s, things began to change. The Japanese cars were not ugly. Admittedly, they were not as smart looking as the American models, but they were at least stylistically neutral. They had a reliability achieved through quality management, not through removal of what some Americans still stubbornly insisted were important features, such as gas gauges. By the time the oil crisis hit, Japanese cars had achieved style, and Americans abandoned their American gas-guzzlers forever.

It took Japan 15 years to build its quality automobile manufacturing industry, beginning back in 1950. It took the American automobile industry 15 years to (almost) catch up. The 1992 J. D. Power initial quality study showed American cars having 136 problems per 100 cars versus 105 problems per 100 cars for the Japanese cars—and this was

---

1 Ads showed the car's "remarkable styling progress" over time, with pictures of 10 or 15 cars from subsequent model years, all of which looked identical. The copy would then point out that if you looked closely, you could see how the shape of the taillights had changed slightly between two model years.

2 Actor Peter Falk tells the story of a studio executive who bought a Volkswagen in the early sixties. When he drove to the lot, he bragged so much about his expected mileage, they decided to play a bit of a trick. For the next three months, each and every day, someone would sneak down to the garage and add a half-gallon of gas to the car. The engine never sputtered, and the owner's admiration of the car's mileage became positively worshipful.

down sharply from the 300 defects reported by the Americans at the beginning of the 1980s (Main 1994; Dobyns and Crawford-Mason 1991). The Americans at this point are increasing their quality faster than the Japanese, even as the Europeans begin to trail behind.

Déjà Vu Over Again

The world software industry is as vulnerable today as the American automobile industry was in the mid-seventies, when time finally ran out. We are building bigger and bigger software packages, with more and more powerful "engines." We have tailfinned "features" that would put a 1959 Caddy to shame. We've done the auto industry one better too. We don't just have our tail fins stuck on the back of our software cars. We have tail fins all over the place: front, sides, beneath, with more than a few applications featuring tail fins coming up right out of the seats. (I'm sure we've all used these applications from time to time.) What does it matter if things fall off now and then? It all sure looks bright and sparkly.

Things worked fine in Detroit as long as everyone else was also spending their time on tail fins instead of on cars with good mileage that anyone could drive easily and that would get them where they wanted to go without breaking down along the way. When mileage and reliability suddenly came into vogue, a whole lot of people faced a whole lot of unemployment while the industry struggled to get back to quality.

Where will the new, high-quality software come from? It could come from the United States, Japan, Europe, or India. It could come from China, Burma, or South America. Software is part of the world economy, and anyone can elect to become a winner. Wherever it comes from, it could take the rest of the world 15 years to catch up— 15 of the most unpleasant years of their lives.

Our industry has enjoyed a few golden moments when systems were cohesive, coherent, and controlled, when average people could feel confident that they could "drive away" their new computers without worrying about whether potholes riddled the software and the learning curve looked like something from the highway to hell. The HASCI system was probably the earliest "clean" interface, appearing even before the Star. It lasted around two months before market pressures forced its developers to allow a flood of incompatible, ported software to submerge it into chaos. Star and Lisa were both carefully constructed, controlled environments that didn't do much—and did that at a snail's pace. The market voted "no" before any potential chaotic flood could even begin.

The Macintosh probably had the longest run as an absolutely pure system—around 18 months. This period was due primarily to what was seen at the time by many folks at Apple as an incredibly stupid decision on the part of Steve Jobs: he forbid cursor keys on the keyboard. The practical result of the decision was that developers found it impossible to dump a lot of old software on the new machine. Instead, they had to start over, building "mousable" applications from the ground up. It gave the machine an important childhood, a time for developers to gain experience in visual interface design without fear their competitors would port them out of existence. Nonetheless, by two years out, the dissipation of the Macintosh interface was in full swing: cursor keys had appeared, and with them came the ports.[3] Macintosh hardware and software were growing in power and complexity by leaps and bounds, and interface and software reliability were trailing behind. Apple, once so far ahead of the pack, is now scrambling to maintain its lead.

The 90–10 Rule

According to the 90–10 rule, the last 10 percent of a project requires as much development time as the first 90 percent. The way it was explained to me was that this meant that one should put aside significant resources to ensure proper completion of the last critical 10 percent of a project—that portion that results in a high-quality "fit and finish."

Somewhere along the line this interpretation got turned on its head: some bright stalwart suggested that since the last 10 percent of a project takes up half the resources, companies could save a lot of good

....
3 As one of those responsible for the decision to add the cursor keys, I will argue that the keys were necessary and that childhoods must end. Nonetheless, the philosophy that drove Jobs to early protection was a good one, and people would be well advised to emulate it on new systems in the future.

money by simply not doing the last 10 percent at all! Just think of the savings! Can you even imagine such a concept even occurring to someone at Toyota or Nissan? "Gosh, what if we just kind of stuck the door on the car without worrying about getting it just right? Maybe it would fit, maybe it wouldn't. We could get the new model out three months earlier, and we could always figure out a way to make the doors fit better on the next release." Unthinkable—and yet the 90–10 rule flashed like wildfire through the industry as computer companies throughout the world attempted to feed the seemingly insatiable demand of the eighties with new, new, new features at all cost. And it was to get worse.

The 80–20 Rule

Someone decided that if you could get away with shipping products that were 90 percent complete, why not ship them 80 percent complete? Products started going out with incomprehensible manuals. No problem; no one reads them anyway. Customers had to spend more and more time assembling their systems out of a myriad of disconnected parts. No problem; users and system administrators have nothing better to do. Developers abandoned reliability testing. No problem; now actual end users will test the products, resulting in more widespread testing than ever before.[4]

Quality did not go out the window on a whim. Developers faced severe market penalties for going the extra 20 percent distance. Microcomputer manufacturers faced stiff competition from low-quality, "disposable" computers from garages in China. Software features and power had been exploding at such a rate that, were developers to really bear down on fit and finish, they could soon find themselves one, two, or three generations behind the competition in all those little check boxes worshipped by buyers and reviewers.

Pretty soon things got really out of control. Software managers, in rushing to market with the latest features, told their people to ship software with known bugs. Big bugs, little bugs, annoying bugs, mysterious

....
4 Power users soon learned never to buy any piece of software with a version number that ended in point zero. After all, version n.0a would be out in a week, and the one that works (sort of), version n.01, would be out in less than a month.

bugs. As soon as a release would leave the shop, all the programmers would go frantically back to work to find fixes, even as the managers were hiring scores of people to handle the complaint calls and figure out work-arounds. Then, just when all the users had gotten used to the bugs—even grown fond of them—the managers would rush out a new release with a brand-new offering of bugs, which would require everyone to rush back to start handling the new bugs. Still no one noticed anything was wrong. In fact, all the software houses seemed happy. Most were making money, so why shouldn't they just keep drifting down this nice, gentle river? Perhaps because of that roaring noise just up ahead.

Human productivity on computer systems exploded between 1978 and 1984. Since then, with a few notable exceptions, it has stagnated— for two reasons. First, input hardware has stagnated. Second, we have not improved the quality of human–computer interactions. Rather, we have stood by and watched as they have deteriorated in the face of increasing task complexity, to the point where now people spend most of their time trying to battle their computer into submission instead of accomplishing their task (Landauer 1995).

Customers are waking up. The people who make the buying decisions on computer systems and software are becoming aware of the real costs of ownership. A 1992 survey pegged the annual cost of ownership for a standard PC at as much as $21,500 per year (Nolan, Norton 1992). That's a lot of money for a $5,000 computer.

Where's the money going? A disproportionate percentage can be traced to direct and indirect training costs. Direct costs might entail people taking time from their regular jobs to attend training classes. The indirect costs are more complex. Users waste time pressing buttons and flailing through manuals, trying to figure out what went wrong with the machine, when the problem is that they have inadvertently triggered some unknown and less-than-obvious system state. They waste time wandering around looking for a warm body in another office to ask for help. Finally, when they find someone who can help, the other party ends up wasting time, too. This peer-to-peer training is expensive. The 1992 study from Nolan, Norton & Co., "Managing End-User Computing," examined peer-to-peer training at ten large corporations, including Chemical Bank, Ford Motor, and Sprint (Bulkeley 1992). The study found that, while the known, visible costs per PC varied from $2,000 to $6,000 annually, the hidden peer-to-peer costs ran from $6,000 to $15,000 per year.

Bulkeley reported:

> "We all just about fell out of our chairs when we saw the amount of mutual support," says David J. Baker, a process consultant for Sprint who participated in organizing the study. "Everyone knew it was taking place, but when we guessed what the amount would be beforehand, we missed by a factor of 65."

Information services managers are putting a lot more emphasis on total cost of ownership than on initial capitalization. They are willing and able to spend more money for software that will ultimately cost them less money to maintain. They are no longer willing to accept software that may look good on spec sheets but results in poor human productivity and high overhead.

The Japanese Turnaround

In 1950, statistician and engineer W. Edwards Deming visited Japan, bringing with him a vision for how the Japanese could turn around their ailing industries, known throughout the world for shoddy goods, and build an economic powerhouse through the application of quality management. He had attempted to carry that same message to the United States, but Americans were too busy pumping out quantity to be bothered with Deming's flighty ideas. The Japanese were not too busy; they listened, and they implemented.

Until the United States opened trade with Japan in 1868, the Japanese had always created quality goods. American traders didn't want quality, though. They demanded the cheapest goods the Japanese could turn out, and the Japanese complied with the strange requests of these foreigners, though not happily.[5] They were more than ready to return to their traditional ways when given the slightest encouragement (De Mente 1993).

....
5 The Japanese people wouldn't touch any of the goods made for the Western markets. They thought we were nuts for wanting them, but they assumed we were just too stupid to know the difference. Of course, they were right.

Deming gave the Japanese modern tools that would enable them to reestablish quality. He taught them how to prepare statistical charts on every step of their manufacturing process, so they could see and understand how and where their processes could be improved. He showed them how to restructure their management and their work force in such a way that they could engage the full talents of every worker in the quality struggle. He also taught them something new: that perfect quality is never accomplished, so they would have to strive toward perfection forever through continuous improvement.

Within 5 years, Deming's message had transformed Japanese industry. Within 10 years, Japanese goods were considered among the best in the world. Within 15 years, the Japanese had begun the virtual takeover of industry after industry. The rest of the world would shout and stamp their feet in a great hue and cry of "unfair, unfair," but it was not unfair at all. Consumers around the world appreciated the quality of Japanese goods and would pay whatever was necessary to get their hands on them.

Which leads me to perhaps the most important part: in most cases, people paid *less* money for Japanese goods than they did the products of their own countries. This, because of one other little secret that Deming shared with the Japanese:

Quality is free.

Quality saves money, lots of money. All that money spent on scrap and rework and printing manuals that are little more than extended bug reports. All that money spent on telephone hot lines. All that money lost because customers don't come back, don't dare buy another product for fear of having to face a similar experience. All these expenses, which represent an enormous cost of doing business, go away (M. Walton 1986). And continuous improvement guarantees that profitability will keep getting better.

An Attitude of Quality

*I*n the mid-1980s, Ford Motor Company was experiencing an unexpectedly high level of warranty service and customer complaints on one of its transmissions. As it happened, while Ford manufactured some of the transmissions, they had also subcontracted some of the work out to Mazda. When Ford examined the record, they discovered that virtually all the failures had occurred on the Ford-manufactured units, even though both transmissions were to have been built to the same specifications.

Ford pulled ten of their own transmissions, disassembled them, and measured each part. Every one was within specification, just as it should have been. Ford was using a zero-defect process put in place in the early 1980s just to avoid the kinds of problems that now seemed to be occurring. It was mysterious when Ford began measuring parts from the disassembled Mazda transmissions. Their gauge now failed, showing the same monotonous readings from sample to sample to sample. They brought in a repairman to fix the gauge, but he could find nothing wrong. Nothing *was* wrong. The Mazda parts were not simply within specifications; the Mazda parts were perfect. Most Ford transmissions also worked perfectly, with parts that were off in one direction being balanced against parts that were off in another, but when enough parts randomly ended up off in the same direction, the overall transmission would be all but unusable (M. Walton 1986).

In the late 1970s, Sony was producing televisions in two cities: Tokyo and San Diego. Part of the manufacturing process was to fix the preset color saturation at what had been shown in user tests as a pleasing level. Specifications called for the level to be within 30 percent of ideal. The American sets were all within that 30 percent, but they were uniformly distributed within it. The Japanese sets were not distributed; they were clustered—in the center—and they looked the better for it.

When I first went to Japan, I had one question on my mind. I asked it a dozen different times, in a dozen different ways, but I never got even the hint of an answer. (That's a strange thing about the Japanese. You can ask a question, and you feel that warm sense that comes over you when your curiosity has been completely satisfied, only to realize they haven't said a word that's responsive to the question.) I asked, "The quality that is so much a part of your products: is it the result of rational rules and procedures, or is it something that comes from your heart?" No answer. I asked, "If your boss came to you and told you, 'We are no longer interested in quality; just build things as fast as you can,' what would you do? Would you follow the new procedures, or would something inside you want to continue building quality?" No response. Their silence *was* the answer. The heart cannot speak, and, in the Japanese, that is where quality lies.

Many Americans (and more than a few Japanese) have come to believe that the Japanese are simply better at quality than Americans. But you don't have to look any further than the example of the Saturn automobile to see this just isn't so. This car is a joy to own and drive; it is safe and reliable, and the buying experience is so much nicer than that of buying a Japanese car (or any other kind of car) that there is simply no comparison. (One should not blame the Japanese. Their cars are usually sold by the same soft-shoe artists who sell almost every car in this country, for as much money as they can con, cajole, and squeeze out of their customers. Saturn dealers don't do any of that stuff, because Saturns are sold at a fixed price by noncommissioned workers, who are there solely to help.)

The 85–15 Rule

Quality is a methodology, but it is even more an attitude. According to Dr. Deming, 85 percent of the responsibility for quality lies with management; 15 percent, with workers. Unless management adopts an attitude that improving product and service is more important than making quick money, unless management decides to embrace a philosophy of pride in workmanship, unless management decides to break down the barriers to cooperation and teamwork, to cease rewarding managers not for producing goods properly but only for shipping them on time, quality cannot and will not be achieved. Management must not only set the example but encourage and reward workers who respond. In Japan, 93 percent of workers believe that if they work harder and smarter, they will be rewarded. In the United States, the figure is 10 percent. U.S. workers believe that the bosses and stockholders will profit from any improvements, but they themselves will not (Dobyns and Crawford-Mason 1991).

Quality is an immersive experience. Getting your feet wet doesn't help; it's all the way or nothing. Deming refused even to show up at a company for an initial consult unless the CEO would be there for the meeting. It didn't matter whether that company was Joe's Pizza Parlor or General Motors. No CEO, no meeting.

When Deming came to Ford Motor Company in 1980, two years after Ford's CEO had declared quality to be "Job One," President Donald Peterson was there to greet him, to listen, and to act. Ford's first quality automobile was the Taurus. It was not a perfect car, but it moved Ford a long way, and it showed Ford that quality could and would pay off. Ford saved over $400 million in the preproduction phase alone, using concurrent engineering to eliminate the kinds of waste that had routinely occurred before. Instead of the production people getting their first look at the car years after the designers had designed it, months after the engineers had committed to hard tools, they sat down at the table on day 1. The designers knew for the first time the kinds of problems the production people faced. The engineers began specifying parts that would not only work but were easy and efficient to fit into place.

The modern quality movement started out with statistical analysis, and it is still driven today by statistical methodologies, but statistics is only a tool to find the problems and show the progress. The real changes must take place in human attitudes and approaches, starting with management and spreading to the workers. Ford learned this, and Ford has had increasing success changing the face of its workplace.

What can we learn from all this? We are in a crisis of management, and it is time to change. It takes courage to insist on quality, but it only has to be kick-started once. Once that first release goes out bug free (or at least heavily bug resistant), the pressure is off on the next release. All those hours spent chasing down old bugs can be invested in avoiding new ones. As Deming reminds us, just as poor quality begets poor quality, good quality begets good quality (M. Walton 1986).

The finest American television set before the Japanese invasion was Zenith— a company that believed in quality. In fact, the company slogan was, "The Quality Goes In Before the Name Goes On." Zenith made a quality product but failed to continuously improve it. By the mid-1970s, it was as far behind as every other American electronics manufacturer and, like everyone else, turned to Asia for their newest product, the VCR. Zenith bought complete, assembled, and tested Sony recorders, replaced the Sony nameplate with its own, and slipped them into a box. Ironically, on the outside of the box, Zenith continued to proclaim proudly, "The Quality Goes In Before the Name Goes On." Today only the Japanese manufacture televisions for America.

We need to get back to quality in our industry, we need to initiate continuous improvement, and we need to start now. Where should you start? With your boss. If you don't have a boss, quality is entirely up to you.

Into Action

Today many computer companies have already begun the turn toward quality, adopting the ISO (International Standards Organization) 9000 quality standards or striving for the Malcolm Baldrige Award. These efforts usually start in the production and service ends of the company and only in the late stage begin to affect software quality. Even when they do, early quality efforts usually focus on reducing bugs, not improving the overall quality of the product offering.

If there is a quality movement anywhere in your company, you are being offered the best opportunity in a decade to do something serious about the quality of your company's software. Once quality as a buzz-word has made its way into the executive ranks, managers who for years have turned a deaf ear on human interface considerations suddenly show new interest. How can you be the one to lead the charge? Quality is a formal discipline. Learn about it. Read the following books and articles:

Diggins, John Patrick (1988). *The Proud Decades: America in War and Peace, 1941–1960*. New York: Norton.

Dobyns, Lloyd, and Crawford-Mason, Clare (1991). *Quality or Else*. Boston: Houghton Mifflin.

Main, Jeremy (1994). *Quality Wars*. New York: Free Press.

Taguchi, Genichi, and Clausing, Don (1990). "Robust Quality." *Harvard Business Review* (January–February 1990): 65.

Walton, Mary (1986). *The Deming Management Method.* New York: Putnam.

Then put into action a formal software quality program.

If you can't measure it, you can't manage it.

This Western business maxim replaces intuition with numerical analysis. Statistics are a driving force in the quality movement; only by close measurement can we ensure we are actually achieving continuous improvement. The downside of measurement is that we tend to focus only on that which is measured, ignoring anything left out. For example, most software houses measure only bugs and revenue, and revenue is a lagging indicator, with changes showing up when it is far too late.

At Sun, our software quality movement started out tightly focused on bug reports. Human interface problems were reported but were relegated to if-we-can-get-around-to-it status, and, as we've all discovered, anything on that list can remain there forever. Moreover, the majority of human interface problems are never even reported. They remain hidden dissatisfiers—nuisances that constantly irk their users but not enough for them to do something about it.

The first release of the Common Desktop Environment (CDE) is a major step forward in the UNIX world, but it brings along some very old baggage. For example, the mail system offers a Reply to Sender button that opens up a new mail window with the address and title fields filled out. It then places the text pointer not in the message field, but in the address field. If you didn't want to reply to the sender, you wouldn't have chosen the option, so why is the cursor in the address field?

The cursor belongs in the message field, since that is in line with user expectations and, in the overwhelming majority of cases, is exactly where the user wants to start typing. Under CDE, perhaps a million users a day will have to perform an extra mouse click to begin their responses. If people respond to three e-mails per day, that's 600 million extra target acquisition and clicks per year. At an average time of 1 second, this "feature" will cost the economy 166,000 person-hours per year.[1] That's equivalent to 83 people spending their entire work lives doing nothing but clicking on message windows. (Compare that to the time it would take to correct the code.)

CDE is not alone. America Online version 2.5 has an address book icon that users instinctively reach for when they've finished typing the messages and are ready to select a recipient. However, if you click on the address book before leaving the message field, an error message explains that you first have to put the cursor in the address field. Why? Isn't it obvious that's where I want the cursor to go? Why not just move it there for me? Multiply these examples of "one extra little mouse click" by the tens of thousands of human interface errors that dot today's software landscape and you begin to see the terrible cost of ignoring such problems.

These mouse clicks probably have a greater impact on total cost of ownership than many high-priority bugs hidden within the products, and yet even if a user were to turn them in, they likely would never find their way to a high rung on the bug ladder, because human interface bug tracking just doesn't work.

We have to establish new metrics that will cause a different approach to change. We have to fill in the middle ground between bug tracking and revenues by doing field analysis and user testing.

Measure ease of learning, ease of use, ease of installation, ease of maintenance.

Begin by developing a baseline. Get out in the field and watch users perform with your and your competitors' software. Look for the inefficiencies and record them, both numerically and on video. Show your company in graphic detail what the "out-of-box" experience is like. Show users struggling to learn and perform operations on your system that are easier on the competition's. Show system administrators struggling to install new software or wasting their time teaching their users how to overcome features that should never have been there in the first place. Develop field study and user testing procedures you will be able to repeat down the road to see how well your company has progressed. Then deliver the results to management.

....
1 I'm being generous. It takes around 2 seconds to acquire a mouse and perform a move and click. In this case, I'm assuming the user already has the mouse.

Work with your quality officer, if you have one, to see that addressing "ease of" issues becomes as important as fixing bugs. That means tying improvements to managers' bonus and compensation packages. Otherwise nothing will change. Then talk to the managers about changing the culture. When engineers at Apple made mistakes in the human interface, the problems were usually caught by other engineers. Even if no human interface expert had ever looked at it, at Apple, the CDE bug would have been caught long before the product ever got to alpha, let alone got to market.

A conventional wisdom has developed in the human resources community that adult workers will not change. This is silly. University of Southern California professor Jerald Jellison points out that our behavior is constantly modified by changing circumstances. An example he uses is the attention-seeking individual driving at 80 miles per hour down the highway who instantly loses all propensity for attention seeking upon spotting a black-and-white highway patrol car in his rear-view mirror. His behavior changes immediately, and he seeks the shelter of the nearest semi. A few minutes later, the same individual may get a flat tire. Upon discovering his spare is also flat, he will revert to attention seeking, doing his best to flag down the next black-and-white. Engineers can change too. They will develop a sensitivity for quality the very same day their managers stop talking about it and put it into action.

The software design community has been watching quality degrade over the past ten years. The quality movement gives us the leverage to fight back—if we act now and we act smart. Bring the problem out of the shadows by giving managers the measurements they need. Then stand ready to offer them the solution.

Reliability

*I*n July 1994, I visited Toshiba Fuchu Works, the home of Toshiba elevators, funiculars, and software. Toshiba's software development process did not at first glance seem appreciably different from our process in America. Toshiba has a series of defined steps, such as research, specification, general design, detail design, and coding, that are not particularly different from ours (although many American developers put coding first). When we dove a little deeper, though, a real difference showed up. Between each step of the software process, the Toshiba people have design reviews. They call these interstitial spaces "hold points." Should some portion of the development be behind, should bugs be rearing their ugly heads, the folks at Toshiba stop and do something about them.

> *Bugs are not inevitable.*

When Toshiba people find out they have a problem, they actually stop and fix it. How marvelous! How refreshing! How weird! We used to have "hold points" in America. NASA used them until shortly before the *Challenger* disaster, by which time our hold points had become more like "talk about it, then go ahead anyway" points. Perhaps it is time to return.

> *Build systems that inherently reduce the likelihood of unexpected interactions.*

Many of today's software failures are brought about by individually bug-free pieces of code interacting in ways that could not have been easily predicted. Our microcomputer hardware designs are reliable in themselves: microcomputers rarely break down. However, our hardware architectures are not preventing fatal software interactions. Nor has our system software been protecting one piece of code or one application from another. The movement toward better protection has begun; we need to see that it is accelerated.

Encourage commercial, well-tested objects and applets.

Neither object-oriented systems nor Web-based applets, by themselves, will result in a perfect world. If volume end users must "roll their own" objects and applets, their libraries will become replete with just-good-enough objects of little robustness and little universal appeal. System houses must take active steps to see that a community of healthy, independent object and applet developers grows up in their shadow, supplying other developers and volume end users alike with well-thought-out and thoroughly tested modules.

Manuals

Stop spending money assembling fat manuals. Spend it on sleek software instead.

Our industry spares no cost to supply comprehensive manuals with software systems, but sees as wasteful having to "squander" money on software designers and up-front prototypes and tests. Our manuals tend to be thick, clumsy testaments to this lack of early planning.

Goal: Reduce manual sizes by 90 percent.

The primary job of a technical writer should be to work early with the designers and engineers to reduce drastically the amount of material that has to be explained to users. Manuals should dwell on the task, not how one accomplishes the task, because the way to accomplish the task should be obvious and intuitive. Writers should be judged heavily on their skill at working with the team to reduce the need for writing, not for the pounds of paper their resulting work weighs or even for the clarity of their writing itself. We have far too many delightfully clear manuals written for hopelessly murky software products.

Why aren't writers doing this now? Management: Change your procedures.

Service

The last two decades have seen Americans go from an acceptance of mediocrity to a demand for excellence, and business has responded. Twenty years ago, American cars were of dreadful quality; today they are virtually on par with the Japanese and continuously improving. Twenty years ago, Americans were eating cast-iron corn, insipid coffee, and watery chocolate bars. Today corn picked within the hour can be found at thousands of roadside farms; high-quality, custom-blended coffee is displacing canned, "bricked," and instant blends of dubious heritage; and Dove Bars thrill the palate with flavors previously found only in fine European chocolates.

The era of mass production is drawing to a close. People don't want products that don't fit anymore. They want custom-made tennis rackets, and they want them now. They want custom eyeglasses, and they want them in an hour, not a month. They want bicycles custom-built to their own exact dimensions, and, in Japan, Panasonic is quite prepared to comply. People want perfectly tailored suits that don't cost an arm and a leg; within a few years, tiny radars will scan your body to build a 3D image, and a computer will take over, cutting cloth for a suit that will fit exactly.

Companies that can respond to these kinds of needs are fast, flexible, and display a positive lust for quality. They are populated by people with a mission—people who are empowered to solve problems, to innovate, to get things done. Walk into a Nordstrom's department store sometime, and see what real service feels like. Think it's a matter of markup and money? Try a Wal-Mart, or a Men's Warehouse. It's an attitude.

One of the chief weapons in improving service is the computer. Last year I flew to Santa Monica close to a dozen times, always staying in the same Loews hotel, featuring fine food, lovely oceanview rooms, and seemingly faultless service, but there was always something missing. Because their check-in clerks seemed to come and go, no one ever got to know me. Every time I checked in, I was a perfect stranger. I began to dread the check-in process.

On my very last trip, the hotel had updated the software in its computer. When I announced who I was, the clerk typed in a few characters from my last name, looked up at me smiling, and said, "Oh, yes, Mr. Tognazzini. It's so nice to see you again!" I knew she didn't know me from Adam. And I knew exactly how the trick was done, because I've been designing such tricks for 20 years. Nevertheless, I felt I was finally being welcomed home.[1]

In the past few years, commercial developers have begun to abandon live technical support; and users are now finding themselves wandering through the labyrinths of voice-mail hell. I have returned several software products this year that did not work out of the box and for which I was unable to contact anyone who could help. Several more products that failed further down the line are sitting on my shelf. In none of these cases will I be ordering the next release. Consumers are five times more likely to stop doing business with a company for poor service than for poor product quality or high cost, and it costs five times as much to obtain a new customer as to keep one (Boyett and Conn 1991).

In the early 1990s, Saturn had to launch a massive nationwide recall of its cars. This could have been a public relations disaster, but instead Saturn turned it into an event, inviting customers to come down to the dealership on a warm weekend afternoon and share a barbecue while the problem in their cars was made right. Each dealership had games and prizes for the kids and converted what might have been a bleak trek to the mechanic into a trip to the county fair. Saturn didn't lose customers; it gained them.

In the early days, when a local car show was to be held in Detroit, Saturn sent out letters to local owners asking if any would be willing to take a stint in the Saturn booth, for zero remuneration, and talk to potential customers about how they felt about their cars. The Saturn folk figured they needed a 5 percent response to get the number of people they needed. The response was 95 percent. In June 1994, Saturn held its tenth birthday party at the factory in Spring Hill, Tennessee; 44,000 Saturn owners showed up to help them celebrate.

Saturn owners feel good about every aspect of their cars. Not only is the car itself a quality product, but the buying experience is actually pleasant, and maintenance is just as nice. And what about the people supplying all these good experiences? They feel good, too. If you wander around Spring Hill, Tennessee, it's easy to spot the Saturn workers. They are the ones wearing Saturn shirts, Saturn pants, Saturn coats,

....

1 Now if only I could get these hotel people to stop trying to read my name from their computer screens when I order breakfast. If someone's name is Smith, they should say "Smith"; if Johnson, "Johnson." If Tognazzini, they should just say, "Sir."

and Saturn jewelry. They take pride in working for a company that takes pride in its product.

If service is important for consumers, it is vital for businesses dealing with other businesses. The tourist-area restaurant with poor food and lousy service goes on year after year because there's always an abundance of new victims. The business world is far smaller, and anonymity does not prevail. My wife tells the story of the first two microcomputer vendors who approached her company, delivering samples of their wares. Within a few months of their arrival, both systems suffered technical problems. When company A was called, the customer representative told her company to "see your vendor." When company B was called, they were asked only one thing: "Do you need a new machine this afternoon, or would tomorrow morning be all right?" Her company now has thousands of computers, all from company B.

Tom Peters draws from a Forum Corporation report to show that 70 percent of businesspeople who drop a supplier do so not because of the quality or price of the product but because of lousy personal service (Peters 1994). Improving service requires contact people to be on the road, meeting folks and catering to their needs, not sitting back at the office filling out forms or fighting their computers.

Some people read these service statistics as a license to ignore manufacturing costs and product quality. This is a dangerous strategy indeed. In the next few years, as more and more companies climb aboard the quality bandwagon, service disparities will disappear, and product quality will gain the upper hand. Now is the time to push quality forward aggressively, emphasizing both product and service.

Reliability and the Software Design Process

Some managers see human interface as a necessary evil to be tacked on during the last three weeks of the engineering cycle. Others prefer to wait until the first bad review. Both strategies are less than effective. Human interface design must occur before coding begins. Too often, the software designers arrive when the building is complete, summoned to pick out the color of the drapes. This is a difficult task when the engineers, in their efforts to provide the strongest possible building, have eliminated all the windows.

Effective applications, like effective buildings, are designed from the users in rather than the technology out. Who are the users? What are their needs, desires, abilities? What talents and training will they bring to the party? Until the team knows the answers to these questions, they cannot design responsive software.

Software designers and usability testers are trained to perform user and task analyses to pin down these answers. Just as engineers spend 16 or more years of their life developing an education that will enable them to do magic in the mysterious inner world of computer science, human interaction people spend their time learning about people and developing the skill to improve their interactions with machines.

The importance of good human interaction design in building reliable systems cannot be overstressed. In 1967, Philco offered a two-year warranty on its color TVs, secure in the knowledge that company engineers had developed a safe, reliable hardware platform. Certainly the hardware *was* solid—but the human interface needed work. Philco had failed to provide automatic frequency control, a feature that locks the color into place as a viewer flips channels. Instead Philco customers were expected to play with the fine-tuning control to dial things in, a task that called for a fairly high-level understanding of color signal processing. Philco's customers didn't understand, and the warranty calls for in-home tutorials went through the roof. Philco responded by announcing to service dealers that lack of automatic fine tuning was not considered a defect, and no more money would be paid in recompense. But the dealers still had to make the home visits, and the customers were not about to pay. Philco now began receiving tens of thousands of warranty charge slips reporting a wide variety of phantom hardware problems, invented by the dealers to cut their losses. Philco quietly went out of business.

A small investment in analysis, rapid prototyping, iterative design, and user testing at the beginning of a project can pay major dividends at the end. Design and testing professionals will not cost you time and money; they will save you time and money. Remember, if you're doing it right, quality is free.

Kansei *Engineering*

*I*n the seventies and eighties, Japanese cars were transformed from tiny square boxes into smoothly curving shapes, as their engineers and designers turned their attention to style and delight. When driving a Mazda in Hawaii last year, I periodically caught some sort of movement out of the corner of my eye. It turned out to be the air-conditioning vents in the center of the dashboard. The engineers had designed in a motor to sweep the louvers back and forth gently, stirring the air to eliminate hot and cold spots. Was this necessary? Perhaps not. But it was a delight.[1]

With their blend of quality, comfort, and style, Japanese luxury cars became an enormous force in a traditional American and European market. (What could be more luxurious than a car that doesn't break?) But quality is about continuous improvement, and the Japanese moved on.

Since the year A.D. 618 the Japanese have been creating beautiful Zen gardens, environments of harmony designed to instill in their users a sense of serenity and peace. Zen, the Buddhism of Japan, had abandoned the traditional path to enlightenment—studying and memorizing scriptures—and instead attempted to recreate the original circumstances that led to the enlightenment of the Buddha. He, you may recall, reached enlightenment not by studying or by mortification of the flesh (he had spent a couple of years pulling out his hair strand by strand, to no avail), but by removing himself from the world of formal learning to sit quietly beneath a Bo tree. There he meditated, clearing his mind of all the chaos and fury of the world, until enlightenment came upon him.

....
1 Particularly given Mazda's reputation for quality. Were I the owner of the car, I would not fear it to be yet another feature designed to break just past the warranty period.

The Japanese garden was brought to life as a surrogate for the Bo tree. Every rock and tree is thoughtfully placed in patterns that are at once random and yet teeming with order. Rocks are not just strewn about; they are carefully arranged in odd-numbered groupings and sunk into the ground to give the illusion of age and stability. Waterfalls are not simply lined with interesting rocks; they are tuned to create just the right burble and plop. Plants are bent and twisted, roughed into shapes that echo ancient trees clinging to wind-swept mountains.

Kenichi Yamamoto, president of Mazda Motor Corporation, explained *kansei* during a speech at the University of Michigan: "There is something general about the tactile, sensual, and therefore psychological relationship between people and their physical environment. People have learned to associate certain sensations and certain emotions as part of their overall feeling of well-being" (Taguchi and Clausing 1990). *Kansei* speaks to a totality of experience: colors, sounds, shapes, tactile sensations, and kinesthesia, as well as the personality and consistency of interactions.

When Mazda built the Miata, they wanted a car that would echo British sports cars of the past. That did not mean turning out a replicar with a modern engine and frame. It meant reproducing the driving experience. Bob Hall, in Mazda's Irvine, California, R&D center, launched the project, choosing as his inspiration Colin Chapman's 1962 Lotus Elan Roadster. Its development was taken over by Toshihiko Hirai in Hiroshima. In approaching design, it was not the shape of the fenders that Hirai-San felt would do the trick, but the feel of the steering wheel, the grip of the seats. To capture a feeling of *kansei,* the designers applied a technique called "concept clarification." Hirai-San said, "We spent as much time refining the basic idea of what we called the lightweight sports car as we did on the car's actual development."[2]

Hirai-San has been further quoted: "[The designers] fought to remain true to those ideas. Their guiding principle was the feeling 'of oneness between man and horse'" (Gross 1989).

They built the car, but something was wrong. It looked British, it felt British, it even smelled British, but it was entirely too quiet. They went after the exhaust system, redesigning it to create that marvelous

....
2 This technique of carefully building a clear, shared vision was also responsible for the purity and effectiveness of the original Macintosh.

low-throated burble of a British engine at low RPMs. The illusion was complete.

The *kansei* computers of tomorrow will offer users a simple, tightly integrated, and, above all, natural environment that will facilitate users' work while making them feel comfortable and at peace. Let us look at a few hardware and software considerations.

Hardware Kansei

If we are to immerse people's senses in the computer experience, we must move to high-bandwidth displays; 256 colors may be a vast improvement over the 1-bit displays of old, but they are no substitute for the lushness of a 24-bit environment brought to life by a master graphic designer. One only has to catch the briefest glance of a program like Convolver to appreciate what a substantial difference universal 24-bit color will make. With 24-bit color at hand, we can then move on to higher resolutions and true 3D.

Sound is important to the *kansei* experience. Many people now enjoy computer systems with quality 16-bit sound, but it is not yet standard, so many software developers neatly avoid the extra work of building smooth, high-fidelity-sound fields.

Touch is vital in human-to-human communication in establishing connection and rapport. We will need to supply users with pads that transmit pressure and position, through which people can touch each other's hands (or whatever).

Kansei spaces are continuous and without seams. You do not go to one Japanese garden to enjoy rocks, another to enjoy water. Today our computer users are surrounded by specialized boxes: a computer here, a scanner there, a printer down the hall. *Kansei* hardware environments will blend these disparate elements into a unified whole. An example is Julie's sensitive surface that eliminates the need for a separate scanner. Another element we integrated into Julie's workspace design, though not shown in the film, was her printer. It was not down the hall. Just as Julie could rub real paper into cyberspace, she could drag a sheet of her cyberpaper into real space by sliding it off the right edge of the display, where it would "reappear" from a printer slot just beneath.

Many software designers have abandoned hope of moving beyond the limited hardware devices of today. They are in the position of the carpenter armed with only a hammer, to whom everything looks suspiciously like a nail. As an example, software designers in the catalog shopping industry have been working for years to streamline the order-taking process. Customers are now given customer numbers, printed on subsequent catalog issues. By reciting the number, customers can often avoid the labor of having to recite their addresses and having to spell their last names (which can take some of us a considerable amount of time). Recently some merchants have been able to store credit card numbers in encrypted form for subsequent purchases. When a customer places a new order, the ordertaker sees only the last four digits of the card, enough to ensure confirmation but not enough to allow theft or fraud.

Wrong, wrong, wrong, wrong, wrong. The proper solution to catalog phone order sales—long overdue—is an intelligent phone with a card reader built in. Upon connecting to the merchant, the buyer could press a single button to transmit his or her complete name and address. When satisfied with the order, the caller could swipe his or her card through the reader. (Later the reader would be replaced by a slot for a smart card holding electronic cash.)

Software designers must stop looking at the world as a giant software nail. They must begin the active search for and acquisition of new hardware tools that will reempower users in the coming decade. *Kansei* is not hardware or software in isolation. It arises from a harmony of both.

Software Design and an Attitude of Kansei

Where does *kansei* start? Not with the hardware. Not with the software either. *Kansei* starts with attitude, as does quality. The original Xerox Star team had it. So did the Lisa team, and the Mac team after. All were dedicated to building a single, tightly integrated environment—a totality of experience. Even with the crushing burdens of the software explosion of the past ten years, the Macintosh interface has held up remarkably well.

Windows, to date, has been lacking in *kansei*. Windows has been a false illusion sitting on the modality of DOS below. The choppiness of the experience spreads far beyond the confines of the display. Contrast it with the Macintosh, designed from the beginning for plug and play. The reality of dropping in new software or hardware often falls far short of the ideal, but the philosophy, the attitude, has been there. To date, the Windows world has been strewn with incompatibilities and disruptions. Only now is it being brought under some control.

In the future, people will need to work naturally at their homes, on the train, on airplanes, and in fast-food restaurants between appointments, with full access to their information space and their friends and coworkers. Their computers will become part of their lives, as natural an extension of their minds as a pen or pencil is of their bodies. They will need the kind of harmonious environment that the Starfire film portrays.

KPT Convolver, recently released by HSC Software, is a marvelous example of *kansei* design. It replaces the extensive lineup of filters that graphic designers traditionally grapple with when using such tools as Photoshop with a simple, integrated, harmonious environment (Figure 16.1).

In the past, designers have followed a process of picturing their desired end result in their mind, then applying a series of filters sequentially, without benefit of undo beyond the last-applied filter. Convolver lets users play, trying any combination of filters at will,

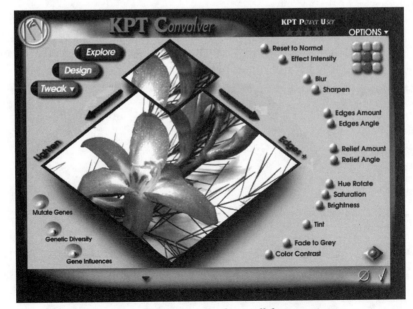

Figure 16.1 Convolver. This composite shows all features at once.

either on their own or with the computer's aid and advice. If, upon applying color contrast late in the game, it becomes amply clear that the change you made earlier to reduce the sharpness is no longer working out, the sharpness can be increased without any loss and without affecting anything that came after. Both time and space lie at the user's complete control.

Convolver is also beautiful. Kai Krause has taken advantage of the guaranteed 24-bit world of graphic design, applying the full powers of his brilliant graphic talent. If you would like to examine a seminal instantiation of tomorrow's look and feel, pick up a copy. It should be a standard product in any software designer's library.

To reempower our users, we must design and construct illusions with substance, believability, and appeal. (More about this in Chapter 34.) We must build a new generation of smooth, open, *kansei* environments. We must remove the confining walls of today's application-centered world and build wide-open spaces where people can work, play, learn, and create in comfort and without struggle.

When Mazda brings out a new model, they mold a new user illusion to fit. They don't add a turbocharger, then hack out a hole in the existing hood to provide room. Engineers, stylists, and designers work together from the beginning to see that not only does the turbocharger fit within the body but that the body shape itself conveys the car's newly increased speed and power. The first cars off the line don't have loose doors, open seams, and body panels missing. Every new design goes back to the basics of *kansei*, appealing to every sense in a simple, natural way. We must nurture our own designs in the same way, moving away from topsy-turvy twists and turns toward smooth, *kansei* perfection.

PART 5

Starfire Applied

The first goal of the Starfire project was to generate a wellspring of ideas for Sun's own future systems. We went far beyond whipping up a few graphics for the film. We designed a complete user model for an integrated, casual, powerful, world-spanning, continuous personal cyberspace. The chapters in this part lay out the details of the Starfire project, from the driving principles of the design to the shape of many new proposed objects.

In the next decade, the students of today, shaped by influences from MTV to *Wired,* will begin the journey outward into the creative and compelling world of pure electronic design. Particulars of the Starfire interface will be superseded. That's progress. However, its philosophy of integrated environments, casual collaboration and communication, and the proliferation of objects and services are important concepts that will likely stand the test of time. The industry has a lot of work ahead.

CHAPTER 17

Integration

*I*ntegration implies a drawing together, a harmonizing, of every facet of the computer experience. Integration is a central tenet in building a *kansei* environment. Starfire is a study in integration, combining the elements of videophone and computing, offering compound active documents that combine the bits and pieces of perhaps dozens of documents that might clutter desktops.

People and Their Computers

Over the years our operating systems have become increasingly complex. Those who have grown with them are often unaware that what was already a steep learning curve has now become a virtual wall. Earlier efforts at simplification have been piecemeal: a NameTool here, a visual interface element there.

By increasing the richness of user-computer communication, we will be able to strip away the modes, the buttons, and the switches that have turned the task of interacting with a computer from a friendly dialog into a fight to survive. As computers increase in awareness of context, and as we build useful and practical agents, our interactions will move from command to conversation.

Starfire is a complete environment, enabling the average user to work within it without ever dropping through the cracks into the operating system. That is not to say that people will be locked out of the system. It is to say that every detail of the visible interface to be built will be designed in such a way that people will be fully empowered to get their work done quickly, easily, and efficiently.

Where people must deal with the system, performing such tasks as installing software and troubleshooting normal problems, they will be provided with a clean, well-lighted "basement," with automated tools and clear instruction.

Macintosh users today perform the following tasks without any technical support:

- Install hardware boards inside the computer.
- Install system software.
- Install fonts.
- Install printer and other device drivers.
- Install applications.
- Install and maintain local networks.

Expert users—people with a technical bent and a few months of experience under their belts—routinely do the following:

- Set up and maintain file servers.
- Troubleshoot complex networks and track down system conflicts.
- Recover from serious disk crashes and other unscheduled events.

All computer users should be able to carry out these tasks, with significantly greater ease than Macintosh users today. If those working for large companies choose to continue their dependence on system administrators, that's fine: the system administrator's jobs will be that much easier than today, and each system administrator will be able to support four or five times as many machines.[1]

Documents

Starfire is a document-centered interface: multiple tool sets may be brought to bear on various regions within a single document. The user can create, in the same "active document," a drawing, a painting, a video clip, text, and graphics while never leaving the document. Not only is the user's model simplified, but the great proliferation of

....
[1] The myth exists that Macintosh systems are not maintained by system administrators. This is not true: there is generally the equivalent of one-quarter a person for somewhere around every 50 people. That person is not a professional administrator but rather that technically oriented man or woman four cubicles over.

fragmentary documents needed to build serious reports and presentations is eliminated, reducing housekeeping and the need for elaborate filing schemes.

The Starfire vision also erases today's sharp division between documents and containers, replacing it instead with a wealth of new objects sharing the characteristics of both. (More of this when we get to Chapters 19 and 20.)

Services

Ironically, with the advent of object-oriented systems, objects long in the users' world will disappear, in favor of services.

Today, most of the capabilities of the computer are captured within individual objects, called applications. Tomorrow, many of these capabilities will become universally available. Let me offer a real-world example of the power that arises when this transition occurs.

Until A.P. Giannini founded the Bank of America around the turn of the century, banks had only a single building per city. If you wanted to do banking, you went downtown. Giannini introduced the concept of branch banking by scattering small banks all over San Francisco. People were a lot happier. In fact, they were so happy, they didn't know they still had a problem: they could get money only between 10:00 A.M. and 3:00 P.M. on those few weekdays that were not bank holidays, a total of, as I recall, 33 open days per year (34 if the bank toughed it out on Groundhog Day). Bank ATMs cured the hours problem, making people even happier, but only because they didn't realize they still had a problem.

It seems that certain people, on a lark, would sometimes spend every bit of cash they had with them and would actually have to turn down badly needed goods and services, like chocolate bars and roller-coaster rides. This tragic situation began to be alleviated in the late eighties as banks dropped tiny electronic bank branches down beside every cashier at grocery stores, Las Vegas casinos, and Disneyland ticket booths. This "debit card" system allowed banks to extend their infrastructure beyond the confines of traditional banks and into the very heart of commercial America.

We still have a few minor problems with our banking, like getting mugged when visiting the auto-teller in the middle of the night, but even these problems will fall away as digital cash comes online, and we fill up our smart cash cards at our own computers.

Remember that recently discovered giant fungus in the Pacific Northwest that lives beneath several square miles of the woods? It isn't *in* the forest, it *is* the forest. It provides a ubiquitous mushroom service to every square foot of its area.

Banks have become the fungus of the nineties.

In the same way, services in the next generation interface, such as dictionaries, thesauri, and mail, will lie in wait beneath the surface, ready to pop up whenever and wherever users or their tools may call upon them. You will no longer compose mail in an e-mail tool. You will compose it using any stationery you please, attach an address, then drop it on an icon of a mailbox, where it will be routed by the most appropriate (or your explicitly indicated) means: e-mail, fax, or snail mail.

Universal Tools

How many text processors are on your computer? You probably own a full-blown word processor, but text processors are also to be found in graphics applications, spreadsheets, and every other application where characters are to be entered. Every one of these text processors is subtly different. When I double-click on a word using Microsoft Word, the text processor selects both the word and any space that might follow. When I carry out the identical action using America Online, the space is left behind, necessitating an entirely different strategy.

Rich text processors, as well as rich graphics processors, will become universal tool sets, available to every piece of stationery you possess. (A version of these processors must be supplied as part of the system, but users should be able to replace those supplied with their own objects or links to favorite applets.)

People and People

Video phone is a given, but linking people with sight and sound is not enough. Future users will want simple collaborative objects, such as electronic white boards, but collaboration must be integrated far deeper into the system. We must support multiple users, manipulating the same objects simultaneously. We must design systems to allow anything that appears on one screen to be offered to a large group of people for simultaneous manipulation.

You saw in the Starfire scenario many instances of collaboration. All were seamless. We took collaboration to be a fundamental property of the system, an underlying service that will be as easy for developers to offer to as it will be for users to use. (This may be a bit naive. Nothing has ever been easy for developers to develop to, but hope springs eternal.)

Almost everything that we use a computer to do has an inherently collaborative purpose, such as sending e-mail, preparing a document for eventual distribution, or accessing a database of information that has been collected and organized by someone else. We must eliminate obstacles to smooth collaboration by including communication, sharing, and representations of people and places in future environments.

Collaboration is a complex, socially negotiated process. Computer environments should provide enough information and cues about collaborators so that they can communicate effectively and efficiently. Cues will range from showing people's hand, eye scan, and cursor positions in a shared drawing tool to information about who changed what and when.

All documents can be shared

Just as any physical document can be shared with other people, so all electronic documents will become sharable with others. Here are some of the forms that sharing can take:

- *Interactive sharing.* Multiple people viewing and editing a document at the same time.
- *Baton-passing sharing.* Multiple people viewing a document, but only one person actively editing it at a time.
- *View sharing.* One person broadcasting a view of a document to multiple people (e.g., a lecturer showing slides).
- *Asynchronous distribution, review, and revision.* Authors' distributing a document for several people to review, then integrating their comments into a revised version.
- *Asynchronous sharing.* Several people working on the document at different times. (They need to be aware of changes that the others make.)
- *Asynchronous broadcast.* Distributing a document (for example, a newsletter) for others to read when they want to.

- *Sequential circulation.* Routing a document to a sequence of people for some action (for example, approval signatures).
- *Screen sharing.* Sharing entire contents of displays, not just specific documents.

Privilege, Powers, and Security

Hypermedia will soon become both more casual and commonplace. Many, if not most, of our documents, from memos to formal reports, will soon harbor hidden, foundational information. This may range from spreadsheets supporting a visible chart to earlier drafts retained for historical reasons. If we design systems so that readers can explore as deeply as they wish without restriction, we will be removing control from someone else—the owner or author. We must therefore examine the reader's rights in the light of the rights of others.

We need to support various levels of privilege applicable to documents, portions of documents, and other objects, whether for simultaneous use or sequential use. What follows is a proposal for the rights of various players:

- *Owners.* Owners automatically have author privileges. Owners are the only people empowered to add new authors to a document. Owners might also be able to prevent authors from adding reviewers and readers to the circle of privilege, but the default condition might well allow authors to send out reviewer and reader versions.

- *Authors.* An author would have full control over the contents of a document (or subdocument, should multiple authors want to protect their individual work). Authors could alter any or all parts of a document and normally could send out reviewer and read-only versions to people outside the circle.

- *Reviewers.* A reviewer could not change the underlying document. A reviewer could mark up a document and add annotations (voice, video, whatever). Reviewers' markups would be in the form of visible, executable gestures. For example, an editor could use a deletion ~~deletion~~ gesture, such as the one you just encountered. Such a gesture is stored as a gesture and displayed as a graphic object, but since the editor is in reader mode, it would not alter the underlying document itself. Authors (or owners) could then, if they agree with the sentiments expressed by the gesture, execute those gestures, permanently altering the document.

- ***Annotators.*** Some people will be given the power to add highlights and comments to other people's work.

- ***Readers.*** A reader might have been given the controls necessary to view information in alternative forms, such as seeing a chart as a bar chart rather than a pie chart, or exploring additional information of interest. A reader could also alter the readability of a document. This might entail using a different layout view, with larger fonts. It might involve temporarily "dialing back" the background on contemporary documents, like those found in the pages of *Wired* magazine, that swirl color and pattern through their text, raising visual interest at the expense of readability.

Readers could not change the underlying document but would have the power to mark it up, just as they can a personal copy of a real book. Readers could underline favorite sections and add annotations, sticky notes, or anything else to a document for the same reason that readers mark up books today—to create reference marks and mnemonic devices.

Owners and authors would also have privileges for subareas of a document. For example, the chief financial officer of a corporation may be responsible for sending out a monthly report on the financial condition of the company. The officer may want to enable readers to copy, then modify some of the verbiage of the report to "repurpose" it for specialized audiences, but the officer needs to lock the financial figures so they cannot be altered inadvertently or by design.

Because of the various forms of possible sharing, users will need clear and constantly updated feedback as to the collaborative status of a document. (Is this being interactively shared? Can I only make annotations on this document? Can I read only this region? How much of my screen can the other collaborators see?) We will need to provide users with the same subtle and natural cues that people use in the real world to be aware of who's paying attention to what and to whom.

Work Flow

Forms and annotation will support work flow in an organization. People need to send documents and forms to people in sequence or in parallel. They need to be able to keep track of the status of the materials that are being routed around. Work flow control will be used to route documents for electronic signatures. It will be used for change management and work-task distribution and coordination. Tracking, historically part of specific commercial and custom applications, will become either an intrinsic system function or a commercially supplied service.

Computers and Networks

Computers and networks will flow together. Many computers will essentially be terminals on the net. This is not as much of a throwback as it might seem. Instead of being enslaved to a single computer, tomorrow's terminals will be windows on the world. Rather than returning to centralization, they will represent the ultimate in decentralization.

Even those computers that are more oriented toward stand-alone operation will meld fully into the network whenever they touch. Tomorrow's computers will not only gather much of their data from the net, but will gather an equal amount of their capability in the form of applets—tiny tools that flow from the net as needed, then disappear into cyberdust.

The lines between local, corporate, and Internet data will disappear. Applet-driven spreadsheets are as comfortable accepting a World-Wide Web address into a cell as they are a number or formula. (Such Web addresses might be, for example, the live, changing price of chocolate, driving a candy company's costing spreadsheet and in turn the thickness of its bars.) The successors to HTML, Acrobat, and Java can finally eliminate all barriers to data and process compatibility.

Achieving Integration

In the past, these kinds of integration were impossible due to fundamental limitations of hardware and software systems. In the future, any lack of integration will be based on the computer industry's failure to plan, communicate, and cooperate. I will discuss the barriers to cooperation and the steps we need to take to overcome those barriers in the final chapter of this book.

Casual Computing

Starfire is a casual environment. When Julie wanted to place the man beside the car in her illustration, it was not some high-powered event. She just pointed, clicked, spoke a few words, and slid the man into place. The system masked its powerful formal complexity, making her job relaxed and easy.

New computer designs, to cater to the shift toward shared responsibility between management and responsible workers, will need to be far more adaptive and flexible. New workspaces must be far "looser" than the most flexible desktop we know today, enabling people to work more in the matter of finger painting rather than today's paint by number.

> *Any casualness on the part of the user must be supported by an equal and opposite organizational formality on the part of the computer.*

People with personal secretaries can be far more casual than any of the rest of us. The secretaries organize while their bosses play. The bosses recklessly scatter reports on top of bookcases or beneath coffee cups, secure in the knowledge that their secretaries will file them away where they can be instantly retrieved (as long as the secretary is not on vacation).

Research as far back as the Xerox Star project has consistently found that people want structure; they want boundaries. What they insist upon is a vote on what these limits will be. Here are some examples expressing the casualness philosophy.

Casual Document Creation

Today, document processing on workstations is done with highly controlling applications like Frame and Interleaf, designed specifically for page layout personnel rather than authors. These applications not only demand that writing be highly structured, they demand the structuring be done before the writing is entered. More flexible tools exist, but they typically lack a full document processor's power.

Many people assume that the opposite would be ideal—that the best interface is no interface at all, that every document should begin as a piece of blank paper. In reality, this robs people of the freedom to launch into their work, forcing them to design the shape and form of their document first. The answer to freedom within boundaries lies in stationery.

Stationery provides flexibility and portability of form and policy. In the Starfire world, any form of container—active paper, scrapbook, sticky note, business card—may be saved as stationery. Stationery can range from something as simple as a plain piece of paper with some background layout rules, to elaborate forms, bristling with tool sets and armed with an array of pointers to other documents.

Companies will create hierarchies of stationery, with each generation inheriting organizing principles from the stationery above. A company could then, for example, change its standard font in all company documents simply by changing the characteristics of its master stationery (Figure 18.1).

Stationery is as old as the Xerox Star. It works. It needs to become a central feature once again.

Casual Connections

If two people have online calendars and both computers are within "speaking distance," via network or, for portables, wireless or infrared, their computers can communicate, displaying their two calendars superimposed to show combined free time. (You can already do this today, as long as both people share compatible computers. The industry must accept and promulgate standards currently under development so that all computers can speak a common language.)

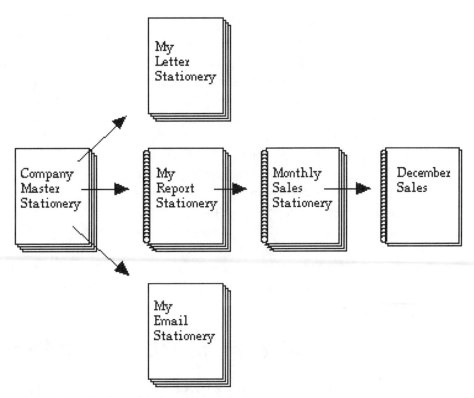

Figure 18.1 *Simple model of stationery inheritance*

Casual Information Creation

Future users should be able to generate information in the most casual
way possible. This must be particularly true of personal information
management. Systems should recognize and differentiate among standard information formats, such as phone numbers, dates, personal
names versus company names (not as difficult a problem as it might
seem—Newton is already doing most of it), and other information the
user is likely to want to "jot down." Personal information managers
can then let a user just start typing, signal the user when the message is
understood, then offer the user aid and counsel to complete the user's
task in as simple a way as possible.

Let's say that you begin listening to a voice mail message. You jot
down the sender's name on your to-do list. At that point, you have no
idea what the call is about. You only know who the caller is. Instantly,
the system fills in the caller's company name, phone numbers,

addresses, and so on, having matched her name against your personal phone book. The caller ends the message by proposing a meeting for 10:30 Friday. As you jot down 10:30, your calendar (as you have instructed it) automatically opens. You click on Friday, and you see that you are indeed free. You press on a single control, and you now have an appointment set in your book.

The calendar offers a subtle prompt that you have not supplied a location. You click on the caller's e-mail icon and have your system generate a message accepting the meeting and requesting the location. Later, her computer calls yours and enters the missing information directly into your calendar, as authorized.

These capabilities assume the existence of a powerful underlying database. People will need to have their calendar, phone book, project organizer, and notebook, as well as a myriad of other documents and functions, all tightly coupled.

Casual Information Distribution

To allow for growth of a paperless world, we will need universal, powerful new file formats. One hundred years after the invention of the telegraph, all standard e-mail on the Internet has added is lowercase text. The growth of the net and the perceived need for compatibility within the rest of the industry are driving the standardization of text, graphics, and other formats, such as video and audio, along with fundamental tool sets for reading and manipulating them. We need to see that the standards become far richer, and we need to do it fast.

Lotus Notes, Adobe Acrobat, Apple Quicktime and Quicktime VR, and Sun's Java applets are joining earlier efforts such as Postscript, TIFF, and TrueType in forming portable and compatible industry standards. Some of these standards are implemented as enclaves. (See Chapter 35.) Lotus Notes, for example, is a mini-environment that offers both services and tools not found outside on the main system. We must design our systems to enable these enclaves to melt back into the system, becoming instead ubiquitous. By their very nature, object-oriented systems will be more open to letting such system- and network-wide services and tools settle in their midst.

CHAPTER 19

Active Documents

*T*oday's visual interfaces offer two primary objects: folders and files. They are designed for two different purposes and are never interchangeable. Folders and their cousins, volumes, act as containers, holding documents and other files. Documents contain data, not other files, with each document type having its own strengths and limitations, as dictated by its creator. (Documents are joined by other specialized files, such as applications and extensions. Some systems also make visible processes—representations of currently running code.)

We based Starfire on a single, fundamental container, with many variations. Some of these variations, such as business cards and tool sets, would be relatively fixed. Others, such as active documents, notebooks, scrapbooks, and folders, would—from the user's vantage point—be mutable at the user's will. The dividing line between file and folder would disappear.

What Is an Active Document?

The active document is the fundamental document form for Starfire. Figure 19.1 is an example of an open active document.

Individual regions are tied to a tool set. In many cases, tools other than those used to create the data can be used to edit. Tools and controls are organized in palettes, which can either be free floating or snapped onto the edge of an active document. Once a tool set is invoked, by clicking on it or selecting a region driven by it, the tool set takes over the palettes and the majority of the menus, just as invoking

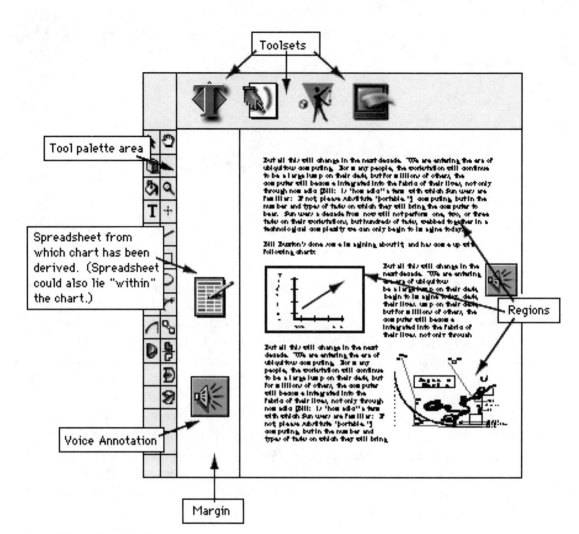

Figure 19.1 *An open active document*

an application today does. The difference is that the tool set is operating within the document, instead of the other way around.[1]

Users can mix and match different media types in a single active document. Each media type is contained in its own region, but the regions can be seamlessly integrated. The boundary of a region can be displayed or hidden, and the background of a region may be white or colored and may range from transparent to opaque (Figure 19.2). These features allow the user to closely mingle many different types of data.

....
1 I first proposed this model to John Sculley in 1985. Apple's OpenDoc is at last bringing it to fruition.

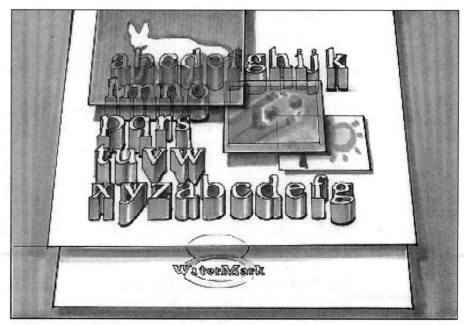

Figure 19.2 *View of an active document showing regions*

Layout Styles

The rules of the document will be dictated by layout styles users attach. Users will choose from a variety of styles, many provided by independent software developers. Layout styles will offer organizational information, as well as a starting style. Users can then open custom style sheets within, as is done within applications today.

Users wanting to create a formal report might choose a page layout style to allow them to create a multipage document with headers, footers, margins, multiple columns, and many other features found only within advanced page layout applications today. They might add a formal report layout style for its variety of special cover formats, table of contents, divider pages, and intelligent indexing.

Tool Sets

Tool sets can be added to an active document or stationery to increase the range of activities a user can carry out in that document. Tool sets are attached by dropping the tool set icon on the document or stationery, either in a collapsed view or when open. The icon of the added tool set appears in the tool set bar. More than one tool set of a kind can be in the bar. For example, the text tool sets from both Microsoft and Frame could be in the bar at the same time. When the user clicks on some text in the document, the tools and menus of the tool set last associated with that text would be shown.

Another way a tool set might be added would be by dragging a clipping built with another tool set onto an existing active document. For example, the clipping may have been constructed using a drawing tool set different from the drawing tool set already in place. The user may want to maintain both tool sets or cast one away. These tool sets may be objects maintained locally or applets scattered across the world.

Buttons and Controls

Buttons and other controls will be available within every container type under Starfire. Their use will range from enabling readers to change the appearance of a chart to full-scale hypertext capabilities. Like other interface elements, we will need to provide consistency among these controls, binding appearance to behavior, so that users can understand and therefore properly predict their behavior.

More Workspace Objects

*D*uring early 1992, the Starfire team investigated a rich variety of container objects that might be found in the workspaces of the future. Some, such as scrapbooks, were home grown at Sun. Others, such as piles, business cards, and clippings, were pioneered elsewhere in Silicon Valley.

Today everything is a file, and everything must be kept in a single kind of container, a folder. The object family we considered would enable people to get a better sense of scale (file cabinets versus folders) and be able to form organizations of information ranging from casual to formal (scrapbooks versus reports). These changes would enable people both to reduce the sheer quantity of files in the workspace and to make more sense of the ones that are left.

Many containers with which the users will interact in the Starfire world will inherit characteristics and behavior from the active document object. This will extend beyond objects normally associated with "paper" (memos, reports, drawings, spreadsheets, mail, etc.), to include the work surface, folders, and tool palettes. For example, the user will be able to doodle on the work surface background or add a note to the front of a folder.

All types of containers will provide a core set of actions. Additional actions will differ among containers. For example, a scrapbook might have a table of contents, and a folder might recognize a "List by Title" command. (The difference between a scrapbook and a folder is that a scrapbook is a more "intimate" container, usually containing fewer objects than a folder.)

Thumbnails will replace generic-looking document icons, providing users with visual cues as to the nature of the material inside a container. Their appearance will go beyond today's thumbnails to reflect the amount of material they contain.

Today's containers look the same whether they contain one or one million files. All Starfire containers, regardless of their view, will provide visual feedback to the user as to their size. From active documents to scrapbooks to file folders, all will look thicker and more complex as they become thicker and more complex. Their shape will help users build a more accurate model of the size and shape of their information space, as well as help them pick out a given container against a background of many others, by virtue of its characteristic appearance.

Workspace Containers

File Cabinets and Beyond

One million files will not, in the real world, fit into a single folder. Starfire users and agents will select objects that reflect the scale of their information collections.

Folders

Folders will gain new features shared by all containers. For example, users will be able to draw on or color the backgrounds of their folders. They will be able to attach sticky notes and scribble along the edges.

Intelligent Folders

Folders can be made intelligent by attaching rules and behavior. What appears in a container might get there because the object meets some criteria rather than by being placed by the user. For example, an intelligent folder might be taught to attract any and all correspondence about a specific project that crosses your desk or even the network. (This capability will not be limited to folders. Folders are just an attractive place to have a lot of unread documents first collect.)

Archives

An archiving folder may contain perhaps two dozen drafts of a document, some auto-saved by the system, some explicitly saved. An archiving folder will automatically mirror the latest version of the document by replacing its own folder-like image with a thumbnail of the document. When the user double-clicks on the folder, the archive will automatically launch the latest version of the document. Normally, users will experience the illusion that there is but a single document, but when they want to refer to an earlier version, they need only use the Reveal command instead of the Open command, and the container will open to show all the previous drafts within.

Commercial Applications

Commercial applications will be magic folders, mirroring a pad of active-document stationery within. Thus, a user will be able to "open" an application just as today, automatically launching a single document. As magic folders, applications can be commanded to reveal their contents. An application will typically contain a pad of stationery and a tool set.

If the user subsequently applies the Reveal command to the tool set, it will show various components within. For example, a word processor might contain a document processor tool set, a page layout tool set, some dictionaries, a grammar checker, a spell checker, a basic graphics processor tool set, settings files, and help files. By placing all these miscellaneous files within the application itself, we will significantly reduce clutter and increase organization. (Today's solution to the problem, aliases, adds a new layer of complexity and actually results in even more files.)

Some special-purpose applications will continue to stand alone, but even these will make every effort to blend into the environment, using the system text processor, graphics processor, spell checker, and so forth, and enabling transfer of resulting information easily and gracefully.

Piles

Piles, first researched at Apple Computer in 1991–1992, allow people to cluster together related documents without any formal organization, then quickly and easily retrieve them from the collection (Mander, Solomon, and Wong 1992).

Clippings

A region inside an active document, when drawn away from the active document, becomes a clipping. A video clip of the Mandelbrot set in its iconic (thumbnail) form, might look like this:

Clippings may be "stored" within an active document or any other container. They share most characteristics of full-fledged documents.

Two clippings appear in their full-size form in Starfire during the scene between Julie and her friend Natalie. Both the "old TV commercial from the company library," and Julie's 3D model of the sports car that she dragged out of her report are clippings. The sports car, like many other Starfire objects, does not arbitrarily display a border.

Sticky Notes

Sticky notes are casual objects that can be pinned or pasted inside, around, or on the front or back of any other container type or can remain independent. Users should be able to create such objects as easily as reaching for a pad of sticky notes in the real world.

For all practical purposes, sticky notes are miniature active documents. They can be multipage and contain regions of any data type. They differ from documents by their visual appearance and the casual manner of their creation and manipulation.

Scrapbooks

Document collections during the course of a project tend to split into two: the formal document or group of documents that will be presented at the end of the project, and the great wealth of source materials, false starts, bits, pieces, and scraps that build up along the way. Active documents offer the user a formal medium of information presentation. A scrapbook is a container for all the fruits of a project, formal and informal, fragmentary or extensive. A scrapbook, in its closed form, might look something like this:

Scrapbooks will have inherently less organization than more formal containers such as notebooks and reports. In an intermediate size, the scrapbook might show a single document per page (Figure 20.1). In its fully open form, a scrapbook might look like the example in Figure 20.2. More pages will be revealed at once by unfolding the scrapbook, its pages being connected together in a fan-fold fashion (Figure 20.3).

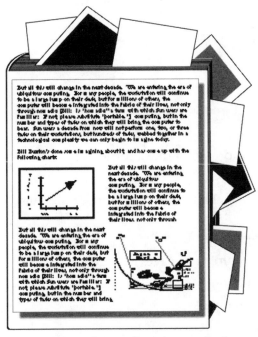

Figure 20.1 An intermediate-size scrapbook

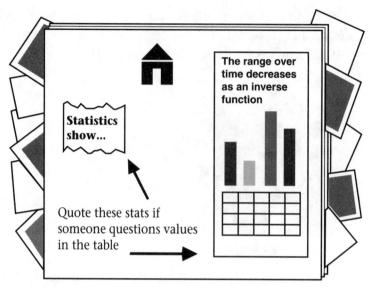

Figure 20.2 *A fully open scrapbook*

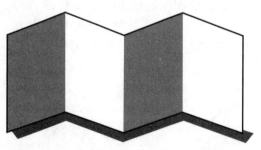

Figure 20.3 *Scrapbook behavior*

A scrapbook can be:

- Created by placing items on top of one another
- Thumbnailed
- Flipped through in its thumbnail form, revealing individual documents
- Opened to reveal a single page
- Unfolded to reveal any number of pages at once
- Browsed through like a book
- Merged with another scrapbook
- Shared synchronously or asynchronously

A scrapbook can contain:

- Whole documents
- Fragments, such as clippings or scraps
- Annotations (text, graphics, other types)
- Icons and thumbnails
- A table of contents
- An index
- Other scrapbooks
- Tool sets
- Editing history
- Items from other scrapbooks
- Pointers (references) to items not in the scrapbook

A user might create a scrapbook that contains all business cards. In thumbnail mode, flipping through the scrapbook would be like flipping through a Rolodex. When open, the user could see a page of business cards or could view the contents of the scrapbook and see all the business cards in list form. This list could then be searched and sorted.

Either a subclass of a scrapbook or an alternate name for a scrapbook might be "project book."

Notebooks

Users might convert active documents into notebooks as a step along the way toward formalizing their presentation. They will be able to select from a wide variety of published layouts, then customize the final look and behavior to fit their needs.

A user will be able to convert an active document into a notebook quickly and easily, without losing any information. Users will also be able to convert notebooks into active documents; information not required in the simpler form will be maintained in the background in case the user wishes to revert.[1] A typical notebook is shown in Figure 20.4.[2]

....
1 Keeping information of any kind in the background raises privacy and security issues. We will need to keep users aware of and informed about any information they cannot immediately see.

2 You will find a still image of a notebook in the source materials at the end of the Directors' Cut Starfire tape. The notebook also briefly appears within the Making of Starfire piece.

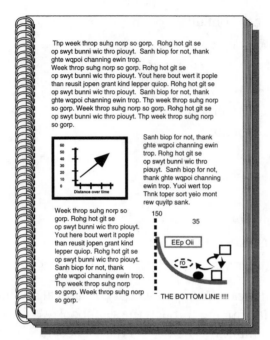

Figure 20.4 *A typical notebook*

A notebook can have dividers, a table of contents, and an index. Users can draw on individual pages in the notebook and can fasten documents, clippings, pointers, and other containers to its pages.

Daybooks

Daybooks are a special form of notebook and have special rules: a daybook cannot be converted to another container type, and anything saved in a daybook remains permanent. Items entered are also automatically time and date stamped. (Write once—read many.) The daybook, a replacement for the bound daybooks used by engineers and others today, will feature an automated signature loop that would be invoked at regular intervals, requesting and collecting witnessing electronic signatures from listed individual readers.

Formal Report

Reports and other formal presentation appearances will also be simple variations of the notebook. A report will be the read-only version of a notebook, automatically removing from the unprivileged's view underlying source material. Julie, when first building her report on the Starfire car, used the notebook format. Only when meeting day drew near did she convert to the more formal, more disciplined view.

People

People are first-class objects in the Starfire world. In the words of Sun's Bob Sproull:

> Let's record information about people: how to talk to them, how to send computer information to them, how to send documents to them, how to make appointments with them, how to print out something on their printer, etc. Let's have addresses for internal mail, U.S. mail, and express delivery; let's accommodate people who are traveling or on vacation or at a temporary address. Let's also make a group a first-class object, so that people can add and remove themselves from groups (assuming appropriate permission), so that groups can enumerate their members, so that groups can establish common practices (e.g., mail to the group is archived in a certain place).

Business Cards

The electronic business card is an example of a person object (Figure 20.5). Unlike the noninteractive communication options on a physical business card (phone number, fax number, e-mail address), the communication options on an electronic business card will be quite alive. For example, clicking on a person's picture in an electronic business card will activate a video phone call to that person; clicking on someone's e-mail address in a business card will bring up a blank e-mail message addressed to the person. Dropping a document on the fax machine on a business card will fax it to them.

Business cards will be widely distributed across the network, appear in databases, and be dropped on people's workspaces during collaborative sessions. They will also be left when leaving voice or video mail. Cards will be able to be queried as to the user's current state to discover if the person is in or out (connected to cyberspace or not) or if the person does not want to be disturbed.

Figure 20.5 The icons chosen by Mr. Smith represent his videophone link, his voice phone link, and his e-mail.

Names

Objects in a Starfire world should be as lightweight as possible. Why demand that users search for a business card rather than simply typing out a portion of the person's name? Bob Sproull expands on this notion:

> We need to provide some kind of naming contexts. When I say I'm going to "send mail to Ivan," I always mean Ivan Sutherland, not because he's the only Ivan accessible via electronic mail, but because I have chosen to make the abbreviation "Ivan" unique in that way to me in any context. In other cases, context may be important: "Peter" means Peter Norvig if I'm addressing myself to an East-coast-labs problem, while "Peter" means "Peter Deutsch" if I'm sending a message to Sun Fellows.

Tickets

As business cards represent people, tickets will represent meetings. Tickets will include the name, date, and time of the meeting, the type of meeting (audio, video, telephone, etc.), and some other information, perhaps whether the ticket is transferable. Tickets to electronic meetings will also have a Join button, which will become active as soon as the meeting begins.

The System

The system will appear to the user as just another object, for purposes of customization and augmentation. Tool sets and services can be dropped on the system, just as they can be dropped on active documents and other objects. A tool set or service dropped on the system becomes available to all documents and other tool sets and services that want to call upon it.

Building Objects

Some containers will be different enough that their designers will want to start off with a brand-new object. Scrapbooks are a likely candidate. In other cases, users (or developers) will simply attach new layout styles to alter the shape and behavior of an existing object. Notebooks and reports are both direct super-sets of active documents and may be achievable by adding layout style.

Escaping Flatland

You swoop down over the sleeping city and glide silently past the huge insurance building on your right. Through a few lighted windows, you can see people still hard at work even this late at night. You bank gently to the left and begin your final descent toward University Medical Center.

As you approach the ground, you see trees coming up to meet you, but you hop lightly over them and slide through the front doors of the medical center just as an ambulance makes its way up the drive. You slip fluidly along the wide corridors of the building until you reach your final destination: the history wing of the medical library.

*I*s this a description of a supercomputer flight simulator? A fiber-network video game? A virtual reality amusement for the next millennium? No, it's the front end for the database depicted in Starfire.

3D

Designers in the future will be encouraged to think in three dimensions. By the year 2000, 3D technology will no longer be an expensive option but an integrated part of computers. It will enhance spatial relationships, aiding organization and memory. It will give us literally a new dimension in defining overall structural relationships. It will enhance realism, making systems more pleasant to use.

Perhaps the most lasting contribution of CD-ROMs will be the flowering of metaphors that they are engendering today. The island of *Myst* and the mysterious laboratory of *The History of the Universe* are the models of the 3D world of tomorrow.

The paper look of documents will shift. Multimedia documents already play havoc with the physical constraints of the real-world documents they mimic. Work at Xerox PARC and MIT's Media Lab is concentrating on new information worlds. Information trees and finite universes of infinite text will stand beside the paper metaphor, offering more powerful views into a complex information world.

Animation

Animation is the fourth dimension in a system image. In recent years, people have been experimenting, mostly unsuccessfully, with animation in the interface. Typical are the animated icons used to indicate that a live process is in the works. The movement of these icons attracts the user's attention away from the current task. (The human vision system is specialized for noticing movement, particularly at the periphery. This adaptation, while useful for noticing advancing tigers, is rather distracting when the eye is constantly pulled away because of the advancing progress of a file transmission.)[1] Two kinds of animation have already proven their worth, and will take their place in future software design.

User-Controlled Animation

If the user initiates and controls the animation, the animation cannot pull the user away from the user's current task, because causing the animation *is* the user's current task.

Apple designers made use of high-speed animation in their pile object to enable users to flash through the contents of the pile. Users could see each document in a pile, displayed in miniature at high speed, by moving their pointing device up or down through the pile. When a desired document was found, sliding the document right or left would lift it permanently into view.

....

1 Microsoft's Bob environment is again experimenting with peripheral animation. It will be interesting to see whether it lasts and whether it will find its way into more production-oriented environments. Perhaps in the end peripheral animation will turn out to be a visual form of loud music, distracting to older folks but comforting to a new generation.

Slow Animation

The real world is not a static, stable place. Things grow up, things grow old. From mountains to trees to horses, everything changes. People have evolved to "read" these changes and to make use of them in understanding the world. Future systems will make use of animation more on the time scale of a banana slug or a sea anemone, animals that get around but take their own sweet time doing so. Our future worlds will also change, in some cases, as slowly as a tree. Apple's e•World information service uses a simplified city as its central metaphor. The appearance of the city changes with the seasons. In summer, it is lush with green foliage; in winter, white with snow.

As we move toward 24-bit, high-resolution color as a standard, we will be able to develop a far richer visual language than seen on today's computers. We will use visual multiplexing to add slow animation to today's static objects. (Multiplexing is a technique of dividing up the possible characteristics of an object and assigning each to a different piece of information you want to transmit. See Chapter 19 in *Tog on Interface*.)

Today a folder holding a single document looks identical to a folder holding the Library of Congress. A document created in 1982 looks identical to a document created last Tuesday. A network information object accessed twice looks just like one accessed a thousand times. Because of this lack of feedback, computer users today must be constantly bombarded with text read-outs of excessively precise measurements of size, age, use, and other characteristics. Consider the multiplexed characteristics of a future folder:

- The base design of a folder will represent either the key file within it or the general class of contents. A user might, for example, have a video clip folder display sprocket holes, while a text clipping folder might have gray lines representing text on its face.

- A folder will display its age since creation or last use by gradually yellowing. (The yellowing, as in real life, would make all other colors—reds, blues, greens, or whatever else—gradually become more yellowish. It would not flip everything to yellow.)

- A folder will display its size by its apparent thickness.

- The documents should show signs of wear, reflecting their history (Hill et al. 1992). A folder will display how often it is accessed by developing a patina of tiny lines and cracks.

People find books by looking for, "You know, that little red one with the worn cover." They use the title for confirmation. Today we offer users little more information about folders than their titles, accompanied by a uniform icon that, being pandemic, signifies nothing. The rich visual interface that will result from multiplexing will enable users to tell at a glance the condition of their information space and to search quickly and effectively for their target.

Simulation

Simulations will become much more important as computer power finally catches up with the task. We will, of course, be simulating physical objects, such as cities or airplanes, in 3D space, but we will add a dimension by simulating social situations as well.

Roger Schank's team at Northwestern University has recently completed a product for a private water company in the Manchester region of England. The purpose of the disk is to teach new customer service representatives how to respond to incoming calls (Figure 21.1).

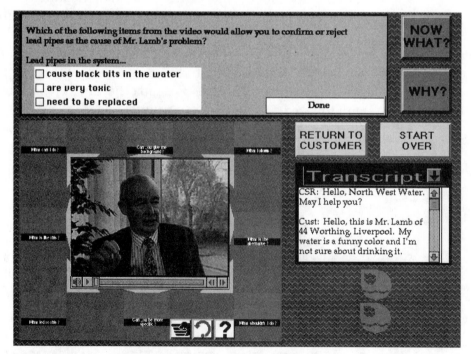

Figure 21.1 *Manchester Water Company social simulation*

Rather than transferring an existing manual to disk with a bunch of buttons to make it interactive (and thus slow you down), Schank's team generated a social simulation. They captured a thousand stories from company employees on videotape—a thousand experiences they then impressed on a CD-ROM. The new representatives carry on a telephone conversation with the simulated customer, with the computer sitting idly by until a mistake is made. Then, and only then, will one of the employees appear in a window.

Let's say the new representative tries suggesting to the customer that his water is "contaminated." A very pleasant woman appears to explain the danger of frightening the customer. She relates the true story of a representative who once asked the customer complaining of bits in the water, "Are they swimming?" She discusses the predictable outcome of the question—sheer panic on the part of the customer—then reinforces the need to avoid causing unnecessary alarm. Either a manual or an interactive document could state "Do not cause unnecessary alarm," but the message sticks through the story format.

Today the user must "speak" to the application by typing answers and clicking on questions. Not too long from now, the apprentice may be able to carry on a vocal conversation with the master, and we will have truly returned, through simulation, to the education system that served us well for the first 2 million years of our existence.

PART 6

Understanding Users

As computing systems have grown in power and sophistication, so users have grown too. Fifteen years ago, we were likely to be expert in the task domain for which we were designing. Today most of us address too many sophisticated task domains to be expert, and users far outstrip us. The user population has undergone other noteworthy shifts. Fifteen years ago, most personal computer users were young and male. Today, users fill the demographic spectrum. Fifteen years ago, almost all personal computers were bought by end users. Many are now bought by corporate buyers who may never see what they have purchased.

If we are to design new systems that will let people and society flourish, we must comprehend users on a far deeper level than ever before. We must understand more about the marketplace. We must understand how we within the computer industry differ from our users, by gaining a deeper insight into our own biases and motivations.

This part looks at users from several points of view. Some offer mood and color; others, pragmatic advice. Taken together, they offer an enhanced understanding of users and the changes we must make to provide for their growing needs.

From here on, I will discuss the particulars of software design much more directly. I have chosen to address people directly engaged in design (since at some point it becomes impossible to write without some concept of a focused readership), but much of what I have to say will, I trust, be useful to all.

Let us begin by exposing a quandary facing all companies marketing to large enterprises—an issue as critical to managers and marketers as it is to software designers.

CHAPTER 22

Two Masters, or The Bifurcated Customer

*T*he need to control is one of the most fundamental of human drives. As a person who spent 15 years in sales and sales training, I can report that ignoring the psychology of the buyer is a sure road to failure.

Those who design for and sell to large enterprises serve two masters: first, the buyer of the product, quite often an information services manager who will use the system seldom, if ever; and second, the people who will actually interact with the systems, known variously as the users, the end users, or the more formal engineering term, "those *$^%#! users."[1] The needs, wants, and desires of these two masters—buyer and user—are often in conflict.

Working for two masters is not an easy task, as a quick review of a seminal paper (a book, really) published (thirty-one hundred years ago) will reveal. I'm referring to that perennial best-seller by Confucius and friends, the *I Ching,* or *Book of Changes.*[2]

....

1 Buyers, even those who use their systems, are still not typical users. As Nielsen (1993) wrote, "Vice Presidents and other corporate executives should realize that they are [not] representative of end users...." While we need to listen to the personal wants and needs of the buyer-users, we also must examine the needs of more typical users. Lowering the training and support costs of the most highly paid occasional-use executive will not offset the kind of savings to be seen in lowering the same costs for 5,000 or 10,000 workers.

2 Even earlier than 3,100 years ago, people had been predicting the future by the means used in the *I Ching,* but by around the middle of the 1100s BC, people began to demand knowledge not only of what fate held for them but of what they should do about it (Legge 1973).

The *I Ching* built upon the idea of an earlier school of Chinese thought—that objects and events are the result of two principles, yin and yang:

Yin is negative, weak, and passive, while yang is positive, strong, and active. The new school flattened the traditional representation of yin and yang, creating a sort of side view:

Yin   *Yang*

Once they had these new "low-rise" symbols, it only made sense to start stacking them up on one another to save space, and, thus, the trigram was born:

The trigrams are eight in number, each with a unique meaning. This particular trigram, the Clinging, represents light-giving fire.

Since the Clinging trigram has two yang, or strength, lines, a Western mind might be drawn to the conclusion that this trigram must be extrastrong. Wrong, Grasshopper. The authors of the *I Ching* realized that two masters and but a single servant represent not strength but conflict, divisiveness, and weakness.

Drawing from this lesson, some developers might conclude that the best approach to merchandising computers would be to eliminate one or the other of the masters.

Macintosh originally had but one master: the end user. This made life quite simple for Macintosh designers: if the system made an end user happy, the designers were successful. Unfortunately, Apple couldn't seem to give machines away to Fortune 500 companies. Instead, Macintosh users in these companies—and there were many of them—had to sneak their computers in through side entrances late at night.

Why did large enterprises have a visceral reaction to Macintosh? The Macintosh was then, and still is perceived to be, an outlaw machine, designed by outlaws for outlaws. Users have full control over their machines, and there is little that a corporate IS manager can do about it, making said managers very nervous. That's why the corporations won't let them through the front door (and, of course, why their outlaw users continue to bring them in the side door).[3]

Keeping Both Masters Happy

The other extreme, serving only the buyer, will sound quite seductive to the salespeople in the crowd (as it will to any buyers reading this chapter). After all, buyers are the ones with the cash. But although buyers are the ones whom designers ultimately have to make happy, much of the designers' efforts will be indirect.

Design teams need to make the end user productive, then report the results of their efforts to the buyers.

Traditionally, designers have stopped at just making users productive. (Some have stopped short of that.) We need to do more. We need to *measure* our users' productivity, not only to test and validate designs but to give sales and marketing people a strong business case for the superiority of our products.

We need to come up with the right set of figures, too. Let's say, through extremely clever design, your design team makes your software easier to learn than the other leading brand. The buyer doesn't care. "Easy" doesn't affect the bottom line. However, "easier to learn" can be translated into specific figures for lowered training costs, and

....
3 Apple's 1985 Super Bowl "Lemmings" commercial didn't help. In it, they marched several hundred blindfolded IS managers—guilty of blindly buying IBM products—off a cliff. Three years after the offensive ad ran, I represented Apple at a conference of IS managers, many of whom were still upset. When I spoke, I decided on a frontal assault: "Approximately one year after the introduction of the Macintosh, Apple decided to approach the corporate IS market. They created a brilliant campaign, called, 'Lemmings,' designed specifically to appeal to the emotions of IS managers [the audience looked at me aghast] by really pissing them off [the audience broke into laughter and applause]." Several audience members told me that, after being angry for three years, they were going to go into a store the following day to look at a Macintosh. It again taught me the value of the old sales adage: "If all else fails, tell the truth."

that is a message your company can sell. Run a comparison of the time it takes to learn your product versus the competition's. Determine whether you can significantly reduce or eliminate the need for specialized tutorial seminars. Look at reductions in peer-to-peer, "casual" training costs. Add those figures up, and get them into the hands of your sales force.

Another area designers attempt to affect is ease of use. Again, buyers don't care whether their users are finding things easy. In fact, the more tortured their employees are, the more return employers see themselves getting for their payroll dollar.[4] What buyers want to hear about is productivity, delivered in the form of quantifiable figures. Fortunately for users, the most obvious effect of software's being easy to use is a strong buildup in measurable productivity. (See Chapter 25.)

When the Masters Disagree

Both buyers and users directly benefit from increased learning speed and overall productivity gains. Let's look at a few places where buyers and users at least *appear* to be in conflict:

Users Want	Buyers Want to
Freedom to move: portability and connectability	Control connections to the outside world and limit portability to provide security
Freedom to choose software	Control channels to negotiate favorable group purchase prices and lower training costs
Freedom to choose brand and system	Control proliferation to lower support training and other support costs[5]

....

4 My editor objects strenuously to this characterization. My editor is rather young and naïve and still believes in the milk of human kindness.

5 You may see a trend developing here. I read an ad many years ago in the daily paper published during the National Computer Conference. An intelligent terminal/minicomputer manufacturer was pitching their systems to buyers on the basis that IS managers needed to staunch the flow of personal computers coming into their organizations "through the back door." (They should have been watching the side door.) The word *control* was used 17 times during the course of the ad. The word *freedom* did not appear.

| Freedom to adapt their system | Control customization to force uniformity to lower maintenance and training costs |
| Freedom from intrusion: privacy | Control legal exposure by searching for and examining potentially illegal documents |

This book touches often on the conflicting needs of IS managers and end users. You will find specific guidelines for balancing freedom and control in Chapter 27 and guidelines on balancing privacy and security in Chapter 36.

Corporate IS managers have a powerful, legitimate reason to control their systems. At the same time, end users have a legitimate need for some elbow room. Good software architecture and design can lower the need for IS managers to exert control, so that users end up with a greater sense of freedom. Working toward making both buyer and user happy can lower overall IS costs and improve corporate productivity.

Boytoys

My wife, the Doctor, recently switched handling the data for a medical research project she's doing from a popular power user spreadsheet application to pencil, paper, and calculator. She is now more productive. Yes, the math is slower, but she is no longer spending 95 percent of her time trying to figure out what power-user feature she needs to get the spreadsheet to stop suddenly filling entire columns with number signs, or how to "trick" her spreadsheet into building a graph with the important data on the X axis instead of in the legend. Is she alone in having these problems? No. They have become so endemic that *Business Week's* cover story for April 29, 1991, was entitled, "I Can't Work This ?#!!@★ Thing!"

What is going wrong here? Somewhere along the line, many technology designers lost track of the real goal: empowering users. From VCRs to clock radios, designers are adding every button, switch, and other power user doo-dad they can in the mistaken belief that the true power of technology is to be measured in the number of features and controls rather than impact on people's lives. Our computer software has tracked the trend. Systems and applications today are festooned with every wangdoodle imaginable, offering users plenty of power to blow themselves up, while at the same time inhibiting them from accomplishing their task.

If the desktop computer is a dark and mysterious closet, the Internet is a positively terrifying, sucking black hole. The advent of the World Wide Web is helping to address part of the problem by making at least the waystations on the net visible, but the sheer immensity of today's cyberspace is frightening to all but a small group of people. Sure, the kinds of tasks users attempt on computers have become more complex, but something else is leading to the increased difficulty of using these machines, something we need to address: we are designing our systems for power users, to the exclusion of everyone else.

Power Users versus Expert Users

In 1985, Apple introduced their extended keyboard, code-named U.S.S. Enterprise, since it shared the approximate dimensions of an aircraft carrier. It had been designed as a companion piece to an IBM clone add-in card that never materialized. It therefore had the full key complement necessary to navigate through the caverns of DOS. It was and remains entirely unsuitable for use with the vast majority of Macintosh applications. It sells like hotcakes. (It sells so well that the orginal 90-key keyboard, featuring infinitely superior human factors, disappeared from the market.) Why? Because even though the keyboard scares the hell out of new buyers, they hope it will scare their friends and associates even more.

Most people want to be seen as power users, but then we have the real thing. Power users typically consist of bipedal, testosterone-soaked life forms between the ages of 18 and 39. Yes, I said testosterone-soaked life forms. At the risk of offending certain politically correct parties, there does appear to be a difference, however minor, between boys and girls. And the overwhelming majority of power users I've come across are definitely male.

Before everyone goes nuclear, let me explain what I mean by power user: a person driven by hormones to want complete and utter control of every function of the computer, even if having such control seriously degrades efficiency and productivity. Tim Allen's character on "Home Improvement," the ABC comedy series, is the prototypical power user. He's the only guy in the neighborhood with a 120-horsepower lawn mower that will do 0 to 60 in less than 7 seconds. It's not much use on his suburban lawn, but it makes a really neat noise when he starts it up.

I knew several guys at Apple who had so many weird public domain extensions in their system folder that virtually none of their applications ran properly. Accomplishing the least task was like walking through a mine field. So what? As far as they were concerned, it merely increased the challenge! They wouldn't have thought of paring down their systems.

Most women see their machines as serious productivity tools, there for the express purpose of helping them accomplish their task. Women want to do their work, not "play computer" (Bulkeley 1994). A lot of men don't want to "play computer" either.

Many people across the board become expert users. Expert users understand their craft and are competent at using the tools that will help them succeed. They may have no interest in tearing apart their tools, either to understand them or to "improve" them. It's the difference between someone who is an expert at driving a car and someone who looks forward to Saturday morning, because that is when he can tear the car apart and perhaps get it back together.[1] The Saturday-morning power user may very well not be an expert driver (although all will claim to be).

Designing for Productivity, Not Power

A few years ago, I went shopping for a battery-operated drill, eventually choosing between two models. One I will label a wimp drill; Tim Allen's character wouldn't touch it with a ten-foot pole. The other was a true power user's dream:

Wimp 3/8-Inch Model	Power User 3/8-Inch Model
Compact	Big, with popular assault-rifle styling
"Regular" power	35 percent extra power for those tough jobs
Two speeds	Infinitely variable speed
Single, built-in battery pack	External battery pack: use one while a second one is charging
Small charger	Large, heavy charger
1-hour charge time	1-hour charge time
Built-in trickle charge	Who needs it? We're powerful!
Five-position clutch	Five-position clutch
Reversible	Reversible
Wall-mount charge stand	Table-top charge stand
2 lb. 6 oz.	4 lb. 6 oz.
$84.95	$159.95

....
1 People have often wondered why Italian cars are so unreliable. It's because so many Italian men just love to tear them apart. They are power users.

I wanted to buy a portable drill because I wanted to avoid having to drag around extension cords to use my existing power drills. (A battery-operated drill is a poor choice for a first drill.) Therefore, I was looking for:

- Power
- Portability
- Availability
- Accessibility
- Functionality

The power user drill had 35 percent more power than the wimp one. An important difference? Not really. My plug-in drill sports more than five times the power of the most powerful battery-operated drill. Thirty-five percent more may be an impressive claim on the side of a box; it makes little difference in practice.

Both drills offer portability, but the wimp drill is significantly lighter and better balanced, enabling a person to carry other tools at the same time with greater comfort.

The lowly wimp drill wins hands-down when it comes to accessibility: the charger base screws to the wall, and the drill is simply dropped into it whole, always there to be found when needed. The power user drill, its battery, and its charger are all permanently loose and can be conveniently scattered all over the house and yard.

The power user drill has two superior areas of functionality. First, it has variable speed, a handy feature particularly when trying to start screws. Having a clutch helps but doesn't solve the problem. I'm pretty good at starting screws, so using the two-speed wimp drill wouldn't be as much of a problem for me as for the new user. This is the same paradox that the Macintosh addressed when it dropped finally from close to $3,000 to more like $1,000: the most casual computer users need the most sophisticated computer and software. The $666 Apple One of 1976 was a fun toy for hackers but useless for the average user. It took a $1,000 Macintosh or its Windows imitator to put a usable tool in the hands of common folk.[2]

The power user drill's second advantage is its ability to have one battery pack charging while the other one is installed in the drill and

---

2 Seventy percent of personal computers will be sold into the home in 1995, a major reverse from the last 15 years, when business was gobbling up greater and greater percentages.

being used. All that would mean to me would be that I have to remove the battery every time I wanted to charge it. I would drag out my corded drill were I to be doing so much drilling as to kill a battery pack.

Both drills charge their batteries fully in 1 hour. (The fact that the power user drill's charger weighs more twice as much doesn't seem reflected in its capabilities, even if it makes it seem more impressive.) But the lower-priced model also has a trickle charger to keep the battery ready to go over time. With the power user drill, the battery I charged three weeks ago is likely to be dead now when I need it. For all practical purposes, a battery-driven drill not used every day and lacking a trickle charger requires a minimum of 1 hour to drill a hole. ("Yes, but it's supposed to be used every day. It's a *power user* drill!")

Stripping off supposed nonessentials because a power tool or software is to be used professionally doesn't cut it. Carpenters get sick. They go on vacation. They don't want to stand around for an hour charging their drill when they return. CAD package users and word processor users also go on vacation. They don't want to spend their first three days back trying to rememorize 1,400 different esoteric commands that have taken the place of a well-designed visible interface.

Attention to detail could be found in every aspect of the smaller drill. Its clutch is a ring wrapping around the front of the motor housing, like the focus ring on a camera, labeled so either left- or right-handed people can read it, then move it easily with a quick twist of the wrist. The clutch on the power user drill is a small knob buried underneath the drill, requiring the user to stop work, turn the drill upside down, and hurt fingers trying to clack the knob into a new position (this for the convenience of the mechanical engineer who designed it, not the user who would work with it).

I ended up buying the wimp drill, because its design team was thinking about me and how this drill would fit into my life when they built it. I knew it would be there—available, accessible, ready to go with no fuss—and that I would be comfortable and efficient when using it.[3]

That's what real people want and need in software. They don't want heavy, clunky, half-thought out features screwed into the side of lumbering software with all the grace of a badly hot-rodded car. *Elegance* is a word whose meaning we're fast losing sight of. Elegance is basic black and pearls, not fool's motley and helium balloons.

....
3 The drill, which continues to serve me well, is a Skil model 2503.

Thirty years ago, computer users consisted of two classes: young male programmers and operators and powerless, minimum-wage females who endlessly keypunched 80-column cards. (Of course, not all keypunch operators were female. I was one of the few powerless male keypunch operators in those days. My cohorts and I quickly escaped, but the women were generally not so lucky.)

Today, two-thirds of personal computer users are women, according to a Logitec poll on PCs and people (Logitec 1992), and millions of those female users are now in higher technical and management positions. Those who are not wandering the labyrinths of cyberspace today will be in the very near future. The majority of users, according to the same poll, are now more than 36 years old. The decision makers—the people who give the nod if a company is going to site-license a piece of software or allow a piece of hardware in the door—are even more likely to be more than 36 years old. The message is clear: we must abandon our boytoys in favor of designing simple, functional, elegant software responsive to all our users. Just where to begin is the next subject.

On the Punishment of Users

A couple years ago, I spoke at MIT, touching on the subject of continuous save, a long-overdue system feature that protects users from losing their work through human error, machine crashes, and power failures. The following day, during lunch at my favorite Boston restaurant, an event took place so outrageous, I feel compelled to share it.

I was peacefully enjoying a green salad of exotic imported California lettuce when one of my luncheon companions, a programmer who had been at my lecture the previous evening, suddenly and quite publicly suggested that continuous save is not a good idea. Warming to my stunned expression, he expanded, saying that it is not only proper but desirable to punish a user for the crime of failing to save work every 10 minutes or so. If the power fails after users have been typing without saving for an hour and a half, they deserve exactly what they get. Maybe it will teach them to save more often.

He then proceeded to squirt citric acid onto a live oyster and slide the squirming result down his throat.

I was shocked, though not so much by what he said. Other developers have, on rare occasion, made similarly misguided comments. No, it was the Mona Lisa smile of contentment that spread upon his face as the oyster groped its way toward his stomach. You could see it in his eyes: he was eating oysters, but he was thinking users.

Continuous Save

Continuous save works just as the name suggests: work is saved to the hard disk as fast as the user accomplishes it.[1] Continuous save as a fundamental property of a system is different from auto-save, featured by some applications. Many applications auto-save only periodically: the amount of work a user thus loses in any particular power failure is a property of how long it has been since the application last auto-saved the work. Typically, an application will auto-save more often than users will save manually (explicit save), but users nonetheless lose work.

Another problem with auto-saving as an application feature is that users may not realize that the feature exists until the auto-saver has written over a good, "permanent" version of a document with a user's temporary, "what-if" version. New HyperCard users routinely lost massive amounts of information when they deleted rafts of cards so they could play with what they assumed was a protected copy of a stack.

Auto-save currently works best in applications based on the notion of a record, a relatively limited unit of data. As the user finishes working with an individual record, it is saved out to disk. Even here, though, continuous save, backed by battery RAM, would protect the current record from potential destruction.

Continuous save, implemented as a standard feature on a system, would prevent the user from accidentally erasing work through a combination of protective features. Since continuous save would be the standard behavior of the system, users would learn its behavior from the beginning. Still, new users might fail to understand the system soon enough, and even experienced users can make mistakes, so continuous save calls for further protections.

Users at any point can set a marker—a checkpoint—to which they can always revert. Such a checkpoint system might result in what appear to be individual, numbered "drafts" of the document. Internally, to save data space, the document could remain a single entity with change resources containing only the differences among successive "drafts." (Of course, if the user copied or moved a draft away from

....

1 Desktop computers should provide the most minimal amount of battery-backed RAM, say 512 or 1,024 bytes, so the user can avoid losing any work at all. Continuous save on portable computers can work differently. Well-designed portables have lots of battery-backed RAM, so that actual writes to disk, with their concurrent battery drain, can occur only periodically.

the original document, the system would then generate a fully independent copy of the draft.)

Checkpoints, however, still don't protect the naive or unwary user against freshly opening a document and performing fatal alterations. Therefore, any time a user opens a document, the system should set an additional checkpoint so the user can revert to the "last saved" version.

Continuous save not only offers the experienced user better control over versioning and improved data compaction compared to the current save system but goes on to offer all users, new and experienced alike, complete relief from the many unpredictable bugaboos of current explicit save systems.

Is continuous save a feature that would be nice but really isn't all that important? I don't think so. While writing the remainder of the chapter, my system locked up on me. What you are about to read has been written twice. Three times, if you count the intermediate draft with all the curse words in it.

"The Computer for the Rest of Them"

Macintosh used to have the slogan, "The computer for the rest of us." Macintosh was not. From the beginning, the Macintosh was designed to be "The computer for the rest of *them*."

Since the majority of our users are not like us, our attitudes, needs, and abilities are usually irrelevant when making design decisions. I was in a meeting a few weeks ago when an engineer dismissed a feature someone suggested including in an application by saying, "Why would I ever need it?" The question is not why *we* would ever need it but why *they* would ever need it.

The Macintosh team, like the Lisa team, Alan Kay's Xerox PARC Altos team, and Doug Engelbart's original SRI team before them, were keenly aware that they were designing not for themselves but for others. All these teams held a common understanding of who their users were, and chief in that understanding was a rock-solid belief that users were not like themselves.

In *Tog on Interface,* I reported on a study I did at Apple showing striking differences in Jungian-type preferences between the general population and Apple engineers. The same differences have been found at other sites (Myers and McCaulley 1985; Sitton and Chmelir 1984).

We are not "normal." We are bright, intuitive, have superior memories. We are also, as Marty Graham (1992) reported in "Nerds Get Revenge— But They Pay a Price," overwhelmingly male. Then there's the matter of our arrested development. According to some local shrink Graham dug up, that's why we are so fascinated with remote-controlled toys and inflatable dinosaurs. (I always thought it was because they are really fun.)

Fooling Ourselves

Most of us all learned years ago that we should not design software for ourselves but instead seek out typical users from our target population. Many of us soon found, though, that dealing with large numbers of typical users was a real bother, so we gradually zeroed in on a handful of people with whom we got along well, who would really play with our new software, and who would give us the most understandable feedback: people just like us.

I came across one developer a few years ago whose sole target user was a guy so much like him they could have been twin brothers. He designed his entire system around what this guy liked and didn't like. His software had more controls on it than the space shuttle. Worse, no one else on the entire planet could make the application work. Even the balance of his own team couldn't understand the monster he had created, although they were too intimidated to say so.

Our drift away from the real user population has become pandemic in the industry. As we have become more skilled, as our friends in the user community have become more skilled, we have lost sight of the millions of users who have not been along for the ride.

In the next few pages, I offer some insightful techniques for getting back to basics. They are written tongue-in-cheek, but make no mistake, they are deadly serious. All of us at one time or another drift away from our users. Each of us needs to take the time on a regular basis to see that we reconnect.

Designing for "Real People"

If we are to abandon designing for ourselves and our alter ego power users, we need to take certain steps. At the first of these we may balk, but we cannot expect to embrace this new world of users until we let go absolutely.

Step 1: Visit Real Users

If you have had no contact with end users in some time, I recommend starting out slowly. Visit a customer site and watch today's users at work. Build up to a trip to a computer store to watch average people, unskilled in debuggers, attempting to choose computer hardware about which they know nothing. When you have become inured to the sight of their overwhelming ignorance, you even may want to venture into non-high-tech stores, to see how our future customers are currently coping in the real world. (This can be a shocking experience, and I do not recommend it on a first outing.)

Step 2: Observe New Users

When I first arrived at Sun, I was given a system attached to a mystery printer. I could print just fine but couldn't for the life of me discover where the copies were coming out. I searched every printer in the building, to no avail. Then I printed out a message asking whoever saw it to give me a ring. I got a call that very afternoon from a woman in New Jersey.

When I contacted my system administrator to correct the problem, he told me changing printers was easy, but he'd come over and help me out this time anyway. He spent 15 minutes typing pure gibberish into my computer while speaking in technical tongues. The only words I understood were, "all you have to do," and "just simply" and "see how easy it is?" No, I didn't see how easy it is.

If you have been using DOS or UNIX for the last 50 or 60 years, you may have lost touch with how much knowledge you have picked up along the way. It may be time to see how the other 99 percent lives.

Step 3: Socialize with Real People

A late-stage step toward developing an internal model of "real people" involves socializing with people whose idea of a good time is visiting an art museum or even going outside. Spend time with them. Nothing worthwhile in the world is accomplished without sacrifice.

Males in particular need to seek out people who are not just like them. They need to try ideas out on women, older people, younger people, people with disabilities, and, most important, people who are not power users.

Step 4: Hire Women

While our universities continue to attract and graduate primarily male engineers, they attract and graduate at least as many female as male designers. You can go a long way toward correcting the gender bias in computer systems by hiring (and empowering) female designers. And look for those few female engineers, too.

Step 5: Listen to Women

We have all read the studies in the last few years that find girls pushed firmly into the background from the earliest years of school. In our field, they too often remain in the background after graduation, no matter how high their levels of talent and skill. Our 87 percent male fraternity is totally out of whack. If we are to fill the needs and desires of our target users, we need to offer our few women a disproportionate influence on our designs.

Step 6: Listen to Software Designers

A design begun in partnership with human interface professionals can result not only in a system real people can use but a system with positive benefits for the most hard-boiled power user.

CHAPTER 25

Ease of Use

A ll this talk about making software safe for the average user might lead people to believe that what we should do to our software is pull out two-thirds of the functionality, all of the shortcut keys, and then make everything conform to some brain-dead consistency standard. Fortunately, it turns out that people really don't want a computer that is easy to use at all; they want a computer that will make them productive, which is where ease of use comes in. ("Huh, I thought ease of use just went out?")

Computer scientist and industry luminary Bill Buxton said at the CHI'92 conference on human-computer interaction that the goal of designers is not to make systems easy to use but, rather, to accelerate the process by which novices perform like experts. I would add, in parallel, that we should strive to enable experts to push well beyond their own current knowledge and capabilities. The question is, How do we achieve these goals without overwhelming users in the process?

Buxton's Law of Conservation of Skills: For every new skill you learn, you must throw an old one away.

Ten years from now, our computers and our lives will be webbed together in a technological complexity we can only imagine today. Bill Buxton has done some imagining about the result of all this, and has come up with the charts shown in Figures 25.1 and 25.2.

Technological complexity will go through the roof during the next decade, while at the same time human evolution will produce a zero increase in our ability to handle such complexity. Only one known cure exists for such a mismatch: ease of use. If we do not start now to

233

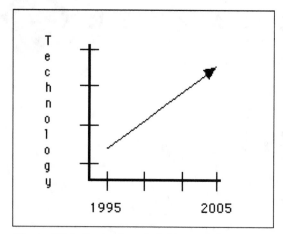

Figure 25.1 *Buxton's projected increase in computer technological complexity, 1995–2005[1]*

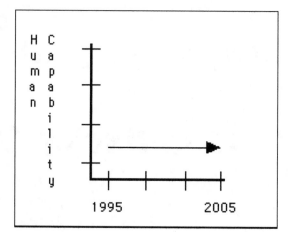

Figure 25.2 *Buxton's projected increase in human capacity to understand technology, 1995–2005*

put massive effort toward making machines easy to use, by the end of a decade they will not be merely difficult to use, they will be impossible.

> *Tog's Law of Commuting: The time of a commute is fixed. Only the distance is variable.*

The U.S. Interstate Highway System was allegedly designed to let people get to where they were going safely, in relative comfort, and in a minimum amount of time. What happened? People just moved farther away from where they work, shop, play, and are entertained. Today in America, it takes just as long and is just as painful to get to work or play as it was in 1950 when the freeway madness began.[2]

Has it all been some grand waste? No. People now have the freedom to select from a much larger pool of jobs. They can live in the country and still drive to the city for a frequent dose of culture. Giant retailers, offering wide selection and low prices, can locate in low-density, low-overhead locations and still garner all the customers they need. We have traded in the speed and ease of use that freeways

....

1 Note the rakish 42.75° upward angle of the rising technological capability. (Bill claims he has proven this angle, through careful research, to be quite accurate. All that remains for him to solve is the unit scale of the vertical axis. For now, he describes it only as "very, very big.")

2 A couple of years ago, Seattle opened a major new freeway. In exactly four days, the traffic was bumper to bumper.

promised for a wide range of personal, cultural, and economic freedoms, resulting in our living more productive, satisfying lives.

In *Tog on Interface,* I identified the two goals of software:

1. Increase human productivity.
2. Increase human happiness.[3]

Ease of use does not appear on this list. That's because it is not a goal but a strategy. It and all the other tactics, strategies, and subgoals of design ultimately can be traced back to these two goals. Ease of use cannot exist as a goal because of the following paradox:

People will abandon the most cushy existence in favor of a comfortable level of pain.

Even those with the strength of character to rise above the power user phenomenon will trade in every ounce of ease of use that we provide in favor of increased productivity and satisfaction. Consider the following short personal history.

Ten Hours of Pain: A Personal Constant

Sixteen years ago, I used Apple II Integer BASIC to write a little program that would let me use the computer as an Etch-a-Sketch machine, with 15 glorious colors and a grand total of 1,000 pixels on the screen. The Apple II was the first microcomputer that didn't require a soldering iron to turn it on, so constructing this game paddle–activated drawing program took only 10 tortuous hours of fiddling with code and receiving syntax errors. The results were a low-resolution graphics program and a great deal of personal satisfaction (Figure 25.3).

Eight years ago, I used SuperPaint to lay out a sprinkler system for my Zen garden. SuperPaint, then from Silicon Beach, was the first program that made it easy to do both drawing and painting in a single

....
3 If the designer is from California, the second goal arises from a deep commitment to humanity and is likely achieved only after long consultations with a personal teddy bear. If the designer is from, say, New York City, the second goal is more likely a purely practical matter: keep the fools happy, and they'll be more productive.

Figure 25.3 *Simulation of typical output from sketching program*

application, enabling me to knock out this project in only 10 tortuous hours. The result was a 1-bit black-and-white landscape layout with lines representing sprinkler pipes, along with a great deal of personal satisfaction (Figure 25.4).

Recently, using Vellum 3D, I created a precision 3D CAD model of an elaborate Japanese roofed gate for my entranceway. At the end of 10

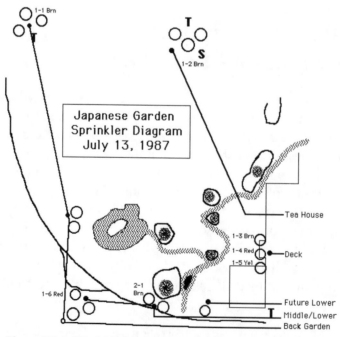

Figure 25.4 *2D, 1-bit drawing of garden sprinkler layout*

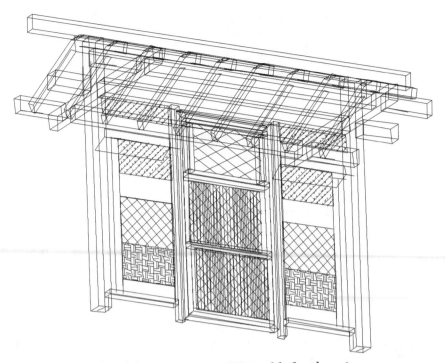

Figure 25.5 *Isometric, wire-frame view of 3D model of garden gate*

torturous hours, the results were a complete set of architectural drawings, a color "movie" of the gate seen rotating in space, and a great deal of personal satisfaction (Figure 25.5). Vellum, with its intelligent "drafting assistant," did the hard work for me, allowing me to concentrate on design, not mechanics.

In each case, I spent 10 hours on the project, I was pushing my own knowledge and abilities to the limit, and I was pushing hard against the application's ease-of-use limitations. But I was also solving progressively more difficult problems and ending up with progressively more useful results.

Eight years from now, I'll be spending 10 hours on some new and exciting project, like using my depth camera to feed 3D, real-world objects into a solid-model animation package, featuring a viewer-controlled fly-through of my latest dream house. Whatever I may be doing, I will be taxing my learning and productivity skill to the maximum, and I will be driving the capabilities of my computer to and beyond the raw edge.

Ease of use does matter. It has nothing to do with building toy applications. It has everything to do with bringing more and more power into the users' hands. Ease of use fixes the upper limit of users' productivity.

Simplification

Ophoto, from Light Source, is the application that first made scanners pleasant to use. It originally replaced Apple's AppleScan, a product that required users not only to give the computer detailed information about their own desires but equally detailed information about the mechanical processes the computer should use. AppleScan was like an old 35-mm camera, loaded down with mechanical features that only an expert could use. Ophoto is a modern 35-mm camera, giving new and casual users the ability to point and shoot, but also enabling expert users to take back as much control as they see fit.

Ophoto increased the power of the user while reducing technological complexity to a single button. Most applications could benefit from similar simplification. Even those that were simple on the first release tend to pick up complexity over time as more and more features are added. Buxton's Law dictates that new features must offer greater ease of use than those that came before. More important, it dictates you must simplify something that already exists to free up mind space for your new expansion. Simplification:

- Requires early and effective planning and design.
- Requires a high level of programming skill and cooperation.
- Can result in a faster time to market.
- Lowers documentation and support needs.
- Results in lowered training costs and more productive users.

Turning resources over to a simplification effort may be a new strategy for many design teams, but it's a strategy we must embrace if we are to succeed.

Users are at the breaking point. They are buying software and leaving it on the shelf because they just can't stand to learn anything more. Soon they won't even bother buying. The answer lies in ease of use. Applying it does not mean scrapping everything you have. Gain it just as you do quality, through continuous improvement. Make every new release show greater ease of use than what came before.

Designing for the Whole Person

*I*n the mid-1970s, television manufacturers began introducing the first all-electronic tuners, replacing the clunky mechanical tuners of old. They supplied them initially on TVs with remote control, suddenly made practical because the remote controls could also be purely electronic. Gone were the heavy relays and motors necessary to turn the tuner knobs mechanically.

A consumer electronics store in San Francisco, Village Electronics, was selling remote control to the industry-average 20 percent of its customers at this time, but it was an uphill battle, for the first mention of remote always produced the exact same "tape-recorded" message from the prospective buyer: "I'm not so lazy I can't get up off the couch to change the channel!" The swift retort, "Oh, yes, you are!" rarely seemed to produce a useful result.

The owner of the store, unhappy with the weak profit margins on the manual TVs, decided to work up a new sales technique for selling remote control TVs, one based on the emerging branch of psychology called transactional analysis. Within two weeks, the store's product mix had gone from 20 percent remote control to 80 percent remote control, accompanied by an overall boost in sales.

Transactional Analysis

Transactional analysis, or TA, was developed as a discipline by Eric Berne beginning in the late 1940s. It gained popularity in 1964 with the publication of Berne's book, *The Games People Play,* followed

241

quickly by Thomas Harris's book, *I'm OK, You're OK*. By the mid-1970s, TA was quickly becoming a central tenet of motivational psychology, that wicked step-sibling of clinical psychology dedicated to getting people to buy things they had no intention of owning.

Transactional analysis is a $20 word for a very simple idea on Berne's part: since very few clinical psychologists are mind readers, why not stop trying to peer into people's subconscious minds and instead concentrate on what they say and how they say it. If you say "hello," and I say "hello" back, we have just conducted a transaction.[1]

Berne intuited a new, fundamental model of the human ego. It is this model that the San Francisco storekeeper made use of in increasing the profitability of his TV sales; it is this model that you can make equally good use of to increase your own product's sales.

The Three Ego States

Berne observed that people have three states of mind among which they move frequently and, in the case of normal, healthy people, fluidly. He named these states Parent, Adult, and Child.

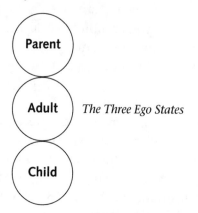

The Three Ego States

The Parent ego state is the site of our tape-recorded messages: "Don't throw that medicine ball, Billy. You could put an eye out." "Sara, how many times have I told you not to...." "Why? Because I said so!" The Parent ego state can be either nurturing or critical.

....
1 Eric Berne came up with such a highfalutin' term solely because he was a Freudian psychoanalyst, and he needed to provide long, long words for simple ideas because it was the only way he could get his colleagues to read his papers.

According to Berne, "'Parent' means: 'You are now in the same state of mind as one of your parents (or a parental substitute) used to be, and you are responding as he would, with the same posture, gestures, vocabulary, feelings, etc.'"

The Adult ego state is pure logic—"Just the facts, Ma'am." It is the state of mind that software teams (other than those building entertainment software and games) usually target, to the exclusion of the others. The Adult ego state responds well to spec sheets and dispassionate sales pitches. Berne says, "'Adult' means: 'You have just made an autonomous, objective appraisal of the situation and are stating these thought-processes, or the problems you perceive, or the conclusions you have come to, in a non-prejudicial manner.'"

The Child ego state is the site of both our playfulness and our tendency to pout. It is, paradoxically, the oldest of our ego states. To Berne, "'Child' means: 'The manner and intent of your reaction is the same as it would have been when you were a very little boy or girl.'" The Child ego state is the one in which adults are most likely to deny spending any time. They do spend time there, though. Look no further than the fact that DisneyWorld is Americans' favorite vacation destination. Is it really just "for the sake of the children"? Faith Popcorn (1992) has identified two trends that point toward our spending more time in our Child ego state. One, which she dubs Fantasy Adventure, leads us to scuba and sky diving and attracts us to theme parks, theme restaurants, and theme laundromats. The other she calls Down-Aging: "Forty now is what used to be 30, 50 is what used to be 40, 65 now is the beginning of the second half of life, not the beginning of the end.... Down-aging is the bridge by which we— adults of all ages—try to connect the carefree baby-boom childhoods we remember (or at least the carefree baby-boom childhoods the media says we're *supposed* to remember) to the not-always-fun adulthood we find ourselves in now." Both trends represent a greater willingness to accept our Child ego state rather than a fundamental shift in human psychology.

Adult males, notwithstanding, continue to go to extreme lengths to hide their childlike thoughts and actions by limiting their play to such socially acceptable outlets as golf, tennis, and drinking. They will invent elaborate pretense and nonsense to create the illusion of always being in the Adult state. Believing such nonsense can cost developers a lot of sales. Read on.

How to Sell Remote Controls

To the San Francisco storekeeper, the consistency with which patrons announced the exact words, "I'm not so lazy I can't get up off the couch to change the channel," was a dead give-away that they were speaking not from their Adult ego state but from their Parent ego state. Therefore, he reframed the sales problem as this: the Child ego state will want the remote, the Parent will do his best to block any spending on such frivolity, and the Adult ego state could, if convinced, swing the deal. (Keep in mind that even though the discussion may sound as though we are dealing with three separate individuals locked up in a single head, we are really talking about three different states—frames of mind—of a single, integrated individual. TA, like most other newly encountered theories, can seem a bit strange at first. One does grow quite used to it with time, and it is remarkably powerful. Bear with me.)

The key, as the storekeeper saw it, was to keep the Parent out of the discussion until he had won over the Adult. Since the Parent was constitutionally incapable of keeping his couch opinion to himself once the remote was revealed, the store owner would keep the remote control in his back pocket, with the customer's Parent ego state bliss-fully unaware of its presence. Then he would deliver a 10-minute sales pitch on the value not of having a remote control, but of having one of the (then) new, all-electronic tuners. No more biannual tuner cleanings at $35 a pop. No more trying to jiggle the control just right so the station would come in. No more having to fuss with a second, separate tuner for UHF, with the strange human interface that used to entail.

He then extolled the virtues of an electronic volume control, which would not produce horrifying static noises after a few years of use, and electronic versions of the rest of the controls—color, hue, brightness, and contrast—that would no longer randomly change settings after a few years of aging.

By the end of his pitch, he had built better than the $100 price differential into the electronic controls; the savings in tuner mainte-nance alone would amount to $175 over the life of the set. He had the Adult, if not sold on buying the more expensive set, at least convinced that it ultimately represented the better value. And then it was time to play his trump card.

He would point to a tiny disk on the front of the set and say, "And now that they have replaced all the mechanical contraptions of old with pure electronics, they can put this little 30 cent photocell in the front of the TV so they can give you this"—at which point he would slap the remote control into the customer's hand. The waiting Child ego state would go wild and start pressing all the buttons on the remote control, while the store owner explained now, to the Parent, that the value in the remote control lay not in changing channels every half-hour but in muting those 180,000 commercials to which the prospective owner and his or her children would otherwise be subjected over the next ten years. With the Adult convinced of the value, with the Child happy with his toy, with the Parent muttering darkly about the wicked ways of advertisers, the sale was made.

The only time his pitch ever backfired was when he sold a set after inadvertently failing to mention the remote control at all! The customer paid for the TV and was quite happy until she saw the store-keeper inserting batteries into a strange plastic wand that came with her new set. When she found out the wand was a remote, she exclaimed—and I quote—"I'm not so lazy I can't get up off the couch to change the channel!" It took another 15 minutes to resell her the TV.

How to Sell Software

When the storekeeper later became an Apple dealer, he discovered he had the same three-in-one customers coming in to buy computers. Their initial line was always the same: "I don't want to play any games. I want this for business." He would always agree with his customer, then watch in amusement as the customer would fight an unsuccessful battle not to be attracted to any of the store computers personed by neighborhood kids engaged in battle with intergalactic warriors. The customer would almost invariably walk out with several games among his purchases.

Your software is bought and used by people who have a childlike side to their personalities. I don't care if you sell statistical analysis packages to aging government accountants. Inside those gray-suited and bow-tied bodies are 8-year-old kids just dying to get out. If your view of the person who buys and pays for your software is that of an adult with a data processor for a mind, you need to expand your view.

The storekeeper retired to Apple in 1978 and soon teamed up with Dave Eisenberg to write "Apple Presents… Apple," the keyboard introduction to the Apple II (see Chapter 34). As part of their training, users were intended to play a game in which they helped a rabbit find his carrot. The marketing people said such a babyish character wouldn't work for business types. The storekeeper added an alternate character with an alternate task: help a Swiss banker find his gold. He then presented the user with the following introductory question, "Would you rather come to the aid of a rabbit or a major financial institution?" He later tested that program on more than 20 CEOs of large companies. Every last one of them chose the rabbit.[2]

Bryce, from HSC Software, can turn anyone back into a child. It allows people with no artistic or computer experience to generate beautiful, mathematically complex landscapes on their personal computers. It allows them to have fun.

I've never lost the lesson I learned in selling all those remotes in my store so many years ago. Writing to appeal to the Child does not entail upsetting the Parent. The greatest fun of all to children is success. Design software that produces immediate, if small, successes, and the world will beat a path to your door. Play with Painter, play with Convolver, play with Vellum, most of all, play with Bryce, and see how quickly you gain a sense of power and control. Then capture that same quality in your own products.

....
2 In hundreds of tests on people from all walks of life, the only people who ever chose to come to the aid of a major financial institution were the secretaries of these very same CEOs. They felt compelled, even though their bosses were not around during the tests, to appear at all times adult and business-like.

A Garden of Design

In the spirit of the Zen garden, I offer a few specimen trees, individual essays that have grown from a single idea into their own unique shape. Some chapters, such as "A Transparent Folly" (Chapter 30), offer designers what may be new ways of looking at the world. Others, such as "Violence in Software" (Chapter 28), "Software That Sells" (Chapter 33), "Flexible Consistency" (Chapter 27), and "The First Step" (Chapter 37) will likely reinforce their current beliefs.

These chapters are important for marketers and managers. The problems discussed, long overdue for resolution, bear directly on quality and can be laid to rest only by management decision.

Flexible Consistency

*T*oday's users are shocked enough as they move from one application to another and find strange and conflicting appearances and behaviors. Can you imagine the confusion in the future should adjoining regions of a single active document appear and respond to users actions completely differently?

No increase in communication will be possible without our cooperating in the design of powerful visual and behavioral languages for our cyberspace world. If the patina of a folder in one instance represents its amount of usage and in another instance is a fixed image, added because a developer thought a patina looked "really neat," communication will break down completely.

Consistency Does Not Equal Uniformity

Don Norman, in *The Design of Everyday Things,* showed a photograph of a nuclear power plant control room based on a naive understanding of consistency: every control in the room looked virtually alike. Very clean. Very neat. Very uniform. Very dangerous. The control room crew, desperate to make potentially hazardous controls stand out, unscrewed the uniform black balls from atop the most critical controls and fastened handles removed from barroom beer spigots. Pulling on a Heineken handle would lower the rods into the reactor, cooling it off. Pushing on Michelob would heat things up considerably.

The Japanese garden is not scattered with rows of identical hedges and shrubs. It is a garden of plants grown as separate and distinct individuals, blending together into a harmonious whole. Consistency does not mean paucity of variation or an end to innovation. Instead, it encourages diversity and innovation, but with planning and discipline.

Meaningful Flexibility

Many of today's systems are staggering under the weight of creeping features. A myriad of little options, each simple in itself, have collectively added up to a bedlam of decision.

> *Make customizations meaningful to the users but safe for the system.*

We need to allow people to personalize their workspaces with family photos and memorabilia. With employees traveling the globe and grabbing the nearest computer in the nearest office, having little touches of home appear in personal cyberspace will cease to be merely a nice touch and will become important to the psychological well-being of workers.

In Starfire, Julie also has control over the location of her mailbox, the number and size of viewports appearing on her workspace, the overall look of her workspace, and all manner of other personalizing things. She has been banned, however, from altering the basic functions of the operating system. Many engineers might call such an act arbitrary and capricious. Information systems managers would tend to disagree.

Operating systems like UNIX empower people to make fundamental changes in their systems, changes that can leave the information services people pulling out their hair. Ellen Isaacs from Sun recently visited a large corporate site where the entire system is downloaded onto each workstation in the middle of each and every night, just to make sure that all systems stay exactly the same. If we are to protect our users from such draconian methods, it is our responsibility as designers to rid our applications of the kind of expensive options to which these managers are responding.

Most people don't want their scrolling behavior redesigned, but sometimes they have little choice. The office computer guru may periodically "improve" everyone's system by adding "really neat" custom features. After a couple of years of these kinds of changes, often easily absorbed by users on site at the time, the interface can undergo such an extensive change that new users find themselves at a loss to learn a system that is not only arbitrary and capricious but lacks a shred of relevant documentation.

The focus on customization of minutia has become pandemic. It is a recognized factor in the serious statistics showing that computers in the office are not raising productivity.[1]

Fortunately, we do not face the choice of zero freedom or absolute freedom (chaos). We can address legitimate user concerns while building policy into systems that limit the range of "user expression" so that users or their peers cannot turn a well-engineered human interface system into an unrecognizable agglomeration of idiosyncrasies. However, before building a utopian world of smooth, responsive design, we need to face one little problem.

Options, once released on the world, are missed when removed.

Options, no matter how silly, take on a life of their own, and inevitably people complain loudly and bitterly when they are removed. The complaints fade, though, if expert users can still accomplish all of their current tasks, even if they must go through some temporary discomfort as they learn new methods. Which brings me to a seeming paradox: We think of expert users in general (and power users in particular) as disdainful of ease of learning, but they instantly lose that disdain when they are the ones who must learn new tricks.

Make new designs clean, efficient, and particularly easy to learn.

When we make changes, everyone becomes a beginner. Expert users have been beginners already. For all their bluster, they don't relish the idea of being beginners again. This guideline will keep the complaints down to a dull roar.

Ashlar's Vellum 3D (see Chapter 25, "Ease of Use") is an application that has cut away massive amounts of traditional choice, replacing it

---

1 I know all this is heresy to a lot of long-time UNIX users, but it's time to move our industry along. The horseless carriage was fun because those early users could affect every part of their cars at will, but those cars didn't get their users to where wanted to go safely, speedily, or even often. If we are to build new and powerful systems, we need more-stable platforms.

with an agent-driven design that is easy to learn and powerful to use. The choices are gone because they are no longer necessary. Traditional CAD can take users up to six months to become competent. Vellum, though completely different from all other CAD packages, doesn't require six months for a trained CAD user to regain competency. In one hour, people feel a sense of mastery over the fundamentals, and after using it for a couple of weeks, professionals surpass all previous productivity levels.

Look at Bryce, from HSC Software. This 3D landscape package enables common folk to outperform artist-mathematicians armed with the most sophisticated, option-cluttered programming systems in the world. What Vellum, Bryce, and KAI Convolver have done for single applications, we must do for the world. Our designs must promote differing style and expression without breaking down the fabric that ties our systems together. Vellum, Bryce, and KAI Convolver prove that systems with meaningful flexibility can be built. They will require up-front design and lots of cooperation along the way but will result in our having happy users who are able to produce far beyond the limitations of their current talents and abilities.

> *Supply tools that make "doing it right" easier than "doing it wrong."*

Developers cannot and will not follow guidelines if they must "roll their own" interfaces. Sometimes developers want to do the right thing but abandon supplied tools because the performance and scope of the tools are insufficient for their needs. System software houses need to form close relationships with key developers to provide the feedback necessary to make sure the system software houses are building responsive tools.

Most programmers and designers want to do the right thing. We owe it to them and to our users to make it easy.

CHAPTER 28

Violence in Software

*H*it. Strike. Kill. Purge. Execute. Terminate with extreme prejudice. Are these action verbs from the latest Tom Clancy novel? Headlines from the *National Enquirer?* No. Just routine vocabulary popping up on personal computer screens everywhere. To get a better picture of the extent of the problem, I published the following letter in my *SunWorld* column a few years ago:

> Dear Tog: Here are a couple of error messages I've seen recently that really stood out, even against a background that's pretty "crufty." Maybe you should start a contest for the worst error message encountered.
>
> **Contestant # 1**
> ```
> Internal error detected
> SIGSENV
> Report this problem to a
> knowledgeable person
> ```
>
> **Contestant # 2**
> ```
> Notifier internal error
> (code # 28) Signal
> catcher called
> recursively: Aborting
> for post-mortem
> ```
>
> *Lin Brown, SunSoft Corporation*

The industry shares a rich folklore about such error messages. My favorite story involved the Macintosh, which, when it crashes, displays a picture of an old-fashioned, round black bomb with a sizzling fuse. I heard of one new user who saw this dire icon and did the only sensible thing she could think of: she ran screaming from the house and called the fire department.

Readers Brian Holtz, Bruce Sklar, Chris Hermansen, Harry Hersh, Martin Hardee, Michael Carpenter, Curt Freeland, Mark Jackson, Kevin Mullet, Alan Balkany, Maria Capucciati, and Ian Darwin sent in a rich selection of error messages, some found on Sun computers, many found on "other leading brands." Here are some that appear designed to frighten:

- `ATTENTION: The idle deamon has spotted you.`
- `Press to Test [user presses down with mouse] Release to Detonate`
- `ka6: death`
- `panic: ubacrazy`
- `FATAL ERROR (VADDR)`

Death, panic, detonation, and *fatal* take their place beside the ubiquitous *kill, abort,* and *execute.* Don Gentner reported, in an e-mail entitled, "Guns don't kill, computers do," that these last three collectively appear 900 times in the UNIX manual.

Next, we have those messages designed to offend:

- `Permission denied.`
- `Wrongo, spazmoid`
- `attempt to use barren object`
- `pc_getfat: use same fat`

We don't have to stop using our in-house jargon. Let's just stop visiting it on outsiders.[1]

Next, we have those messages apparently not designed at all:

- `Mouse buffer flushed when overrun.`
- `This is not a cpio file. Bad magic number.`

....
1 Other professions have, for years, maintained a separate vocabulary for those inside and outside their industries, with only occasional comedic cross-overs. My wife and I were examining a new car several months ago, in the company of an excessively helpful salesman. He insisted on pointing out each and every feature of the car, finally reaching the handle that protrudes just above the front passenger's door, typically grabbed when the passenger and driver are sharing a momentary disagreement about whether the driver should be braking and swerving to miss a tree or not. "And here," he announced loudly and proudly, "you have your 'Oh, sh—' bar.... I mean, your Passenger Side Grip Handle."

- Notifier assertion botched: more than one paranoid user
- WARNING: preposterous time in file system
- Internal Error: child 2926 exited, and I didn't even know I had it!
- Unable to save file. Save anyway (y or n)?
- No keyboard found, strike F1 to continue.
- BadWindow error. Hang on it could get ugly.

Many of these, from the safety of a book, seem amusing, but their entertainment value becomes somewhat diminished when they pop up at 11:00 at night, with the user due to present 30 color slides at an early morning meeting.

Next, we have the messages written by genius engineers suffering from the delusion that the entire rest of the world is populated exclusively by other genius engineers. Reader Eric Bergman dredged up this message in honor of Support-New-Users Week:

> Insertion failed—
> The memory buffer is full.
> If this is an isolated case, you can circumvent
> this condition by undoing the operation you just
> performed, storing the contents of the subwindow
> to a file using the text menu, and then redoing
> the operation. Or, you can enlarge the size of
> this buffer by changing the appropriate value in
> the .X defaults file (Text.MaxDocumentsSize).

Principle: If a problem is such that an error message can describe the exact sequence of events necessary to repair the problem, the system should do the repairing, asking for consent or reporting its actions only if necessary.

In the previous example, the alert could be rewritten to say:

Memory size must be increased to insert this text. If the size of this insertion is unusually large, you can temporarily enlarge the memory allotment by clicking on "Temporary." If you expect to make other insertions of this size in the future, click on "Permanent." Click "Cancel" to cancel the insertion.

Depending on the circumstances, I would probably eliminate the "temporary" option entirely, unless there is an overwhelming reason to support it. Most users will not even understand how large their current insertion is, much less be able to predict how large future ones will be. Causing users to stop their work for 5 to 15 minutes while they seek out coworkers to help them form judgments is not a high-human-productivity strategy.

In applying this principle, be sure to accompany it with the following important corollary:

Corollary: Try to avoid suggesting changes that make you look stupid.

Although it arose in a slightly different context, consider the following advice offered to reader Dave Damkoehler by his spellchecker: This is his original:

It should be as fast (or faster) to capture and share an idea online as it is to sketch a concept on a whiteboard.

And this is the spellchecker's suggested change:

It should be as fast (or faster) to capture and share an idea online as it is to sketch a concept on a wattlebird.

Just getting the wattlebird to hold still is half the battle.

Principle: Construct messages so that the nonsophisticated end user receives a clear, simple message that he or she can understand and follow; then enable the more sophisticated user to glean additional important information.

In the case of on-screen messages, you might enable sophisticated users or system administrators to press a button labeled "technical details" that will unleash any necessary technobabble.

Printed messages should first have a section in English (or other human language) describing what is going on and what the normal user should attempt to do about it. Ideally, the more sophisticated user should then directly ask the original device for more detail. If that is not practical, then the printed message could have a follow-on section, clearly marked as being for advanced users and system administrators, containing additional technical detail.

Even when technical details are revealed only at the user's command, they should still be as close to human language as possible. Avoid abbreviations and eschew obfuscation. Many of today's new users want and need to become technically sophisticated. Let's not make their transition any more difficult than it need be.

Corollary: Ensure that the user has enough information to be able to seek technical support.

One difficulty in making an error message too simplistic is that when the user does try to get help, the helper can't gain enough information to give it. Many applications today print a reference number following a clear English message. When the user calls the company, the technical support person can ask for the number and know exactly what is going on.

Dear Tog:

It is not enough to have "people who are skilled in technical writing compose the actual messages." By then, it is far too late to influence the *reason* for the error message.

What is needed is to have skilled communicators be involved in the program design from the beginning, eliminating wherever possible the need for error messages, and then, only then, participating in the effort to communicate the message required.

And, by program design, this includes the combination of hardware, firmware, software, packaging, distribution, manufacturing and marketing, so that the messages are created with the full understanding of the "user's environment;" and reflect what is actually sitting and sometimes operating in front of the user. . . .

The advantage the 128K byte Macintosh had over the IBM PC, the IBM mainframe, and all the other pretenders to the throne was a real attempt to present a package as a complete whole, to have it operate within known parameters that defined how it was to be used, and every part of the machine from case design through the error messages tried to be a part of this whole. All of the other computers failed even to attempt this "wholeness."

Until ease of use is combined with functionality, there will be no resolution to the problems of error message creation. Even the best writer can not explain a poor design without violence to the language, most likely to the writer, and certainly to the user! The communicators must join with the young-at-heart programmers and designers to create a unified whole that operates without conflict or confusion. Programmers and designers must insist that the door is open for the communicators. The challenge is as simple—and as enormously complex—as that.

Jim Dexter, SunSoft Corporation

Jim raises perhaps the most important principle of error messages:

Principle: First, eliminate the need for the message.

My experience has been that the need for 90 percent—sometimes more than 90 percent—of messages can be eliminated through proper design. Given this condition, why are there so many error messages? I think it can be traced to the relative ease with which an error message can be coded up versus the energy a programmer has to put toward planning and executing a full solution to the problem causing the error. Throwing in a lot of error messages saves programming time and at first glance would seemingly help a project make its schedule while saving the developer money.

Unfortunately, it doesn't work that way, because someone else has to write about each and every message in the manual. The manuals get thicker and take longer to publish, and manual production is almost always the gating item in a software release.

It doesn't end there, because someone else will probably have to write about each and every message in the online documentation, using not only the writer's time but another programmer's time as well. The amount of money being spent today to pay programmers and writers to create online documentation for errors and features that shouldn't exist is staggering—and getting worse. That original programmer, saving 2 hours or even 2 days of work by throwing in a quick error message, is sitting at the top of a pyramid of waste that may end up sapping 10 or 20 times that amount of time in documenting and maintaining an unfortunate feature.

None of this even addresses the enormous costs error messages visit on our customers, in training, in peer-to-peer help sessions, and loss of productivity. Jim Dexter is right: we must open channels of communication between writers, designers, and programmers and build enough time into programming schedules to correct errors instead of announcing them.

> Tog,
>
> Your error message stories brought to mind my own favorite example of computer-human interface-slapping. Out of nowhere, my workstation froze and my console showed this message:
>
> ```
> ie%d: no carrier ; giant packet received
> ```
>
> Is the Post Office using my machine? Is the front desk trying to tell me there's some heavy lifting to do? Did...I...do...*bad?* When I was able again to use my machine, I turned to the online documentation of what went wrong. Here's a portion of the message: "Provided that all stations on the Ethernet are operating according to the Ethernet specification, this error should never happen."
>
> So, they created and documented a message to describe something that "should never happen," and—because it should never happen—failed to give any information about solving the nonhappening problem. I, of course, apologized to the computer for my unspeakable display of illogical suspicions, and promised never to bring up the subject again.
>
> Then I hunted down and edited a tech writer.
>
> *Dave Damkoehler, SunSoft Corporation*

I'm not going to comment on either the cop-out error message or Dave's potentially criminal editing job (depending on the time of year this occurred, tech writers may have been out of season). What I would like to comment on is Dave's aside: "when I was able again to use my machine...." It's almost unbelievable that the following principle needs to be expressed explicitly, but here it goes:

Principle: Choose a practical medium for delivering your message.

Dave's is not the only example of impractical delivery media I have come across. Take the experience of Jeff Butera, a math graduate student at North Carolina State University. Jeff reported that when his printer stopped printing and he reloaded it with paper, he then and only then received an important written message on the very first new sheet: "Printer out of paper."

Why We're Here

Computers, like most other Western institutions, started out as a male bastion, ruled by an inordinately young crowd with lots of youthful enthusiasm. These kids adapted to their use the most violent language they could find, enjoying the reaction of those outsiders of either opposite sex or greater age who dared to aspire to their priesthood. The grand tradition of horrifying elders continues into modern times with the adoption of such wonderful terms as UNIX, with its obvious pun relationship to a word that can spectacularly threaten young males (a powerful example of "whistling in the graveyard"), and, more recently, SCSI, which of course is pronounced "scuzzy," to make it as ugly as possible. Boys like that.

Many users have accepted male teenager vocabulary as part of today's rugged computer rite of passage. Most of them, having already passed the test, will even defend its use—a familiar phenomenon among any group of early adopters. Regardless, we must stop using violent language now if we are to democratize access to cyberspace.

The era of aiming vocabulary and notices at 19-year-old male technology freaks is passing. Some computer vendors have virtually eliminated the kind of notices on their individual PC platforms that crop up on the Internet and on older operating systems. The absence of caustic messages results in a greater willingness on the part of users to explore and learn their systems on their own. This lowers training costs, a clear competitive advantage.

What We Need to Do

Common sense is the best guide to developing application interfaces for today's users: Write notices in clear, concise English or other human languages. Avoid arcane jargon or offensive language. Notices should:

1. Identify the problem.

2. Give users enough information to ensure the user can solve the problem.

3. Optionally, identify the notice with a reference number or other cryptic code that will enable a "more knowledgeable person" to offer further advice in the case of naive users or catastrophic failure.

4. Tell the truth.

Moving away from emotionally charged language should not lead us to euphemisms: if there is a fire in the server, tell people! In the United States, motorists wrongly attempting to enter the exit of freeway off-ramps used to be greeted with a message in small black type that said something like, "We Think You Should Know that Entering Here Could Cause Certain Unfortunate Results." One of the great steps forward in U. S. automotive safety was replacing these signs with big red signs saying, "Go Back. You Are Going The Wrong Way."[2]

In cases where the notice may be the result of the system or application having lost its mind, offer the alternative possibility that the message giver has gone berserk.

This last guideline is particularly important. Users soon lose faith in a system that offers up bogus explanations for what is wrong. One Macintosh application became famous for claiming that a certain file was not on the disk, when in fact the file was sitting right next to the application claiming it was missing, in full view of the user. The problem was that the application supplying the message had gone completely off track but was blissfully unaware that anything was wrong. Had the message been a little less definite about the source of the problem, people might have had an inkling of what to do.

Error messages that cannot be handled quickly and easily are, for all practical purposes, place-holders for uncorrected bugs. In the future, fewer and fewer "more knowledgeable persons" per capita will be on tap. Experienced users will need to handle almost any problem, and, in many instances, error messages will be their only map.

....
2 Note that the user is told what to do about the error even before the error is explained, as opposed to the old message that offered no particular course of action at all.

Developers must begin applying the same rigorous methodology to designing notices that is applied to program design. Designers and programmers should develop the general content of notices (after eliminating the need for as many as possible), but the actual messages should be composed by people skilled in technical writing. Then test the messages to find out if typical users can understand and successfully respond to them. All members of the development team, including marketing people, writers, quality assurance testers, and managers, share the responsibility of delivering clear, inoffensive, and effective error messages.

Software reviewers, it is time to lower the boom. Many independent developers with whom I speak have complained to me about reviewers who seem to slide down competitors' checklists of features—some of which don't even function—and give them great reviews even when their software is all but impossible to use. (James Gleick, in the *New York Times Magazine* for June 14, 1992, devoted a lengthy article to this phenomenon.)

After all these message horror stories, I want to share a sterling example of how messages should be written. It came from AppleLink, a communications service I have usually lambasted over the years. The message was not perfect, but it was refreshingly open and honest:

> The maximum amount of text that a Macintosh "text edit" window can display is 32767 bytes. The Macintosh front end to AppleLink is unfortunately implemented using that window type. Please break up your correspondence into pieces that are smaller than 32767 bytes, and resend it (we know this is a pain, so we're working on it and hope to fix it soon).

Fix it they did.

Successive Disclosure

*I*f we are to support all users without overwhelming novices or boring experts to tears, where do we start? Expert users want and deserve direct, sophisticated access to their machines. Successive disclosure is one technique that can fill their needs without overwhelming the new or casual user.

> *Principle: Disclose new and ever more powerful techniques and features only as users need and can understand them.*

> *Corollary: Functions should be accomplishable through the simplest technique possible consistent with high efficiency.*

The original Macintosh was so sensitive to the needs of the new users that anyone using it for more than around a month ended up hopelessly frustrated. UNIX, on the other hand, threw every single possible option in the new user's face simultaneously, then demanded that the new user understand each option well enough to decide whether it is needed.

> *Never present an expert-user option in such a way that normal users must learn all about it in order to know they don't need to use it.*

Microsoft Word has an advanced pasting facility—so advanced that after ten years of using the product, I have yet to explore it. However, that's OK, because I have never been required to explore it, since Microsoft Word also has a perfectly ordinary Paste command, too. Had they lumped both pasting techniques together, I would have had to learn all about Paste Special without any apparent need.

Make the simple case simple.

The original Macintosh installer required users to know enough about the Macintosh to be able to decide which files they would and would not install, all for the benefit of a few expert users. The current installer has a Custom button for the expert user, and the other 99 percent of users no longer have to learn anything.

Make the complex case simple too.

Once Macintosh users venture into the inner recesses of the installer, they are on their own. The installer knows what a normal installation will require but offers no indication to the expert user. Rather than modifying the normal case to fit one or two special requirements, the expert user must start from scratch, often guessing at what the system needs.

Do not require advanced techniques to perform nonsophisticated functions.

Following this guideline does not preclude you from offering more experienced users faster, more direct ways to accomplish the same tasks. However, before you start supplying shortcuts, make sure you've given the standard method your best shot. Many applications on the market today suffer badly from their designers' and engineers' expending way too much energy on shortcuts. Were the same time invested in improving the original design, many times the shortcuts would have proven unnecessary.

We should provide nooks and crannies in our software so users will stumble upon new possibilities only as they gain the confidence and experience to make use of them. The model is that of a neighborhood with a wide main street off which lie interesting little side streets and shops. Users can spend all their time on Main Street until they choose to explore.

We do not need to wall off users from advanced techniques. Users want to avoid sudden, overwhelming confrontation with advanced features, not have their software treat them like fragile fools who must be protected at all costs. Designers often find the thought of erecting hard walls seductive; after all, we want users to get up and running quickly. However, hard walls tend to backfire. They result in users' having to learn a "training-wheel" interface, only to abandon it later for a significantly different "grown-up" interface.[1]

Designers sometimes employ another technique I call the "giant switch." Users play along in their sandbox interface with few menu items and few options until they feel confident, then throw one switch that unleashes every single power user feature at once. Successive disclosure is gentler, revealing new powers and possibilities piecemeal, and in response to the user's needs.

How does one design a system that incorporates successive disclosure? Remember, the goal is to provide a flat, easy-to-use main street with interesting offshoots.

Features the new user needs should be "within arm's reach."

They should be visible, intuitable, and build upon rules the user will have learned through experience.

Features new users do not need should be placed in the background.

This guideline can prove difficult to implement. Designers face many different trade-offs; successive disclosure is but one. A designer who focused all attention on successive disclosure might end up with an interface that only a new user could love. Instead, design your software for the advanced user, then apply successive disclosure to the result. For example, look at Figure 29.1, which shows the Image menu for Photoshop 3.0 for the Macintosh.

The menu is roughly divided into two sections. The activities from Map through Effects are repetitious ones that directly affect the working area of the document. From Image Size on, the options are more in the nature of long-term housekeeping. So far, so good. The most-used items are near the top, for faster access.

The bottom half of the menu, after leaving Effects, is laid out perfectly for successive disclosure: almost everyone can guess at what

---

1 When I first learned to use chopsticks, at age 18, I was taught the "kid method," which entails using only the thumb and first two fingers. It is quick to learn but results in a certain lack of control. Nonetheless, I became comfortable with it. Later on, I discovered the cognoscenti snickering at me for using the kiddie system. I've attempted to switch over to the far-superior four-fingered method, with mixed results. As the Dvorak keyboard fiasco taught us so many years ago, people do not give up established habits lightly.

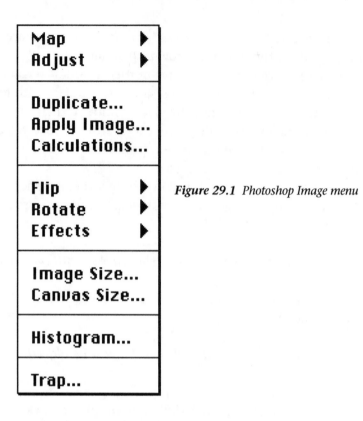

Figure 29.1 *Photoshop Image menu*

Image Size refers to, but how many of you, my technically sophisticated readers, understand what Trap is? Or care?[2] You don't have to. It will hang out down there at the end of the list until you get good and ready. You don't have to keep tripping over it on the way to other features.

The top half of the menu does not follow successive disclosure principles. Most people will grasp Flip, Rotate, and Effects after seeing the hierarchical menus that accompany them. (Flip, for example, offers two options: horizontal and vertical. Not much room for ambiguity there.) Most people, however, will not grasp Map, which occurs first on the list, even after reading some of its available options, such as Equalize..., Threshold..., and Arbitrary....

New users come in two types: those unfamiliar with a specific application and perhaps the system on which it runs, and those unfamiliar with the task domain—the subject matter. The top half of the menu is

....

2 Trapping is a process whereby the edges of adjoining color areas are purposely expanded into each other so that when an image is later printed using four-color presses, white gaps are not left between areas due to poor image registration.

perfectly appropriate for people who arrive at Photoshop already expert in graphic design; the manipulation that one must carry out once one chooses Threshold, for example, is neither unfamiliar nor complex. The problem arises when users new to graphic design don't have a clue as to what Threshold means.

This does not mean that Map should be moved. The first item on a Macintosh menu is second only in acquisition time to the second item, which is first. (Go figure.) If Map is used often, it should be in a fast-access position. However, designers should be aware that they may be compromising their users' first-day experience.

Design software so people unfamiliar with the task domain can learn it.

Computers can do a lot more than empower people to do today's work. Computers can prepare them for tomorrow. We seem to want to divide software strictly between the domains of productivity and training. All applications should aid training, from "toy" flight simulators to Photoshop to Excel. One of the joys of my owning a computer has been its leading me into new fields of knowledge and endeavor I might never have otherwise discovered. How many of us knew how to land on an aircraft carrier, to augment images, or to manipulate spreadsheets 15 years ago? How many of us know now? Our software has taught us.[3]

Assuming every user arrives at an application as a task domain expert not only limits his or her ability to learn and grow, it limits sales.

Active Successive Disclosure

Teachers build their careers around active successive disclosure. They challenge students to attack and master progressively more difficult tasks and techniques as the students become capable of handling them. We can do the same thing. Some efforts have been made to have little messages popping up on the screen, saying things like, "Did you know that you can make your four-color reproductions come out better by using trapping?" Some programs have timed the messages to arrive

....
[3] I assume I could land on a carrier based on my demonstrated skills in Hellcats over the Pacific, although I am not too anxious to put it to the test.

right in the middle of some highly complex cognitive process, ensuring that the user will forget what he or she was doing and will have to start over, a technique that can be avoided.

Quicken, from Intuit, optionally displays a different helpful hint every time the program is launched. The hints not only help users discover new and hidden program capabilities, they serve to entertain, keeping the user's attention while the boot procedure continues.

KPT Convolver from HSC has an "award system" that brings up little cards as people extend their reach into new areas of the program. These cards don't just offer hints; they award the user with stars. Yes, stars. Just like in grade school. Each star is accompanied by some nifty new gadget expanding the power of the user. I was amazed at how hard I found myself working to uncover all the rewards.

As with other forms of user help, the more knowledge the help system has about the user, the task domain, and the user's history with the application, the more welcomed and more effective the help will be. A user known to have never explored the Trapping menu option in Photoshop, when launching four-color separations, will appreciate being told about trapping, since it is vital to successful color printing. However, having the application still carp about trapping the 307th time the same user selects four-color separation will likely lead to equipment defenestration, or worse.

The Advanced User Manual

We can also accomplish successive disclosure through the miracle of the written word. The Texas Instruments SR-52 programmable calculator, released in the mid-seventies, came with two manuals, the second of which was the most effective manual I have ever seen. The usual beginner's manual explained in detail the operation of every possible option, but without, as so often happens, explaining why someone would want to use it. (Explaining why is key to enticing users new to the task domain.)

I quickly put aside the second manual, because I had no idea what the author was talking about. A month later, however, after programming the calculator for a couple of hundred hours, I opened the second manual again, discovering that during the intervening period, the text had magically rearranged itself, allowing me to comprehend everything it said.

The second manual was written by and for people who had had enough experience using the SR-52 to have fallen in love with it. The author—who was first an expert on the SR-52 and second a fine writer—carried readers deeper and deeper into the inner workings of the machine. The manual was written with an affection and vitality that I have never seen exceeded. As a beginner's manual, it would have been a disaster, but as an advanced-user manual, it was worth its weight in gold.

Any application or system that will be used regularly deserves an advanced-user manual, either online or in print. To turn out an advanced-user manual, begin with a writer who is well versed in the task domain, has some experience with computer systems, and is a competent communicator. Then have him or her follow these guidelines:

Get lost in the software for perhaps a month.

You do not write an advanced-user manual by cogitating on what an advanced user might need. You write it by *becoming* an advanced user.

Recognize and record learning transitions as they occur.

Be aware of the big "Aha!" experiences that mark the passages to comprehension. Record them in such a way that those that come after can reexperience them with far less effort.

Talk extensively about the "why," and put it in the expert's context.

Tantalize the experienced user by going beyond the pedestrian use of features.

Experts do not necessarily use tools as originally designed. The autoharp, we learned in school, is held flat on one's lap and gently strummed with a pick held between thumb and forefinger. "Real" auto-harpists wouldn't be caught dead playing this way. They strap the auto-harp around their necks, using their left hand to press the chord keys arrayed along the right edge of the instrument. They then pass their right hand over their left to strum the strings, which are also now conveniently located on the wrong side of the instrument. They use finger picks on three fingers and, rather than taking the easy way of strumming chords, pick individual notes. They end up looking like pretzels because their arms and hands are utterly intertwined, but they produce music quite impossible within the original designer's intent.

Similarly, software expert users "play" their applications in ways the designers may have never considered. Photoshop's Channels command, for instance, was implemented as a serious way of interacting more deeply with a single image by separating the image into primary colors. But you can do something much more fun with two images: Shoot two photographs, moving the camera laterally between shots. Bring up both images in Photoshop, using Channels to select only the red channel on each. Copy the red channel from one of the photos, and paste it in replacement for the red channel of the other. Voilà! You now have a red-cyan 3D image that will pop out at you when you view it with your kid's 3D comic book glasses. (You could use your own comic book glasses, but why risk scratching them.)

Finally, why write when you can get your customers to write for you?

Provide a mechanism for emerging experts to feed back tips and techniques they have found most useful.

This can be done through an online data-collection system or by your company's actively soliciting feedback. Collecting feedback, however, is the easier half of the exercise. Be prepared for the time and effort you will need to roll it into future versions of your application and documents.

A Transparent Folly

One of the perennial buzzwords of human-computer interaction is *transparency:* a good interface should be transparent to the user.

On a recent trip to Madrid, I used a shower in my hotel room that featured a shower-bathroom interface that was completely transparent. The shower door was made of spotless, clear glass that lay back flush with the tile wall. No frame, no handle, no nothin'. For the first two mornings, I sprayed water from one end of the bathroom to the other. Since I couldn't see the transparent interface, I didn't know to close it. On the third morning, my wife gently inquired as to whether I might not want to use the shower door.[1]

When people say an interface should be transparent to the user, they are referring not to the interface between human and computer but to the interface between people and the work they are attempting to accomplish. The idea is that the computer should not become an impediment to the users' accomplishing their goals. For example, an on-board flight computer should not interpose itself in such a way that the pilot, whose job it is to keep the aircraft one or more feet above the local terrain, fails in that task. Such an interposition could be accomplished by the programmer's demanding that pilots type in the command, "pull up!" rather than enabling them to pull back on one of those old-fashioned sticks.

The problem with the concept of transparency is that it doesn't help me as a designer. True, it does define a goal—the computer should

....
1 This is not quite as insane as it sounds. I designed our shower at home not to need any kind of barrier, and it works quite well. I assumed they had attempted the same thing but with a less successful outcome.

not get in the way—but that goal leads to neither strategies nor techniques for accomplishing it.

Let's look instead at the proposition that interfaces should be opaque, the exact opposite of transparent. On a simplistic level, this would seem to imply that the interface should cut the user off from all knowledge of what is going on.[2] Here, however, I am using the concept of transparency—or the lack thereof—to describe the relationship between the user and the computer, not the user and the task. In this view of the world, users do not see the computer at all, seeing instead an artificial projection provided by the computer.

The UNIX console is an example of an interface displaying high transparency between the user and the computer; the engine cab on a steam locomotive is another. In both cases, users are in direct, immediate command of every conceivable function (if they have a clue as to what to do). Engineers in each case report a powerful sense of satisfaction derived from their control, not so much of the task domain but of the great machine itself. That this sense of control is somewhat illusory can be seen from the simple fact that the mightiest locomotives are missing a control considered standard equipment on even the lowliest of compact cars: a steering wheel.

Good graphical user interfaces (GUIs) work in an entirely different way. Instead of confronting the user with the reality of myriad dials and switches, the user is offered a metaphorical model, a projected pseudo-machine that may bear little resemblance to what an engineer would perceive as the real thing. Around 20 years ago, the airplane industry figured out that advanced military cockpits had become more complex than any human being could fathom. They realized they needed to move away from the steam engine model, toward a metaphorical model instead. The result was the "glass cockpit" of today, with hundreds of analog dials replaced by a few TV screens (CRTs) displaying disarmingly simple graphical representations of all critical flight conditions.

Not that the changeover came easily. At first the pilots balked, demanding their steam gauges back. The glass cockpit designers responded with an alternate view, displaying on the CRTs pictures of the old dials. However, after around 6 months, the pilots abandoned

....
2 Such a scheme, using punched cards, was implemented on many of the early computing machines, much to the dismay of those of us who used them.

the dial views forever in favor of the far more information-rich metaphorical views.

The "transparency" advocates would argue that the advanced CRT views offer great transparency between user and task: the pseudo-view presented on the graphic displays more closely matches real life than the steam gauges before it. This has been accomplished, however, by completely cutting the pilot users off from the reality of the instruments that actually collect those data. Reality has been replaced with a communicative but thoroughly opaque interface.

The Macintosh, Windows, and Mosaic interfaces are similarly opaque, whereas DOS and UNIX were not. Interfaces like Starfire, with all their apparent transparency between user and task, will be the most opaque of all.

C H A P T E R 31

Designing Artificial Communications

*I*n *Being Digital*, Nicholas Negroponte suggests people disliked talking
cars because they, "had less personality than a seahorse." While I
could hardly argue with such an assessment, I think the problem went
deeper. Talking cars have failed because they were pedantic, cloddish,
and, way too often, just plain wrong. They would tell you to put on
your seat belt when the belt was already in place. They would repeatedly scream at you for having your keys in the ignition when the ignition is absolutely the finest place for keys to be when you're trying to
unload your sister-in-law and her five kids at the airport in the 2.3
seconds allowed before the airport police start screaming at you to
move it along.

> *Observation: People will assume a higher level of perception,*
> *intelligence, and manners on the part of a machine (or person)*
> *that speaks, compared to one that signals.*
>
> *Guideline: Use voice only when you are confident that your*
> *messages will be responsive, accurate, and useful and that the*
> *delivery system will operate within accepted rules of etiquette.*

What would this guideline have meant for talking cars? They would
have refrained from telling you to fasten your seat belt if it was already
in place. They might have told you once that the door was ajar but not
repeated it every 2.3 seconds for hours on end. They might have
warned you once that your headlights were left on, but then would

have been polite enough to turn them off if you didn't respond after 3 to 5 minutes (allowing you time to get in the house).

In the not-too-distant future, computer systems will have a large amount of integrated information available to them, allowing software agents to present a far better illusion of perception and intelligence. Consider the task of a calendar manager program. Let's say you have a 3:00 P.M. appointment in an adjoining town that has historically taken you 45 minutes to reach. At 2:00, your calendar manager might begin perceiving your office, where you are working. It might first check to make sure that you are not on either audio or video phone. It might then ascertain whether you are alone. If you are not alone, it might then listen for speech, so it will not interrupt. Then it might speak up and let you know that you have a 3:00 meeting for which you will probably have to leave in 15 minutes. (If you are alone, it might give you particulars about the appointment. If someone else is there, it would simply remind you of a meeting with significant travel time, thereby protecting your privacy.)

Perhaps the calendar manager finds that you are not in your office. Perhaps you are on the road to the adjoining town or are actually in the town at a different appointment. The calendar manager would then delay the reminder until a time closer to 3:00.

We could kill voice-delivered agent technology even as it is aborning, if, like the car manufacturers, we were to jump the gun. Today some calendar managers, lacking the contextual information to pull off a system like the above, pepper us with a series of textual warnings: "You have a 3:00 meeting in 1 hour. You have a 3:00 meeting in 55 minutes. You have a 3:00 meeting in 50 minutes." These systems can be irritating enough. Adding voice would leave them broken. Can you imagine having a human assistant who would break into the middle of a conversation you were having with a client to declare repeatedly in a loud voice, "your door is ajar," or, "you have a 3:00 meeting in 55 minutes"? Such a person would be updating his or her resumé long before 3:00 rolled around.[1]

----

1 Please do not suggest that I program in my own notice after computing how much travel time I will need. If I could subtract :45 from 3:00 I wouldn't need a computer. Besides, I might have had an earlier appointment in the distant town—later canceled—and therefore preprogrammed only a 15-minute warning. If a calendar manager is unaware of geography and travel times, it cannot really manage a calendar.

The Danger of Artificial Communication

Talking cars may have gone away for a while, but talking airplanes are on the rise. On a recent trip to Denver, my fellow passengers and I were entertained during final approach by a loud, masculine Voice of God emanating from the flight deck, "You are too low! Pull up now!" The airplane was having a little chat with the captain. The captain pulled back on his yoke even as 237 passengers pulled back on their armrests, and the plane glided in for a perfect landing.[2]

If you are going to play God by offering artificial communication, you had better be accurate. Consider a Voice of God that tells the pilot to pull up and to the right to avoid a mid-air collision just as the head-on aircraft has been told by the competing brand of voice control to pull up and to the left. Boom! Or a military radar system that does away with all those annoying little blips that take so much training to interpret in favor of nice little airplane icons that can make becoming a new radar operator as painless as a trip through Hamburger U. This is a really fine approach unless, whoops, every so often the system makes a little boo-boo, and a commercial airliner pops up looking just like an armed enemy fighter plane on an attack run.

With artificial communication, we are asking users to put their trust in a simulation we have created to take the place of a more direct form of feedback. We carry an awesome responsibility to ensure that these simulations are truly reflective of the conditions at the time.

Use simulations to amplify or replace other less comprehensible or dramatic forms of feedback, but only when you can build fail-safe features into your system to prevent error and misuse.

Letting loose a loud, masculine voice in a cockpit is far more effective than counting on a captain to be watching the right instrument at the right time or to understand and instantly heed one of perhaps

----

2 The aircraft designers might be faulted for embarrassing the captain, but their trade-off was to make the voice soft enough that it potentially could be ignored should anything have gone wrong with the aircraft like, oh, say, the roof having peeled back or something. For safety sake, they need to go with the Voice of God approach.

dozens of warning buzzers or idiot lights. That effectiveness, however, is predicated on the captain's following the order without question, requiring enormous faith on the part of pilots. Every time we use artificial communication in interfaces we are asking for faith. Faith is built from a series of good experiences over time. One bad experience, and faith goes out the window.

The final warning before an airplane plows into the dirt used to be, "Pull up! Pull up!" It was changed. It turned out the first response on the part of the pilot was to think, "My goodness gracious! What is going on!" Somewhere in the middle of "goodness," the plane slammed into the dirt. Now the warning is even more primitive: "Pull up! Don't think! Pull up now!"

Before we ask users not to think, we better do a powerful lot of thinking ourselves.

CHAPTER 32

On High-Altitude Computing

I am writing this chapter at 50,000 feet on an airplane, using a new portable computer that I have managed to get on loan under the guise of doing human interface research. So far on this trip, I have researched the problems of playing the computer version of PGA Golf at high altitude. It does not seem to have improved my game, although I do seem to be able to loft the ball a little better.

After two weeks of living with the portable, I have discovered my style of using the computer has changed both because of the environments in which I have been attempting to use the computer and because of limitations of the supplied pointing device, a trackball.[1] These have led to my depending much more on the keyboard than I have previously.

Here are a few guidelines I whipped up while waiting for an electronic foursome to play through. I trust they will make your applications portable savvy and justify my further playing of golf on airplanes.

Expect users to make more errors.

Portables are held on laps on airplanes, trains, rapid transit systems, even buses. People will be making mistakes, and applications need to be particularly sensitive to the kinds of errors that can occur. We need

....
1 Trackballs are not bad devices, but they just don't do as well as mice. On the other hand, mice are not too practical at the back end of the plane here in cattle class, as you are likely to elbow the football player squeezed into the seat next to you in your efforts to drop a document in the trash—which could give whole new meaning to the term *catastrophic data loss.*

to head off the errors wherever possible and provide simple, straightforward recovery when they occur anyway.

Expect users to make more errors when selecting from menus.

Make sure that users selecting the wrong item will become aware of that fact. For example, do not place the menu items Open and Delete Document next to each other, then offer virtually identical dialog boxes that require identical actions on the part of the user.

Test applications on portable computers using subjects who are advanced in years or otherwise less physically able.

Any physical limitations of the user are magnified when the effectiveness of the pointing device is reduced; lowered coordination, hand tremor, and other effects make precision movement extremely difficult. We are a young industry, and most of the readers of this book are younger than many of their users. The fact that you can wheel around the interface with no problem is in no way predictive of whether others will also be able to run an application using a portable's pointing device. Pay careful attention to actions that cannot be carried out successfully by test subjects, and either reduce the need for precision or offer efficient, effective keyboard alternatives.

Here are a few guidelines aimed at trackballs.

Applications must be forgiving of fingers losing contact with the trackball button during drag operations.

The user's finger can lose contact with the button because of a peculiarity of trackballs: with the mouse, the fingers holding the mouse and the finger perched over the mouse button move in concert as the mouse moves over the physical desktop. With the trackball, the finger or palm moving the ball moves relative to the fixed position of the finger on the trackball button. Even with large trackball buttons, fingers can easily lift momentarily from the switch during the effort to manipulate the round trackball during a drag operation. Punishing users by having their documents seemingly disappear forever when they accidentally release the button while perched over a folder is a tad unfriendly. Not offering an Undo option to drag it back up is positively obnoxious.

Applications must be forgiving of incorrect initial mouse movement because the trackball is difficult to control during "take-off."

With the trackball, the initial direction is difficult or impossible for many people to control. This problem becomes particularly acute in some graphics programs.

Graphics programs that support the Shift key for constraining mouse direction must be fully forgiving of users' starting off in the wrong direction.

This guideline has always seemed to me a matter of common sense, and yet many paint programs continue to set the constraint direction with the first movement to an adjacent pixel. These applications are impossible for many portable owners to use. (I tried to use one, released ten years after this problem was first noted, and was completely unable to predict the direction a constrained line would take.)

Where practical, algorithms should not lock in a constraining direction until the moment the mouse is released. For example, if the user has drawn a 3-inch-long horizontal line and, while still holding down the mouse button, moves much above 22.5 degrees, you should jump the line up to a 45-degree slope.

If memory is available, applications should reside in memory instead of paging in, to save on power (and the user's time) by not spinning up the hard disk all the time.

Where it is impractical to have the entire application in memory, great care should be given as to how to segment applications to reduce hard-disk access to a minimum.

One strategy to reduce the apparent time to hard-disk spin-up is to keep in memory enough of each logical segment to keep the user occupied while the balance of the segment is brought in. For example, in a spreadsheet application that can create a chart, hit the user instantly with the dialog requesting information about what kind of chart the user wants, allowing time to bring in the charting segment while the user is trying to figure out the difference between a bar chart and a scatter graph.

Code for enabling users to open menus and other operations should always be available. Users become frustrated when it takes almost 5 seconds just to see the available options in a menu.

Notify portable users when you are turning on the hard disk.

When a hard disk is spinning up in a high-noise, high-vibration environment such as an airplane, pauses for hard-disk spin-up are easily interpreted as system crashes because all movement ceases without any audible feedback. Inform users with a subtle but clear visual indicator.

These guidelines will prove useful beyond the needs of portables. The trackball guidelines can provide for the needs of people with limited hand mobility and coordination, regardless of the device they are using. The hard-disk guidelines are as needed by those who are hearing impaired as they are by people overcome by temporary noise.

Software That Sells

*P*ainter, from Fractal Design, seemed to take over the computer paint box market in a matter of minutes. Why? Because using it was a pleasurable experience from the moment people launched it. Because after 2 hours of using the other packages of the time, people felt confused, frustrated, and out of control and still had no grasp of what the other packages could or could not do. Because Painter was and is an application designed to *sell*.

72½ Hours to Victory

The critical time in the life of an application lies from a half-hour before it is sold to three days later, when the check clears. If your software cannot be demo'd without embarrassment by a salesperson of passing intelligence, if its benefits cannot instantly be perceived by a customer, if the first day or evening spent learning it is about as much fun to users as driving a nail through their foot, sales may fall short of early projections.

Programmers, designers, and even product marketers tend to leave to others the task of seeing that a piece of software is snatched off the shelves by customers. Little thought seems to go into making the products themselves into sales tools. True, sometimes a feature or 20 are shoehorned into an otherwise fine product so the reviewers' checklists will look really good, but usually little attention is given to making the software reach out and grab new users. Painter reached out and grabbed the graphic design community, leaving the competition in the dust. Your product can do the same.

Painter doesn't even have to be turned on to be attractive. It is a paint program, so it comes in a bright, shiny, gallon-sized paint can. Not only does this attract attention on a dealer's shelves, but when users are showing off Painter to their friends, they inevitably end the demo by saying, "And catch this, Dude, it comes in this bright, shiny, gallon-sized paint can!"

When it's running, Painter is even more attractive. Its graphics are clear and concise, but they are also bright, flashy, and enticing—enticing enough to catch the eye of the most wary shoppers and gently seduce them to sit down and try it.

Success Experiences

Consider the initial experience with older 24-bit paint programs. After rushing home from the store, the user plunged 15 disks into the drive in heady anticipation, anxious to select a nice piece of charcoal and start sketching. Sure, no problem. All the user had to do was specify it:

Are we having fun yet?

After less then 10 minutes of first using Painter, I felt successful and empowered. Rather than expecting me to apply my vast knowledge of physics and art (not!) to the construction of custom paint brushes, Painter presented me with the following palette of familiar tools:

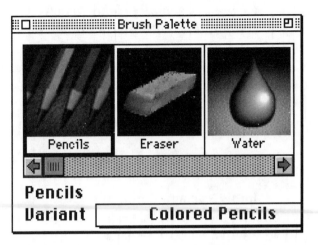

By scrolling, I got to these other familiar tools:

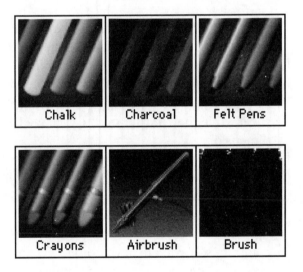

Recognizing my limitations, I selected the crayon tool and fell to drawing the same house, tree, and flower I have been drawing since the traumatic days of second grade, and they looked just as they always have! I could not have been more pleased! In 10 short minutes, I experienced success.

Guidelines for Software That Sells

Customers should be able to accomplish a familiar task, comfortably, within 20 minutes.

I don't expect to be able to use every feature and accomplish every advanced operation in 20 minutes, but I do expect to accomplish some very real task and feel good about the experience. The following guideline can help accomplish this goal.

Begin in a familiar domain.

If this is an application for artists, then make them feel at home by offering them charcoal versus watercolor, not low-percent-moisture versus high-percent-moisture.

Offer familiar tools and behaviors.

If the software is a more advanced version of a current product, it should emulate the current product where possible.[1] For example, if you expect people to manipulate tables of data with three dimensions, consider displaying the first two dimensions as a spreadsheet. People can spend their first 20 minutes creating a two-dimensional spreadsheet while they muster up the courage to launch into the third dimension.

Make existing work transfer into your application easily and intelligently.

The early adopters of computer technology have already bought computers. If you are developing new and more powerful tools for people, a large percentage of your users will be drawn from those already using a less powerful tool to accomplish the same task. It is not enough for your application to open up old documents. It must do so intelligently, so that people can take advantage of your new, more powerful features with a minimum of fuss.

....
1 The emulation may be limited by factors beyond your control—like a team of intellectual property lawyers from the owner of the current product showing up in your outer office.

I explored a hot new application recently that let me do a straight, dumb copy of old data. Then I discovered to my chagrin that manipulating those data into a form where the application could make it stand up and dance would have required more than 100 separate cut-and-paste operations. It wasn't worth it. I went back to my tired, old standby.

Give people an intellectual upgrade path.

Create manuals (or sections of a manual) just for people coming from your old product or your competitor's product. Hire writers who are expert in the earlier products; then have them record their experiences as they learn the new product.

Salespeople should be able to learn, in less than 30 minutes, a 5-minute demo they can give without fear of embarrassment.

A lot of software is still sold by actual humans. Painter offers a special brush called "Artists," which comes in several flavors, such as Van Gogh and Seurat. These brushes are the equivalent of the drum box on the electronic organ down at the mall: they enable a salesperson with the most minimal of training to turn out "instant art" that looks halfway decent.

Test constantly on users unfamiliar with the new product.

In Chapter 2 of *Tog on Interface,* I talked about the dangers of the creeping learning curve, occurring as one new object or behavior is added day after day, month after month. I too often see developers who have created really wonderful new capabilities but have completely lost sight of how much time they, the developers, have put into learning how to use it. You must test constantly on new users. Field sites, alpha sites, and beta sites will deliver a wealth of useful information, but if you want to find out what happens during the first 20 minutes of using your product, you have to try it out on someone new. Chapters 14 and 36 of *Tog on Interface* explain in detail how to do it, and how to do it cheaply. So do it!

Initial success experiences are what sell software. Users, unless unusually motivated, are rarely willing to toil 10, 20, 30 hours or more before they feel the faintest glimmer of competence. Make them feel successful, and they and their friends will be back for more.

PART 8

Beyond the Horizon

In this final part, we will look at not only the expanding horizon of the future but the expanding horizon of the art and science of software design. The software design field has for too long looked inward for answers. First, we will explore the lessons learned by magicians over the last 5,000 years and how we can apply them in our own work. Then we will move forward into the future, exploring techniques that can help project the shape of emerging markets. In "Brave New World" (Chapter 36), we will consider privacy, a precious freedom our society is in danger of losing forever. Finally, "The First Step" (Chapter 37) lays out the most fundamental change our industry must take now, if we are to achieve the promise of the future.

Magic and Software Design

Software designers are struggling to generate more effective illusions for purposes of communicating to their users the design model of their applications (Heckel 1991; Laurel 1991; Norman 1983, 1986, 1988; Rubinstein and Hersh 1984; Shneiderman 1992). At the same time, they are confronting serious issues of ethics: When does an attempt to create an empowering illusion become trickery? When does an attempt at anthropomorphism become cheap fraud (Laurel 1991; Shneiderman 1988; Tognazzini 1992)?

Our profession has drawn its lessons primarily from psychology, computer science, and graphic design. While these have supplied much valuable material, we are still busily recreating organized knowledge in our field that Laurel points out has been well understood for thousands of years.[1]

Perhaps no field other than magic is tied so closely to the field of graphical interface design. The people working at Xerox PARC in the 1960s and early 1970s were aware of the principles of theatrical magic when creating the first graphical interfaces, to the extent that David Smith named the interface itself the "user illusion" (Kay 1991). We are

....
1 Our profession sees itself as being on the cutting edge of discovery, but in many instances this is just not true. At a computer convention I attended a few years ago, a paper was roundly criticized in the hallways for being a rehash of work done in a related field almost ten years ago. Ten years! Shocking! A story made the rounds some years back about a fellow from a Silicon Valley database company who went to the Vatican to talk with them about moving their library indexing system onto computer. He asked casually one evening whether they ever lent out books, rather than being a reference-only library. The fellow from the Vatican responded, quite straight-faced, that they had tried such an experiment for several years during the late 1400s, but it just hadn't worked out.

designing interfaces for an interface system based on magic, yet there is almost nothing written about it in our literature. (An exception is a single page by Heckel.) Magicians have been struggling with the principles, techniques, and ethics of illusion for at least 5,000 years (Burger 1991). There's a lot we can learn from them.

This chapter is not exhaustive. On the contrary, it barely scratches the surface. My goals are to introduce other software professionals to the teachings of this parallel profession of magic and to excite interest in what I believe to be a powerful set of tools for software designers. I have been an amateur magician for as long as I've been a professional software designer and have applied the principles, techniques, and ethics of magic routinely in my design work. I have found them to be invaluable.

Eerie Correspondence

It's hard to read through a book on the principles of magic without glancing at the cover periodically to make sure it isn't a book on software design. These books clearly delineate the basic principles and techniques that support graphical user interfaces:

- *Consistency.* Books on magic technique dwell on the various aspects of consistency—for example, "Consistency is the key to conviction . . . . No matter how effective an inconsistent part may be, the damage that it does to the routine as a whole more than offsets whatever advantages it may have in itself" Nelms 1959). "Irregularities destroy naturalness and conviction. When naturalness disappears, and when something unnatural is evident, the spectator's attention immediately becomes vigilant and alert. In the normal course of events, this is disastrous to deception" (Fitzkee 1945).

- *Unity.* "No first-class success in any type of entertainment, whether it be in the form of a motion picture, a stage attraction, a novel, a short story, or any other type of diversion, can be achieved without endowing the undertaking with some degree of unity, no matter how fragile the connecting thread may be" (Fitzkee 1943).

- *Keep it simple.* "The Japanese define an artist as 'one who has the ability to do more and the will to refrain'" (Nelms 1959).

- *Use of real-world metaphors.* The magician's tools should be disguised to look like objects in the real world. "If these things are common things, objects with which the spectator is familiar, this spectator will accept them in terms *as he knows them.* He will assume the device to be the same as the common article with which he is acquainted" (Fitzkee 1945).

- *Technique of user testing.* Nelms (1959) gives a complete précis on user-testing, including the importance of choosing spectators from the target population: "If you try to dramatize a routine for a brother conjurer, you will merely bore him—unless he sees something in your routine that he can use in his own act. . . . When you work out a routine for laymen, test it on a friend who knows nothing about conjuring. Ask for his detailed criticism. Then try your routine on another friend and get his opinion. If several laymen find fault with the same spot in your routine, it is bad." He goes on to detail the pitfalls of taking the spectator's diagnosis too literally: "A layman's diagnosis of what is wrong will usually be false and will often be absurd, but he almost always puts his finger on the point where the problem lies."

Sound familiar?

Virtual Realities

Both software designers and magicians create virtual realities. We bring ours alive on computer displays; magicians bring theirs alive on the stage. We capture our "performances" in code so they can continue to occur long after their writing; magicians traditionally appear live. We depend on our knowledge of the mechanics of computer technology, the aesthetics of graphic design, and the science of psychology. Magicians depend on their knowledge of the mechanics of their tricks, the aesthetics of showmanship, and the science of psychology.

Mechanics

Amateur magicians start out struggling with the mechanics of magic, and most never get beyond working with rigged gimmicks, like marked cards and "magic" milk pitchers. Competent magicians can work fluidly with apparatus, so that the spectators are unaware that the card seemingly dealt from the top of the deck came from the bottom, or that the rabbit that seemingly arrived from out of nowhere had been residing in the magician's pocket, munching peacefully on carrots. Magicians must be competent at the mechanics of their craft, yet such competency does not make someone a magician, any more than knowledge of a rapid-prototyping system makes someone a software designer. It sets the stage and makes everything else possible. (Of course, we software designers have a distinct advantage over our magician friends: we can depend on programmer colleagues—confederates—to do our technical trickery for us.)

One interesting difference exists between the mechanics of magic and of software design: while we are struggling to hide from our users the vast complexity of our electronic reality, magicians are attempting to hide how trivially simple their tricks are. We've all been told that magicians never reveal their secrets because it is "a magician's sacred obligation . . . to keep the secrets of his brotherhood" (Jillette and Teller 1959), but there is another, more practical, reason: people get very angry when they discover they were so completely taken in by such simple ruses, and they invariably turn on the magician.

Showmanship

Showmanship seems like an unimportant aspect of software design, but an exploration of how it applies to magic reveals some unexpected results.

What is this thing we call a human interface? Lawyers will tell you it's the "look and feel" of the software, but when you press them, they will be at a loss to explain what that means. (They will also bill you $250 for their failure.) Don Norman calls it the "system image," the physical embodiment of the designer's "design model" (Norman 1983, 1986, 1988). Rubinstein and Hersh (1984) call it an "external myth." Ted Nelson (1980) calls it "virtuality." Alan Kay and his cohorts at Xerox PARC, in deliberate reference to magic, called it the "user illusion" (Kay 1991). All of these words are descriptive, yet all are abstract and therefore somewhat elusive.

Magicians work to produce illusions, but they don't call their stage presentation an illusion; they call it an act—a good, down-to-earth term you can get your hands around. It comes equipped with expectations: we know that an act should inform, excite, and entertain us. If it doesn't, we know what to do about it, which might or might not involve computing trajectories for rotten fruit, depending on the poverty of the performance.

Look at the most famous contemporary magicians: Doug Henning, Paul Daniels, Penn and Teller, Siegfried and Roy, David Copperfield. All are consummate showmen. Indeed, an examination of David Copperfield's tricks shows them all to be rather old and prosaic, but he performs them in such a theatrical style and on such a grand scale that we are enthralled. Most magicians, with a suitable trap door, can perform Servais Le Roy's turn-of-the-century "Asrah" illusion, making a comely young person disappear in thin air, but David Copperfield has made a 100-ton steam locomotive disappear into thin air. Most impressive.

Many principles of magic showmanship are directly applicable to software design. Here are just a few (Fitzkee 1943):

- *Character.* "No chef would prepare a dish without seasoning. Character is the seasoning which makes your entertainment dish palatable. Everything has character, even though the character be weak and uninteresting. Your job is to develop a quality of character in your routine that makes it tasty to the spectator. Otherwise you have a mere assembly of ingredients—tasteless, unsavory, unappetizing, lacking zest."

- *Smoothness.* "Perfect smoothness is necessary to any routine. In no other way will your act seem finished to the spectators. Smoothness, which is a word meaning you have planned thoroughly and well, gives confidence both to the performer and to his audience."

- *"Get to the point.* Be brief. Keep interesting them. Quit before they've had enough."

Showmanship has an important place in computer software. It certainly was a conscious component of the Lisa and the Macintosh. As one example, we didn't adopt the trash can for file elimination just because it fulfilled the requirement of a "real-world" metaphor. We chose it because it seemed "neat," and we kept it because other people loved it.

Showmanship does not mean, to use Ted Nelson's term, "adding ketchup" (Nelson 1991). It implies the application of a deep understanding of human nature to the task of making software seem vital, involving, and fun. Negroponte (1991) remembers

... scholarly papers (circa 1972) that argued against color in the displays. They were filled with tables, control groups, and the like, proving that color could be confusing. Today, I hear of similar studies that speech and natural language are not appropriate channels of communication between people and computers....

I certainly understand that I don't want the pilot of a 747 to land an airplane by singing songs or a doctor to perform open heart surgery by humming into his apparati. But I can't fathom any cause to avoid richness in communication, especially as computers become ubiquitous and are part of the quality of our daily lives.

Magicians learn showmanship the hard way, by standing on a stage, receiving instant and often painful feedback from a live and lively audience. One way people can learn how to inject showmanship into software designs is through a similar, if less painful, mechanism: by dragging prototypes to customer sites, computer stores, club meetings—anywhere one can find an audience.

When setting out to design "Apple Presents . . . Apple," the first in-box microcomputer tutorial back in 1979, Dave Eisenberg and I forwent the goal of teaching everything about the computer in favor of the more attainable goal of teaching a few fundamentals in such a way that new users would become interested and confident enough to want to learn more on their own.

The application started with an "attract mode" that gently cajoled the reluctant user to "just press the Return key." It continued with a building set of "success experiences," until after approximately 5 minutes, even the most fearful users were usually zipping away inside the application, feeling fully in command. During its design, we tried the application on more than 300 people, making it more lively and interactive with every pass. Within 6 months of its release, the Apple independent dealers identified it as their most valuable sales tool: they reported it made prospective owners love the computer and that the sale was then easy.

Not everyone will immediately agree that showmanship in spreadsheets is as important as showmanship on a Las Vegas stage, but consider this reality: software must be bought before it can be used (except in India and Italy). Showmanship does not imply the injection of irrelevant frills and fancies. It is the gentle seduction of the users, leading them to accept, believe in, and feel in control of the illusory world we have built for them.

Psychology and Dichotomy

"The art of illusion" writes Henning Nelms (1969), "is at least 95% applied psychology.... When [modern conjurers] use more than one part of trickery to nine parts psychology, they cannot hope to create the maximum impression."

The act *is* the entity in magic. The mechanical devices and techniques are there solely to support the act, showmanship is there to enliven the act, but psychology makes the act work.

Actually, there are two simultaneous acts performed in magic: the one the magician actually does—the magician's reality—and the one the spectators perceive—the spectators' reality. The magician's reality consists of all the sleights of hand and manipulation of gimmicked devices that make up the prosaic reality of magic. The spectators' reality, given a sufficiently competent magician, is entirely different: an alternate reality in which the normal laws of nature are repeatedly defied, a reality where the magician, as well as his or her tricks, appear supernatural.

On the surface, this defiance would seem in direct contradiction to software design, where we more often engage in making our "supernatural" machines appear natural. However, at a deeper level, both camps spend their time doing the same thing: making people believe one thing is going on when quite another is really taking place. The Macintosh has no actual, physical trash can, and no amount of rummaging around inside with a screwdriver and a pair of wire-cutters will reveal one.

This dichotomy, this concept of two simultaneous acts—the real and the perceived—is both key to magic and the most important link to our own work in design. In the course of working with hundreds of people assigned to design software during my career, most of them programmers with no formal knowledge in human-computer interaction, the most critical concept I have found missing has been the dichotomy of the programmer's "reality" and the user's "reality." (I have put *reality* in quotation marks in both places, because what the programmer sees as "real" in the computer is just the system image provided by the systems engineer or hardware engineer. Our computers consist of realities within realities within realities.)

Magicians' spectators, with the exception of young children, are adversaries, there for the specific purpose of finding the magician out. Magicians often reflect their adversarial relationship in their vocabulary—for example, "The deception the magician seeks to accomplish is an attack upon the spectator's mind. Specifically, it is an attack upon his understanding" (Fitzkee 1945).

Because of the natural suspicion of their spectators, magicians have had to develop the psychology of the illusion to a high level. If we apply their techniques with our users, who are not suspicious (unless we insist on "burning" them a few times), we surely will achieve a believable result. Let's look at a few key techniques magicians use to generate their simultaneous but alternate, reality.

Misdirection

Misdirection, says Fitzkee (1945), is "the psychology of deception and the application of craft and artifice for accomplishing the magician's objectives." Fitzkee identifies six techniques for causing misdirection: simulation, dissimulation, ruse, disguise, monotony, and maneuver. Let us examine just the first two:

- *Simulation.* "Simulation is a bewildering way of saying that something is made to look like what it is not" (Fitzkee 1945). Simulation is our most powerful misdirection tool in software design. It is the underlying principle of Norman's System Image, Rubinstein and Hersh's "external myth," Nelson's "virtuality," Smith's user illusion. Professional designers use it for the express purpose of creating a dichotomy with the programmer's reality.
- *Dissimulation.* "Dissimulation means the act of concealing the real fact by pretense" (Fitzkee 1945). A trash can instead of a dialog requesting track and sector identification for zero overwrite is simulation. A nicely laid-out dialog box for requesting file name identification for file removal is dissimulation. The essential reality is fully present; it is just being covered up.

Simulation and dissimulation are both important magic techniques. The magician who wishes to simulate a coin's disappearing into thin air from his or her right hand had better be proficient enough at dissimulation that spectators don't notice the coin actually sliding into a pocket from the magician's left hand. However, dissimulation is there to cover up, not to startle and amuse. For example, in the Asrah illusion, the assistant slides through a trap door but still appears to be lying on the platform. Dissimulation. Dull. It is when we as spectators believe we see the assistant, shrouded in silk, slowly rising into the air with no visible means of support, following the beckoning of the magician's wand, that we become interested. Then, when the magician suddenly whips the shroud away, to reveal nothing but empty space, we are left dumbfounded and amazed. Simulation.

Amateur designers are far more likely to cover up a reality than alter it, but so are professionals who are deprived of sufficient resources to "do the right thing." In the early days of Lisa and Macintosh, we at Apple were given all the resources we needed, and we used simulation widely and effectively. Now our entire industry seems bent on power at the expense of everything else, and programs and interface systems are showing the symptoms of dissimulation. For example, Apple's confusing System 7 feature, Publish and Subscribe, was essentially raw technology, with just the lightest sugar coating (dissimulation). In contrast, human interface and graphic designers designed Apple's QuickTime video animation tool from the ground up as a simulation responsive to the needs of its users. They repeatedly tried out the software on real users under real conditions, to see whether the design illusion was realistic, productive, and responsive. It ended up being all three.

Attention to Detail

Magicians continually stress that illusions don't work without attention to detail:

> When a magician simulates placing something into a container—any kind of a container, a hat, a tube, a can, a box—he goes through the exact motions he would make if the object were actually placed in the container. His attention is upon the hand apparently containing the object. It follows along as the object is placed in the container. The opposite hand, holding the container, adjusts itself to accommodate the additional weight. The performer's attention then follows the apparent presence of the object. Meanwhile, as he would if the object actually were placed in the container, he ignores the hand which formerly seemed to, or actually did, contain the object.
>
> ... No matter what type of simulation is used, no matter what the simulation is for, the magician is acting out a role. He must do this well or the simulation will not be effective. He must do it convincingly or he will not convey the impression he is trying to accomplish. He must do it naturally or it will seem artificial and will arouse suspicions (Fitzkee 1945).

Magicians talk about the "delicacy" of the illusion: a bit of light escaping from what is supposed to be a dark box or the errant corner of the assistant's dress protruding from the trap door destroys forever all hopes of maintaining the illusion. Fitzkee (1945) cautions the performer to be "particularly careful that his handling of all of his properties, *in every respect,* is in keeping with what they are purported to be, *at all times.* If they are handled as if they are what they seem to be, this contributes to convincingness and conviction.... Naturalness is the most powerful weapon at the disposal of the magician when he seeks to deceive."

The spectator doesn't have to know details of the deception to know deception occurred, thereby destroying the illusion. In fact, the spectator can be dead wrong in his "explanation," and still the illusion evaporates. Fitzkee tells the story of a time when he was filming Howard Thurston performing the Levitation of the Princess Karnac, in which the woman playing the princess is actually levitated, without benefit of shroud. Fitzkee, meanwhile, was up in the balcony of the auditorium, filming the procedure, when "several spectators heard the camera operating. They immediately connected the camera with the levitation. I could see them nudge their companions, call their attention to the camera, then point to the activity on the stage. From the way they relaxed and settled back into their seats, I am positive they felt they had solved the mystery" (Fitzkee 1945).

America's Disneyland and Disney World are studies in attention to detail. They are masterful illusions that make people believe in the unbelievable. The illusion does not rest on fooling a single sense. Sight, sound, smell, taste, and touch all receive a flood of concordant information. Many other amusement parks feature theme rides and costumed employees, but as you walk around, you are confronted with the seams. In the land of make-believe, you see a Chevrolet pickup truck not quite hidden behind the magic carousel. While dashing through the Old West, you can't avoid overhearing your stage coach driver talking loudly with the man riding shotgun about his date with Allison at the disco last night.

The better the illusion, the more shocking is any flaw. In 1994, as I boarded the train at EuroDisney, I saw a young male member of the "cast" (as Disney employees are called) riding the rails during his break. The fact that he and every stationmaster at each stop saw fit to chit-chat about their personal lives was surprising enough. What was truly amazing was that he had unbuttoned the top of his eighteenth-century French costume to reveal a most twentieth-century American undershirt beneath. The entire illusion that so many people had invested so much time and energy building up was, at least for the moment, destroyed.

No Disney cast members in the United States would dare walk around with their costumes unbuttoned, and, even if they did, no other cast members would be foolish enough to engage them in idle chit-chat in front of the guests (Koenig 1994). It would be unthinkable. This lack of attention to detail may at least help to explain why EuroDisney was having such a struggle to survive.[2]

Maintaining an illusion on a computer requires the same level of commitment and fervor historically displayed by Disney. And it can be as easily damaged. The Star, Lisa, and early Macintosh displayed finely crafted illusions. Today our system illusions are rent by inconsistencies, program crashes, and unfathomable conceptual models.

Most of us have seen—or even been involved in—software projects where attention to detail was slight or nonexistent, resulting in software with unclear system images, flashing redraws, unresponsive feedback, or, even worse, a dangerous lack of forgiveness. Such breeches result in software that is confusing, awkward to use, and even frightening—not exactly our design goals.

Overcoming Objections Before They Arise

Once an objection, or even a suspicion, arises in the minds of spectators, the trick is finished. Magicians put great effort into making sure their illusions develop in such a way that spectators are not even given to questioning why a certain action is taking place. They do this by providing a motive within the spectators' reality for every action taken within the magician's reality. For example, in the Asrah Levitation, the assistant will not actually be present during much of the performance, having slipped through the trap door. The device that takes the place of the assistant and floats up into the air is made of metal rather than

---

2 Disneyland in Tokyo has no greater quality than Disneyland in America. The only difference I could discern was that achieving that quality in Japan was a good deal easier. The streets at California's Disneyland are clean because of the myriad of street sweepers who trail around behind the guests, whisking their every litter into dustpans before it has hardly touched the ground. At Tokyo Disneyland, I saw no street sweepers at all, and none were necessary: the Japanese don't litter.

flesh and blood. It is therefore given to a certain unnatural stillness. If the spectators slowly became aware of that stillness, they might become suspicious, so to avoid their potential objection, the assistant is first seen to be hypnotized or forced to drink some poisonous elixir, thus seemingly rendering her as still as the apparatus that will replace her. The magician has overcome the objection before it arises.

Hormuz was an early program written in the PILOT language. It featured a character that would "speak" with children through the screen and keyboard. The character introduced himself as an ancient Arabian, then urged the child to "come close to the fire, for the light is weak." He went on, after asking for the child's name, to request the child's gender: "My eyes grow dim with age: are you a little boy or a little girl?" (words approximate). Having established the character as old, having established that the night was dark, the designer is then able to ask what would otherwise be an insulting question of a child. The designer has overcome the objection before it arises.

Believing in the Illusion

Magicians live in both the world of their mechanical tricks and the illusory world they are creating for their spectators, but they believe in the spectator's world: "All of the most successful showman-conjurers agree that you must believe in your own magic; you cannot hope to convince an audience unless you first convince yourself," writes Nelms (1969).

In my experience, programmers face an ongoing struggle to believe in their own illusions. They continually want to slip back into the comfort of their mechanical world down below. In the early days of software, the system image directly reflected every convolution and limitation of the structure of the program, the programming language, and the operating system. Today's best visual interface systems are designed before the underlying systems are built, so that although we continue to design for the expected *capabilities* of systems, we need no longer design to a predetermined *structure*. Instead, we design system images to reflect the structure of the design model (Norman 1986, 1988; Tognazzini 1992). Later, when the programmers lay out the software, they tend toward a structure in general conformance with that of our system image, neatly reversing the historical sequence.

Programmers who have not made the transition to the design model's illusion are easy to spot: they meet any attempt on the designer's part to create a new and interesting design model with, "Yes, but that's not the way it really works." The last thing a magician wants is for his spectator's model of the act to bear any relationship to "the way it really works."

Although we don't share the magician's pressing need to hide this "reality," we often gain advantage by offering the user a well-constructed illusion. For example, ISDN, the all-digital telephone system, can complete a call connection in a few milliseconds instead of the usual 5 to 10 seconds, exchange data in brief, high-speed bursts, then log off, terminating billing charges, after an additional few milliseconds. By being faithful to the realities of ISDN, we could offer users a much faster log-on procedure, but consider how much more we could accomplish by separating the illusion of the interface from the realities of the hardware. With "instant" log-on, high-speed communication, and short-duration transmission, we could create the illusion that the user is always connected. Any time the system saw the user perform a task that requires transmission, such as dropping an addressed document in an out-basket, the system could sign on, send the document, and sign off, all without the user's conscious awareness. As far as the system is concerned, it is saving every precious penny of the user's money. As far as the user is concerned, he or she is "connected" 24 hours a day, seven days a week.

The business of constructing a new metaphor, a new conceptual model, is one of spinning a tightly woven illusion. For example, Starfire proposes that there be only one primary holder of information, the container. The instances of this container would range from the folders of today to the document of tomorrow. Any container can change its form to become any other container. So a document can become a folder and a folder can become a document.[3]

If this interface illusion is taken literally, it requires the software engineer to create a single object so malleable that it can be molded like putty into a dozen different forms. Given the powers of tomorrow's object environments, that might prove to be a possible solution to projecting the illusion, but suppose it isn't. Does that mean that the illusion must be changed to reflect the "realities" of the system? No.

....
3 Like the concept of "views" on systems today, those aspects of a file that are not used by a given container type will be maintained in a separate resource, to be restored should the user want to return to an earlier container type.

Consider that, in fact, we end up with exactly a dozen different hard-wired containers. Not one of these containers is capable of being anything but what it is: a folder, a scrapbook, a notebook, an active paper document. We then build utilities that can do conversions: feed the utility with the name of an active paper document, and it will produce a notebook from it.

We could, within the illusion of the interface, require the user to open the utility, enter the name of the source container, enter the name of the destination container, and press the Process Now button. But we can just as easily have the user select the source document, command, "change to notebook," then carry out the conversion, and replace the old object with the new, seamlessly and invisibly. From the programmer's point of view, what has just happened is that the data from one container have been transferred to another, and the old container has been deleted. From the user's point of view, however, there is only a single object, and that object has just changed form.

Manipulation of Time

Magicians manipulate time, as well as space. Here is one of their ways:

Offsetting time of reality from time of illusion.

Magicians use two techniques to offset the actual time a trick (the essential working of the apparatus) takes place from the time when the spectators think it takes place: anticipation, where the magician does the trick early, before spectators begin looking for it, and premature consumption, where the magician does the trick late, after spectators assume it has already occurred.

I once saw a magician on television, seated before a small, 1-inch-thick table, performing one of the oldest magic tricks known: Cups and Balls, described by the Roman philosopher Seneca in the first century C.E. The spectators attempt to guess under which of three cups (or, in this magician's case, stainless steel pans) the ball lies, while the magician makes sure they cannot. The magician began with the usual sponge ball, about the size of a golf ball, which, when squeezed into the palm, becomes the size of a pea and is rather easily inserted beneath any pan desired. After the people around the table had, predictably, failed to identify the correct pan on a couple of occasions, the ball began to grow. And grow. And grow. By the end of the trick, the man tilted the pan forward, then lifted it away to reveal a bowling ball beneath. (The bowling ball, while no wider than the pan, was a great deal taller than the pan was deep.) The table was not gimmicked in any way. The man had, from all appearances, not lifted any heavy objects. Rather, he had been very busy talking with his spectators when the bowling ball suddenly appeared.

By chance, I had videotaped the performance and was able to study it in detail. The magician had used a technique I call counterpoint. For the entire course of the act, his trickery had preceded its revelation by around 5 seconds. As he would engage in a vociferous explanation of why the spectators had failed on the last round, gesticulating with his hands for emphasis, he was actually placing the load for the next round. The choreography was superlative. Like the rich counterpoint of Bach or Händel, the notes of his own reality blended perfectly with the reality he was presenting to his spectators. All of that man existed in the reality of his spectators—his intellect, his emotion, his gestures, his words, his apparent actions—except some tiny part of his mind, like some little demon, which went quietly about the task of preparing the next trick. It was a beauty to behold, and, try as I might, even examining the tape frame by frame, I could not catch him loading that bowling ball behind the pan.

"Pipelining"—drawing screens, gathering data before needed—is a form of anticipation. Printer buffering is a form of premature consumption. These techniques illustrate that the timing of the user's illusion need not track the reality of the operating system or hardware.

One caveat: illusion is sometimes shattered on computers when something goes wrong. Telling the user that "the document has been successfully sent to the printer" when the document has in fact only been spooled to the computer's internal print buffer would seem like a good idea, but not when a difficulty arises with the print buffer software and the user ends up dragging a properly functioning 100-pound laser printer into the shop for repair. We need to consider the entirety of the user's reality, and that consists of both the expected and unexpected.

Here is the second way magicians manipulate time:

Stretching time to create the illusion of difficulty.

Houdini, the great escape artist, was famous for his Milk-Can Escape in which he was squeezed, half-naked and handcuffed, into a 3-foot-tall vessel brimming with water. The top of the can was securely fastened from the outside with six padlocks, and then the apparatus was curtained off from the spectators. They grew increasingly nervous as they watched the minutes tick by as he attempted to make his escape. By the time some 10 minutes had passed, the tension would build to an explosive level, not at all relieved by the mounting panic seen in the faces of Houdini's helpers. Finally, the helpers would be able to stand it no longer and would tear aside the curtain to smash open the milk can. But there beside the can would sit Houdini, nattily dressed in a suit and tie, calmly reading a newspaper (Henning 1994).

The magician Blackstone told the story of one occasion when Houdini's manager could hear the rustle of Houdini's paper within a couple of minutes of the curtain's closing. The manager whispered to Houdini to keep the noise down, to which Houdini replied, "Tell the band to play louder" (Henning 1986).

Houdini's fondness for reading extended to magazines, too. After his famous escape from inside a locked safe behind a screen, which took mere seconds, he spent the next 15 minutes backstage, idly reading a magazine, after which he dotted himself with water and burst forth, looking properly sweaty and exhausted (Dawes and Setterington 1986).

Houdini understood the importance of not making a task look too easy; the designers at Fairchild did not. Fairchild produced one of the first home video game machines, called Channel F, back in the mid-1970s. It featured a first-rate tic-tac-toe game with a tragic flaw: regardless of how long the player took to plot the next move, the computer would respond within one-half second with its next move. Combined with the machine's skill at choosing the best possible move, this fast reaction left the user feeling puny and inadequate.

Researchers from Robert B. Miller on have been studying the psychological effects of response time on the user (Bergman, Brinkman, and Koelega 1981; Grossberg, Weisen, and Yntema 1976; Henning 1986; Miller 1968; Shneiderman 1992). What the study of magic offers us is a different perspective on the subject: we are looking beyond efficiency and accuracy to the effectiveness of the "act" and its "big picture" impact on the user.

The throwing of the *I Ching* is an ancient ritual involving the repeated casting of yarrow stalks in a meditative atmosphere. The process of a single prediction can easily be stretched to the better part of an hour, and no prediction is to be repeated on the same day. I will offer no speculation on the accuracy of the prediction (although the system was designed with enough ambiguity that the diviner can tailor the results to the question and circumstances at hand). What I will call attention to is the immediate beneficial effect on the subject, who is being honored with a great deal of the diviner's time and attention in a warm, spiritually comforting atmosphere. It is the epitome of "quality time."

One of the earliest programs on the Apple II was an automated *I Ching* caster that could electronically "cast the stalks" in less than 1 second. You could ask one question and get 60 completely different answers in less than 1 minute! It may be safe to say the designer was unstudied in the ways of the Tao.

By applying the magic technique of time stretching, along with a healthy dash of showmanship, we could write a quite different *I Ching* program. It would ask the user many pertinent and perhaps not-so-pertinent questions, "cast the stalks" in a way that was both visually interesting and very time-consuming, deliver results in a quiet, dignified, poetic way, and refuse to answer the same question again on the same day. It would likely be no more accurate in its predictions than its faster cousin; it would surely be less productive, taking hundreds of times longer to use; but it would be far more responsive to the real (if imagined) needs of the person using it.

The designers of Zen gardens stretch time to generate an illusion of space. Those paths of rough-shaped stepping stones that require such balance and concentration are there to slow you down, to create the illusion that you are covering vast distance when, in fact, you are traversing but a few feet. This is a valued illusion in a country where land is scarce and gardens tiny.

When real and perceived speed disconnect.

Magicians purposefully disconnect the illusion of speed from its reality to aid their tricks. We often do it by accident, and to our detriment. The real speed of a computer and the user's perception of that speed often end up quite different. For example, workstations are typically far faster than the Macintosh, but the *experience of using* the Macintosh would often leave one with the impression that the Macintosh is faster. Why? Because the Macintosh designers made sure that the most important object in the user's space, the mouse pointer, would have zero latency, would never lag behind the user's true position. They did this through a combination of very fast software and frequent position updating, so none but the most rapid mouse movements result in a series of separated pointer images. (Most Macintosh users will claim a breakup never occurs, having never noticed it.)

Latency becomes far more troublesome as perceptual bandwidth increases. Virtual reality systems today suffer from significant latency problems, giving them a "mushy" feel and leaving many users disoriented, dizzy, and confused. VR latency does not arise from a dearth of design; the hardware just isn't yet up to the task. During this decade, latency will begin to disappear, and public acceptance of VR systems will rise.

Responses that can be made instantly should be made instantly. When a response will take some time, the user must receive instantaneous intermediary feedback (less than a half-second), then be kept interested and entertained to reduce his subjective perception of how long he's been waiting.

In the 1930s, a major high-rise office building was opened with what soon proved to be too few elevators. After a series of engineering firms were brought in, each confirming that there was no way to speed up the existing elevators or add additional ones, the building owners, in despair, brought in an interior designer. The designer recommended that huge floor-to-ceiling mirrors be installed between each pair of elevators, and the complaints disappeared. People now had something to do while waiting: either gazing at their own magnificent image or peering secretively at others with little fear of being caught.

The engineers had concentrated on reducing objective time; the designer concentrated on reducing subjective time. Reducing subjective time works.

Illusion and the Threshold of Believability

I propose that there is a threshold of believability—a point at which careful design and meticulous attention to detail have been sufficient to arouse in the spectator or user a belief that the illusion is real. The exact point will vary by person and even by mood, so we must exceed it sufficiently to ensure believability. Disneyland and Disney World are above the threshold of believability; county fairs are not. Lucas's *Star*

Wars was above the threshold; *Attack of the Killer Tomatoes* was not. Penn and Teller's cutting a live snake in two, then restoring it, on "Saturday Night Live" was above the threshold; Uncle Charlie's tired, old card tricks at Christmas were not.

The original Star, Lisa, and the early Macintosh all exceeded the threshold. Some of the graphical user interfaces appearing now, with their underlying dependency on dissimulation and their lack of consistency, are falling short. If users cannot trust the system, if they are occasionally but violently thrust into the programmer's reality, they cannot, will not, and should not believe in the world we are making for them.

One need sacrifice no power in building a believable illusion. For years, Macintosh programmers were able to recover from a crashed application by typing arcane incantations in their debugger, while regular users were left with no method of recovery at all. With the advent of System 7, anyone could press Command-Option-Escape to achieve the same result. Recovery is now not only achievable by every end user but is easier for the programmers.

Illusions, to be believed, must not only look but act real. Consider today's databases that have the visual appearance of a book (a popular metaphor in HyperCard and its offspring). Most of these show the same number of pages in the illusion, whether there is one page of information or a thousand. The illusion is not real. It may be a lot more work to program for conditional graphics, but the thickness of a book communicates important information. Denying users this natural way of gauging volume, we then end up supplying the same information in yet another object or dialog the user must battle to do their work.

The Ethics of Magic

"Magicians, if they are strictly ethical," writes Fitzkee (1944), "are morally under obligation to insist that their methods are purely natural."

Stage magicians have been impersonating "real" magicians (such as Merlin) for a long, long time. They've had plenty of time to experiment with the ethics of stage magic and have come up with workable solutions. I present these solutions because I find them applicable to the ongoing discussion of impersonation of people by computers (anthropomorphism).

Shneiderman (1988) argues strongly against having the computer personify a human, although he does suggest that young children might be exposed to a cartoon character for the sake of visual appeal. Laurel (1991) agrees in part, but has expanded her horizon: "I have argued, not for the personification of the computer, but for its invisibility.... The representation of agents or characters is a different idea altogether than the notion of 'personified' computers." She goes on to argue the benefits of visible characters in the interface.

The mainstream of magic is in essential agreement with Laurel's view: "A magician is an actor playing the part of a magician" (Fitzkee 1945). Mainstream magicians find it important that spectators do not leave the theater under the impression that the magic performed or that the magician who performed it is supernatural. This is such an important issue to them that when people claim supernatural powers, magicians flock to expose them. Houdini spent much of the latter part of his life both seeking out a true spiritualist and utterly destroying all the fakes that lay in his path (Gibson and Young 1953). Uri Geller, who claims to bend spoons and start broken watches through spiritual intervention, has had his own personal exposer, in the person of James (The Amazing) Randi, who has taken great pains over the past 15 or 20 years to duplicate any "spiritual" trick Geller attempts with plain old-fashioned magic techniques, much to Geller's discomfort.

A notable exception to the mainstream view of magician-characterization lies within the offshoot of mainstream magic called "magick." Harkening back to the dark days of ancient sorcery, these conjurers carry out acts of bizarre ritual, like decapitation and disembowelment, with accompanying blood and entrails, after which they reassemble their victims and restore them to life. Cameron (1974) writes, "The average magician has long since given up dread—what he requires is a sound Gothic revival!... The silks-from-a-box man rants and raves about the ethics of claiming supernatural powers and insists that the public should be protected from these charlatans and psychic impostors. Rubbish and triple balderdash! Either he is working MAGIC or he is presenting mechanical and manipulative mumbo jumbo—he cannot have it both ways! The usual argument is that the spectator should believe in the magician's powers during his act ... but regain reality at the conclusion of the performance. Stuff and fadding nonsense! Either you are a magician with magical powers or you are not. It is as basic as that!"

My observations of the purveyors of "magick" are that for all their bluster, they are as committed to not leaving their spectators deceived as mainstream magicians are. Perhaps the difference between these conjurers and outright frauds is exposed in this quotation from Matthew Field, from the foreword to Burger's (1991) book on magick: "Magicians get angry at [Uri] Geller because he is, we believe, a magician who does not admit to being one. That anger might be better directed at the fact that Geller uses his magic to promote only himself, leaving those who believe in him, and our world, no better off (and perhaps a bit worse than that)."

Like mainstream magicians, magick conjurers imbue their *characters*, not themselves, with supernatural power. Whether they make an announcement at the end of the show to the effect that, "No, we were just kidding," does not seem important to me. (It does to Laurel, though, who suggests we should make such an announcement *before* our software performances.) What both factions have in common is that there is a character involved, and the audience understands there is a character involved.

Applying the "super-anthropomorphism" ethics of magic to software, I see it calling for Laurel's split between the invisible computer, on one hand, and the robust, visible character on the other. This fulfills the same requirement of honesty: the magician is not supernatural; the character he plays is. The computer is not capable of human intelligence and warmth; the character we create is. People will not end up feeling deceived and used when they discover, as they must ultimately, that the computer is nothing but a very fast idiot.

False Realities

Building demos for unreleased products can be ethical or unethical, depending on how the demo is presented. A magician who forces a seven of diamonds within the confines of a magic act is acting ethically. He and his audience have a tacit understanding that he will be carrying out sleight-of-hand. The same magician who later that night forces the same card while playing a game of poker is a cheat.

One early computer manufacturer kept showing a demo for a word processor for three years. Not only did the word processor never actually make it to market, but it demonstrated features, such as smooth scrolling, that under normal (non-demo) circumstances were not achievable on the target hardware. The result was that a lot of people held off buying for a long time, to the detriment of their customers and competitors.

So-called docudramas on TV strive to make people believe they have witnessed an event, when what they have actually witnessed is a carefully crafted illusion. In the case of video prototypes, we must assure spectators, within the context of the prototype, that the system being shown is not real. Starfire not only does not exist, but much of it couldn't exist for a good ten years, so we wrapped the demo of our proposed technology around an obviously fictional story, a story firmly set a decade into the future. We worked hard to make the technology seem so real that people would feel they had touched it themselves, but we also took pains not to pass it off as anything but a vision.

Computer simulations can take on such a sense of reality that spectators are unable to convince themselves they aren't real. In San Francisco recently, prosecutors replayed their version of the events surrounding a fatal shooting by means of computer simulation— a rigged demo of the first order. They claimed they chose the medium strictly to communicate their version of the events more clearly to the jury, but obviously their intent was to implant in the jury's minds the illusion that the jury members had personally eye-witnessed the crime.

The technique is designed to attack the human subconscious directly, bypassing all the information filters with which evolution has provided us. Orson Wells and the Mercury Theater proved on Halloween, in 1939, when they presented a fictional "War of the Worlds" and terrified half the United States, that there are no disclaimers big enough when the sense of reality and potential harm grow large. "War of the Worlds" was peppered with disclaimers, but nobody heard them.

Conclusion

If, having finished reading this chapter, you feel strangely unsatisfied, I have accomplished my aim: 5,000 years of magic cannot be compressed into a few pages. We have much to learn from the best of the master magicians, and several important resources for doing so. First, Fitzkee's trilogy and Nelm's single volume (all in print) together lay out the organized knowledge of illusion making clearly and precisely. Reading just these four books will give you a firm foundation. Second, while perhaps you were not left so strangely unsatisfied by this chapter that you are ready to become a full-time apprentice to Penn and Teller, you may at least want to become a more active spectator by studying the performances of them and the other master magicians mentioned here. Finally, there is no substitute for direct experience: learning to perform just one or two tricks well will instill many of the techniques and principles I have discussed at the level not achievable by either reading or watching. I have found the experience of learning just a touch of magic to be most enlightening and useful. I urge you to consider it.

One closing word about magic stores: avoid the fancy one out at the mall, run by a dull young person who doesn't know the "French Drop" from "Kellar's Blue Room Illusion." The store you want is old and dingy and has a huge plastic fly in the window. And don't be afraid; as Penn Jillette says, "the seedy side of magic stores is the only good part. I love the fact that the tricks themselves are a rip-off, a lie within a lie. My friend Elliot thinks that if he had been ripped off in a magic store as a child, he might not have been ripped off by getting his master's degree. A sleazeball with sponge bunnies might have saved him a few years and several thousand dollars."

Predicting the Future

*T*he only way to win in the computer game will be to stay far out in front of the competition. With operating systems and applications taking years to develop, unless you can predict where the market will be several years out, you will be working on a product whose time will have passed even before it reaches its first user.

If you glance back at the history of computers, you will find that the major overnight successes, such as the Macintosh interface, were the products of 5, 10, and even 20 years of hard work toward a goal that would have seemed unachievable to most at the time. The first personal computer, created at SRI in the early 1960s by Doug Engelbart and company, cost over a quarter of a million dollars, in early 1960s dollars. It had all the power and finesse of a Macintosh Classic missing most of its memory and much of its speed. But the group at SRI knew where the future was going, and knew that at some point, speed, memory capacity, and economics would cross a magic line and a "computer for the rest of us" could be born. They also knew the gestation period would be at least 20 years, and they wanted to get a head start.[1]

How can one predict where a market for new technology will lie in the future? Market research studies are certainly one method, but they are notorious for missing some of the biggest market explosions of all. Desktop publishing was not predicted to be a market at all, let alone its becoming the booming market it is today. Paper spreadsheets have been around for decades as tools of economic planners and accountants. No market research analysts came forth in the mid-seventies to

....
1 Most new technologies take around 30 years to achieve a broad commercial market.

exclaim that the time for an electronic spreadsheet had arrived. Likewise, the World Wide Web was a bolt out of the blue.[2]

The Immutable Pie

Before launching into the vagaries of prediction, let us start with a given: people have only so much time and so much money. A lot of investors are banking on people shelling out hundreds of dollars per year to pluck information off the net, while others expect to make similar killings with pay-per-view, video-on-demand, sales of CD-ROMs, digital video disks, and a myriad of other hot technologies. People cannot afford everything, and they cannot do everything at once. In predicting growth of a new technology, first measure the competition for your potential customers' time and dollars.

The Pitfalls of Prediction

Other high-tech prognosticators have gone about their tasks in the past with less than sterling results. From their mistakes, we can derive principles to be applied to our own "futurist" efforts.

Markets for new technologies expand as complexity shrinks.

This principle predicts the explosive popularity of spreadsheets, computers with graphical user interfaces, and the World Wide Web. New technologies tend to arrive *sans* human interface. The interface gets added when people decide they would like to expand their market. Before that happens, however, companies often want to forecast whether the effort will be worthwhile, but predicting a future that will later seem so inevitable may be fraught with difficulty.

In 1950, Xerox Corporation (or, as it was known at the time, the Haloid Company) introduced its first copier, the model A. It consisted of three pieces of equipment, with users required at one point to carry the copy with toner barely clinging in place over to a separate fuser

....
2 Within a few years, it will seem to have been a foregone conclusion, and many of us will like to tell whoever will listen that we could have thought of it ourselves, if we hadn't been busy that weekend.

machine, where they would lay the copy on top of a heated asbestos plate to melt the image into permanence. The process was so cumbersome that the machines were sold only to large printing houses and were used only for producing offset plate "masters," which were then put on standard printing presses for multiple-copy reproduction runs.

By 1955, the company was ready to introduce its first easy-to-use plain paper copier, the model 914. Fearing their ability to perform their own marketing and distribution, Xerox managers made overtures to license the product to IBM. IBM, in turn, hired Arthur D. Little to research the market possibilities. Based on observation of the then-current Xerox market, ADL reported back that no increased market existed. ADL's reaching this conclusion is no small wonder, since the existing users to whom consultants spoke universally held a model of the Xerox machine as a great heaving monster that reduced users to the used, in their role as articulated document transporters.

IBM turned Xerox's licensing offer down, after which Xerox execs decided to proceed on their own. They asked Ernst and Young (known as Ernst and Ernst when they were actually young) to reexamine the market for plain paper copying. Ernst and Young, instead of focusing on Xerox's existing cumbersome technology, studied the market for the then-dominant plain paper copying technology: carbon paper. A typewriter stuffed with six layers of onion-skin typing paper interleaved with five sheets of carbon would produce one great copy (the one on top) and several increasingly marginal copies below. Receive from someone a carbon copy you'd like to pass along? Type it over.

Ernst and Young analysts made the same error as had ADL: they assumed the existing market would essentially remain stable. They were, however, at least looking at the real existing copy market, rather than the Xerox offset press market, even if they did assume that the meager level of copying that existed under these strained conditions would hold. They predicted a market of 4,000 Xerox 914 machines worldwide. Xerox nevertheless tooled up for 10,000 machines—cock-eyed optimists that they were—but quickly was swamped by more than 200,000 orders by an avid public lining up to reproduce now that it could be simple and spontaneous.[3]

The Xerox example was not an isolated incident. We've all heard of IBM president Thomas J. Watson, Sr.'s early announcement that his

....
[3] From private conversation with Robert Gundlach, inventor of early key technologies in the xerographic process. The facts are his; the words are mine.

company's opinion was that "the world would eventually need only twelve computers" (Dillon 1986). He was right. How many vacuum-tube computers, filling five-story buildings, able to run no more than 15 or 20 minutes between overhauls, and armed with all the computing power, if none of the speed, of an original Apple II *does* the world need? To predict the future, we must look beyond the limitations of the moment.

The home satellite market was launched in the 1970s. Equipment was bulky, difficult to install, and required constant tinkering on the part of the user. Its user population was limited to early technology adopters, rural residents without access to cable, and people with a real Jones for having 500 channels. When the first direct broadcast satellite system was unveiled in mid-1994, it exploded into the fastest-growing new technology in history. DBS dishes provide fewer channels than the traditional satellite systems, don't cost that much less to buy, and cost more for per-month program fees. Why the large growth? You don't have to be (or hire) a propeller-head to operate it. You turn it on, and it's there.

Radio-telephone service preceded cellular phones by 20 years. Like the older satellite dish owners, radio-telephone users were expected to become intimately involved in the technology, scanning the band for open channels, judging the signal strength based on distance to the transmitter, and finally placing their call through operators who seemed to spend most of their time saying, "Huh? What?" Cellular phones at first were just as expensive and almost as bulky as the high-powered radio-telephones they replaced. What was the difference? A clean, opaque interface offering absolute isolation from the underlying technology.

Initially unpromising technologies will often find their niche.

Danger lurks in announcing that a technology will fail simply because it is so wrongheaded as to be ridiculous.

In the mid-forties, CBS developed a color TV system that consisted of a black-and-white picture tube with a large color wheel, with red, green, and blue segments in it. The wheel, placed in front of the tube, spun synchronously with the picture, so that as the red information was being displayed on the picture tube, the red filter would pass across the face of the tube, and so forth.

The cameras worked out well: a 2-inch camera lens required around a 5-inch spinning disk. The sets were a bit more of a problem. A typical-for-the-time 9-inch television required a disk some 20 inches in diameter. Worse, Corning Glass had predicted an upper limit of 17 full inches in picture tube size, which would eventually require a disk over 3 feet in diameter, spinning at some 900 RPM in people's living rooms. The U.S. Federal Communications Commission nonetheless enthusiastically approved the system as the U.S. color standard, over the flaming objections of RCA and Zenith, whose competing system required little colored dots of phosphor inside the tube itself. It seems that RCA and Zenith had only a three-picture-tubes-and-some-mirrors mockup of their design, and the FCC was in a rush to judgment. Fortunately, cooler heads eventually prevailed, and a couple of years later, the CBS system was consigned to history.

Well, not exactly. The CBS color system was revived once again in the late sixties to send back some of the most famous—and expensive—images in history: live color television from the moon. In that pre-CCD era, the CBS spinning wheel camera with only a single, black-and-white Vidicon was smaller, lighter in weight, and less technologically complex than any available alternative. With the problems of playback handled through a suitable NTSC color translator, the CBS spinning-wheel system finally had its day in the sun.[4]

Existing technologies are tenacious and adaptive.

While people may be slow to predict the growth of high technology, they tend to jump the gun when announcing its demise. DEC and Apple both produced more of their early computers after the pundits announced their obsolescence than they had built before. But such predictions are not limited to our industry.

The advent of television spawned any number of articles predicting the demise of the movie theater. Why would people trek all the way into the city to watch new movies, when they could watch the same class of entertainment on TV at home? The simple answer is that they wouldn't. Both the movies and the theaters had to change. B movies,

....
[4] Rather literally, unfortunately. The very first thing the astronauts did with it was to pan the colorful lunar landscape, getting a great shot of the rising sun, which instantly—and permanently—vaporized the target in the Vidicon.

for young children and adults, disappeared. No more Saturday matinee serials; no more cheap cop movies. (B movies for teenagers saw no attendance drop, but widespread anecdotal evidence suggests the kids weren't watching the screen anyway.)

While the B movie business went to television, the A movie business only increased in depth and quality. Movie houses met the technical threat of television head on by increasing the size and altering the aspect ratios of their screens. Cinerama, Cinemascope, and Todd-A-O replaced flickering black-and-white images with dynamic, wide-screen color extravaganzas. (Theaters also experimented with a wide variety of gimmicks, including "Smell-O-Vision" and 3D, condemning 3D to an early demise by doing it wrong.)

One of television's big draws was convenience: one only had to drag oneself to the couch to be immersed in a variety of really bad programming. Theaters responded by decentralizing and multiplexing. People no longer needed to travel great distances to get their shoes encrusted with sticky popcorn. Now they could fall by their local strip mall and enter any one of a dozen capacious 9-foot by 12-foot theaters, almost as easily as changing the channel. Movie theaters have lived long and prospered.

Radio was supposed to be killed by television too. Certainly television did a bang-up job of wiping out radio drama, but the rest of radio flourished. Today people own far more radios per capita than they did when radio was announced dead. They don't, however, own the radios people aspired to before the advent of television: consoles. Those big, floor-standing wooden boxes disappeared.

The portable radios of the day disappeared, too. Large, heavy, and fragile, they depended on vacuum tubes containing red-hot cathodes as their source of free electrons. Keeping them in batteries was a nightmare. The key to reducing the size, fragility, and power drain of the portable radio was the invention, in the late forties, of the practical transistor.[5] With transistors generating an infinitesimal fraction of the wasted heat of tubes, a six- or seven-transistor radio became a wonderfully efficient alternative.[6]

....

5 An impractical transistor, the first instance of the dominant field-effect transistor of today, was invented in 1928.

6 This heat advantage disappears when one moves from the seven transistors of a portable radio to the 7 million transistors of today's portable computers, requiring users to carry around a battery of batteries.

Most people think that vacuum tubes have long since disappeared. Not true. Just like movies and radio, vacuum tubes have changed to meet modern conditions. In the waning days of the pretransistor era, the trade journals carried news of a new, room-temperature, low-power tube called a cold cathode vacuum tube. It seemed too little, too late, but it wasn't. You've probably got a pretty good collection of these tubes around your house. They never made it as amplifiers and oscillators, the mainstays of radio technology, but they became a fixture as those glowing blue/green alphanumeric displays used in clocks, calculators, cash registers, VCRs, and specialized computers.[7]

The biggest vacuum tubes of all still continue to grace our desktops in the form of ponderous CRTs. After 40 years of promises that flat screens were just around the corner, they, in all their dim, liquid-crystal glory, arrived. Now that we have about played out liquid crystals, an even newer flat screen technology is waiting in the wings. It promises low power consumption and brilliant images. It's a radically new, radically different, cold-cathode CRT.

Technologies divide and conquer.

From all these examples, a definite trend is clear: technologies evolve in multiple directions. They branch, and branch, and rebranch, just as does life through evolution.

The console radio of the twenties has been replaced by everything from headphone radios to 500-watt car stereos to home theaters with five or more loudspeaker systems fed by racks of equipment more elaborate than that of many early radio stations.

The original black and white, 4:3 aspect ratio movies disappeared, but not before spawning off a range of successors from back-of-the-airplane-seat Theater-in-the-Sky to neighborhood multiplexes to seven-story-high, 3D OmniMax screens with sound levels approaching the threshold of pain.

The standard black-and-white 9-inch 4:3 television is now available in a range of sizes from 1-inch images on the inside of your sunglasses to 16:9 12-foot screens in your media center to building-height Jumbotrons in churches and at sports events.

....
7 The red displays are LEDs, solid-state devices. The blue/green ones, however, are genuine vacuum tubes.

The observations suggest that the "glass lump" computer on your desk will indeed go away, to be replaced by the wide-ranging sizes and shapes of computing devices.

Predicting Fallout

Futurists are notorious for missing the big changes in the world. Everyone missed the fall of the USSR. They have been quite successful, however, in predicting the sequelae: the shift from the strong, centralized government necessary for war to weaker, distributed power.

No one predicted the arrival of the electronic spreadsheet, but lots of people were able to recognize immediately what its effect on computers in business would be. Similarly, no one predicted the blazing success of the World Wide Web, but the ramifications are all too obvious.

One can spend an inordinate amount of time and energy attempting to predict the big changes, only to fail. In many cases, we will have to wait for the unpredictable to occur, prepared to gauge its fallout quickly and accurately.

Of course, not all events, however large, are unpredictable. In the computer field, we have at least one "leading indicator" of market demand that has proven quite reliable.

Enclaves

In the early days of the Apple II, all was chaos. Then came AppleWorks, an integrated package incorporating a word processor, database, and other standard applications of the time. It was an immediate smash success. AppleWorks' sole advantage over the competition was its consistent interface. It had no cut-and-paste, no interapplication services, but people were happy enough just to find themselves in a single, consistent world. AppleWorks foreshadowed the success of the Macintosh, which applied a single, consistent interface to every application that entered its domain.

The next enclaves to appear were the giant, all-in-one applications we are living with today. The first I noticed was Wingz, an enclave that combined a powerful spreadsheet with a decent charting package, a weak word processor, and some primitive graphics and page layout capabilities. Wingz provided a niche solution to the specific problems of spreadsheet users. However, application enclaves work under only limited circumstances. For example, if you are writing a report for which you need to derive only a few figures from a spreadsheet, Wingz is not for you; the word processing capabilities are too weak.

Other application makers were quick to catch up. Word processors now contain limited graphics, spreadsheet, and page-layout capabilities. Paint programs will capture and play back movies. Movie-makers have text processors, allowing their use for titles. ClarisWorks offers a range of standard application capabilities that users can bring to bear on a single document. ClarisWorks is not excessively powerful, but it fills the needs of new and casual users quite handily.

These new enclaves did not arise from a need for a standard look and feel; today's GUIs supply that. They were driven by the need for tighter integration; they foreshadow the move to document-centered design.

A third, more recent enclave is represented by Lotus Notes. Within Lotus Notes, people have a rich ability to communicate and collaborate. Outside its confines, those abilities fall away. Lotus Notes evidences both the desire for collaboration and the need for collaboration to become a standard service, available to all users, in all applications, at all times.

The latest enclaves are the visually oriented information and service providers, such as America Online. Turn them inside out, from self-contained enclaves to universal services, and you have the World Wide Web.

Keep your eyes peeled for successful enclaves. They will lead you to the future.

Brave New World

*A*ldus Huxley spoke of a world trapped in a terrible tyranny in his 1931 novel. However, unlike the oppressed people of Orwell's *1984*, Huxley's society voluntarily relinquished their own freedom. No despot from without held them in his grip; they gave up thought, emotion, art, history, and culture, all in the quest for social stability. Along the way, they also gave up privacy.

In his 1958 book, *Brave New World Revisited*, Huxley warned that our society was drifting toward the society of his prophecy far more swiftly than he had ever imagined: "Even in those countries that have a tradition of democratic government, . . . freedom and even desire for freedom seem to be on the wane." He felt we were worshipping at the altar of order, being drawn to it by the twin forces of increasing population and technological advance. We are now in the 1990s. We have seen population growth in developed countries leveling off, but the threat from technological advance is on the march.

People say that we have nothing but the illusion of privacy left in America. To an extent, that's all we ever had. People of sufficient power, be they in the government or business, have always been able to find out almost anything they want. What computers have done is to concentrate and proliferate information that once was private. Today almost anyone can find out about our most intimate secrets, if they want to go to a small amount of work (Consumers Union 1991). In the near future, it may take no work at all.

Many American businesses feel they have the right to search our e-mail, eavesdrop on our phone calls, and monitor our trips to the bathroom. They claim the right to peek at us from surveillance cameras and search through our hard disks at night (Piller 1993a).

Our governments sell information we provide to them under penalty of law to private concerns to better enable them to solicit us to buy products we may not want or need. Retail credit services slurp up data from a wide variety of sources, then shop the resulting information around, even though much of it is riddled with inaccuracies. In 1991, Consolidated Information Service found errors in 43 percent of the 1,500 credit reports it analyzed from the three largest bureaus (Consumers Union 1991).

While American videotape rental records were made private by the 1988 Bork bill, our medical records remain fair game (Ignelzi 1995). "The U.S. is an embarrassment to the privacy movement overseas.... The U.S. stands alone as an example of what a superpower should not do in privacy," writes Simon Davies, director of the Australian Privacy Foundation (Piller 1993b).

In 1990, Lotus in conjunction with the Equifax credit bureau, began developing "Marketplace: Households," a CD-ROM product designed to deliver into the hands of anyone who chose to buy it personal information gathered on virtually all households in America. Thirty thousand people wrote to Lotus complaining about the attack on personal freedom they saw the product represented, and it was withdrawn even before its formal launch. The interesting thing about "Marketplace: Households" and the resulting public hue and cry was that the product did nothing that mainframe applications haven't been doing for years. In fact, "Marketplace: Households" was less invasive than existing credit services.[1] What Lotus and Equifax were doing was breaking an unwritten law in America: "Invade my privacy, but don't shove it in my face." People hadn't seemed to mind their local merchants' forking over $25 or $50 for a complete rundown on every facet of their life, but as soon as common folk, like the neighbors, could plunk down $700 and buy a CD-ROM, people went nuts.

Beyond simple denial, people have not noticed the spiraling down of privacy due to the frog factor: drop a frog in boiling water, and he'll jump out instantly. Stand him in tepid water and raise the temperature slowly, and he'll sit there staring at you while you boil him to death.[2]

....

[1] By a small margin. "Marketplace: Households'" smallest unit was one side of a single block. This was little comfort to those of us who live in rural areas where there is only one house to a side of a single block.

[2] I am taking this on faith. I have not tested it out. (If it "tastes like chicken," why not just eat chicken?)

With our privacy ebbing away so slowly, people long failed to notice the heat, but the frogs are waking up. Between 1970 and 1992, the number of Americans who expressed concern about their personal privacy jumped from around 33 percent to 78 percent.[3]

The Taming of the West

In many ways, the Internet has become a reincarnation of the Wild, Wild, West. It is a place where a cowpoke can do as he pleases and have to answer to no one. Some folks want to change all that. They're ahankerin' to come in and clean up the town, makin' it a place safe to raise young folk. As we go to press, the U.S. Congress is struggling with a bill to outlaw "obscenity" on the information superhighway. Here are the burning issues causing the government to want to take action against the Internet:

- Children wandering the net are being exposed to raw adult conversation and material. If children want to go to an adult chat room today, they must only prove they can press Return.

- If the children don't go to the adults, a few unsavory adults are willing to go to them. The only requirement for membership in a teen or youth chat today is a sincere desire to pretend you're not grown up.

- An unfortunate minority of people on the net today take pleasure in visiting foul language upon the most benign of conversations, displaying a dearth of civilization usually manifested only in public bathrooms.

- Women are complaining about men who pose as female and crash their female-only conversations. Men are complaining about the same guys posing as females in the adult chat rooms.[4]

- Communities of interest want to hold their private rooms private. Today it is difficult to keep the pretenders out. (It is not just the foul-language boys dropping around, either. Gay chats are periodically interrupted by right-wing Christians telling them they will all soon burn.)

....
3 From a 1992 poll conducted by Lewis Harris and Associates, reported by Piller (1993b).

4 I'm sure in this era of equal rights that a few women are pretending to be men. It doesn't seem to be as much of a problem.

The Internet community faces a choice. It can try to hold onto its free-wheeling ways as long as possible. This will result in government's doing what modern government does best: passing progressively more repressive legislation until much of today's cyberactivities have either been driven underground or turned into an elaborate game of cat and mouse.[5]

In 1995, a smoldering fire of censorship was fast turning into an explosion of repression. By mid-year, the same magazine that in 1985, declared the personal computer its Man of the Year was featuring a cover showing a very young child staring at a computer screen in open-mouthed surprise, coupled with the headline, "Cyberporn: . . . Can We Protect Our Kids—and Free Speech?" (*Time,* July 3, 1995). The article did not reveal how so young a child could have stumbled upon so shocking an image in an electronic world that is difficult for even computer-literate adults to traverse, but it did reveal that the full power of the U.S. Senate seemed bent on driving anything not suitable for two-year-olds from the net, without regard for the niceties of free speech or expression (Bloch, Cole, and Epperson 1995). The cybercommunity was not long in responding: "When 84 of 100 senators voted to include the Exon bill in the telecommunications reform package last week, they may have laid the groundwork for the second half of the '90s to resemble the second half of the '60s (HotFlash)."

The community has a narrowing opportunity to launch a preemptive strike, similar to that of the satellite TV industry. The movable dish market (as opposed to the newer DBS systems) is wide open, offering everything from 24-hour-a-day televangelists to back-hauls of blacked-out sports to hard-core pornography. People have complained about the excesses of the satellite world, but the government has taken no action. Why? Because the industry implemented an electronic parental lockout system. The program providers rate their offerings, and the parents lock into their receivers the ratings level their kids are allowed to watch.

Net ratings, set by parents through software, could keep the kids in check on the network too, lowering the threat of government intervention immediately, since the argument in favor of censorship is that "we must do something to protect our children." A consortium of companies including Netscape, Microsoft, and Progressive Networks was due to announce just such a ratings system by the end of 1995 (Quittner

....
5 Attorney Phillip K. Howard (1994): "By exiling human judgment in the last few decades, modern law changed its role from useful tool to brainless tyrant."

1995). Privacy and freedom would be preserved while still providing for a reasonable degree of social order. Meanwhile, companies like SurfWatch, of Los Altos, California (motto: "We surf and protect"), are providing a subscriptions ratings–lockout service, surfing the net in search of new pornographic material and protecting their subscribers' children from it in much the same way companies have been protecting individual users from computer viruses in the past.

Parents, of course, still have to do their part. A number of alleged incidents of children stumbling across the wrong things or the wrong people have occurred on America Online, a system that provides an effective parental lockout system but only if parents use it. Some parents have complained that censorship options are too difficult to understand. The solution is for service providers to have self-censorship already preselected when people set up accounts.

Social Anonymity and Authentication

The balance of the problems may require a different approach. They can be traced to anonymity. Anyone on the net can pretend to be any age. Anyone can jump into a chat room, scream uppercase obscenities, then be on their way, eliminating their screen name behind them. Some people call for an end to anonymity, a solution that would rob us of much of our privacy. Less drastic measures can do the trick.

We enjoy anonymity in real life, but it is qualitatively different from the absolute anonymity of the net. True, when we wander the streets or enter a store, we are not required to display identification or shout out our names, but we are there in person, and, short of our wearing a ski mask, people will, given sufficient provocation, be able to identify us later. Even in a ski mask, many of our characteristics remain visible. People know if we are male or female, tall or short, skinny or fat, young or old.

A study of Japan shows the corrosive power of anonymity in breaking down social convention. A Japanese businessman within his familiar social environment acts with a level of politeness unequaled on the face of the earth. However, within the anonymity of a crowd, the same gentleman found only minutes before bowing repeatedly to his colleagues may roughly shove people aside to force his way through (Rowland 1985). Today the net is a lot like that.

Absolute anonymity results in zero accountability. It appears we may need to reduce the absolute anonymity enjoyed by cyberpunks today if we are to maintain some semblance of a polite society. This should not and must not result in equal and opposite repression. We have the opportunity to create a system that allows people to vary their anonymity based on preference and circumstance, just as is done in society today, by implementing digital authentication.

Developing digital authentication is a necessary step in enticing commerce onto the next, since companies seem reluctant to open up their stores of intellectual property without some record of who is traipsing around. They also want to be paid and would like to ensure accountability.

Digital authentication will be an outgrowth of digital signatures, already in use. Authentication will expand on signatures by making available, under users' immediate control, confirmed identification and billing information.

Digital signatures are issued by a private concern, not the government. Today they can be applied for by mail, leaving the door open for pretense and fraud. Systems using digital signatures today store the software in the host computer, be it workstation, PC, or PDA. This opens the door for people to steal others' digital signatures via the net. To protect privacy, the software needs to be moved out into an external device. My colleague, Whitfield Diffie, inventor of modern cryptology, calls for a move to a credit-card-sized smart card that could be inserted temporarily in whatever device asks for a signature. In an e-mail exchange, Diffie identified three essential elements:

- A device that is trusted to hold the secret information that enables the signing of your signature. That object must also do the most critical part of the signing so that it never has to share that information with anyone.

- Something to prevent the use of the device if it is lost or stolen. I imagine a password, but a fancier one might recognize finger-prints, like the badges in "Star Trek."

- An individual action, such as pushing a button, for each signature, indicating that you want it to sign. This prevents the work-station, under another's control, from making free use of the device to sign things. You might still be fooled about what you were signing, but the fooler could only misdirect one signature for each document you thought you were actually signing. Since the real documents would remain unsigned, you would eventually notice.

In the future, people probably will have to get their digital signature and authentication cards by showing up in person at a private registration office, armed with documents proving who they are. It will not be particularly onerous; a driver's license and credit card carry the needed information, and people will have to apply only once.[6]

Age Authentication

The pressing problems of the net can be solved by adding age to the information collected. With authentic age data available, those wanting to enter an adult chat could insert their smart card to prove they are over the age of consent. Anyone wanting to enter children's restricted chats could be required to prove they are, indeed, a child. No longer would phantoms be able to slink across the net into our children's bedrooms at night.

Digital authentication would not mean an end to anonymity. People would typically use their real name on the net when conducting public business or spending time in open public gatherings but use a private "handle" for when they visit the net equivalent of bars and after-hours joints. (The link between real name and handle would need to be strictly protected.) Only under specifically defined circumstances might they be "carded," and then the information would be used strictly—and temporarily—to confirm age, mirroring the way carding works in real life, where names and other information are neither noted nor kept.

We could record other information in an authentication card. If we were to store people's current gender, potential partners would stand less chance of being fooled. Gender information could also be used by gender-specific forums to prevent gate crashing. The problem is, where

....
6 Adult-oriented bulletin board systems already require prospective users to send in proof of identity, but, of course, it is difficult to compare the photocopied driver's license picture with someone on the other end of a text connection.

would we stop? Should Presbyterians have a right to keep Baptists out of their forums? If so, we need to add religion. Do gays and lesbians have a right to keep out straights? If so, we need a box for sexual preference. Do African Americans have a right to keep Asians from horning in? If so, we need to add race.

Expanding beyond age would set us on a dangerous course. People are already handling the problem of gate crashing. Services offer private club rooms with password authorization, and even the most dedicated gender crosser can usually be exposed with a few piercing questions (Phlegar 1995). Expanded authentication might wipe out the problem entirely, but at what cost?

Someone who feigns a different gender and does it well might be able to slip unnoticed into the other gender's world. So what? Perhaps people have a right to see how the other half lives. On the other hand, gate crashers of all types who chose to disrupt would, through authentication, find themselves discouraged. People might not know who they are, but they would know how to send them a message. A few thousand people on the Internet dropping them a note might cause them to desist. (People will sometimes jam someone's e-mail box today, but now disrupters can just change handles or providers. Authentication could be designed to make hiding from social sanction a lot more difficult.)

The U.S. Supreme Court has ruled that people have free speech rights to anonymity (Cavazos and Morin 1994). Our society needs to ensure that this right is upheld in our new electronic networks. We need strong privacy laws, beginning with a law that will forbid providers from giving our real names to anyone except under court order. Then we must ensure that no "creeping authentication" takes place, where more and more often we find ourselves having to reach for our smart cards without good reason.

We need to protect our freedom, and we need to protect our children. Age authentication could do both, and the argument that the Internet must be made surgically clean would fall to dust.

A darker scenario could be in the making. Authentication as a protector of freedom works only if it can be implemented before an era of repression begins. If the conservatives succeed in their effort to enforce a new prohibition of ideas on the net, many people will seek the protective coloration of anonymity. Were authentication then imposed, a new industry in bootleg authentication cards would flourish as the net was quickly reduced to an electronic speakeasy.

Stifling legislation as far-reaching as some of the current proposals would be about as successful as Prohibition on alcohol consumption was in the 1920s. It would eventually be declared unconstitutional by the Supreme Court, but that might take years. In the meanwhile, it would produce a new underclass of high-tech criminals, an element that would be with us long after otherwise-law-abiding citizens no longer required their services.[7]

Financial Anonymity

While we may actually need to move toward less anonymity in social situations, just the opposite is true of our financial life. Today our pattern of spending is an open book, available for perusal by the government, private industry, and any private gumshoe with a few friends and a terminal. Law enforcement is overjoyed. It's becoming progressively more difficult for criminals to move money through the system without leaving a trace. The IRS is equally ecstatic. On April 15, 1994, Coleta Brueck, project manager for the IRS's Document Processing System, outlined plans to trace every citizen's income and spending patterns so thoroughly that the IRS will be able to send citizens their own tax returns, filled out and accompanied by a bill.

Right now, any number of firms, from three-person shops to Microsoft itself, are working away designing digital money. Most of these schemes do not ensure anonymity, which is of little surprise. Most of the people working on the schemes—banks and computer companies—make a good sideline profit in selling the very kinds of information that anonymous money would eliminate.

The technology exists to provide fully secure but untraceable digital cash.[8] David Chaum, working from Whitfield Diffie's earlier invention, has created just such a system that is mathematically proven. Its anonymity cannot be broken, no matter how powerful the decryption

....

7 Organized crime in the United States, spawn of Prohibition, is bigger and more powerful today than in those freewheeling days of the Roaring Twenties.

8 A digital cash system is defined by Steven Levy (1994) to be where "money is in a fungible, universally accepted, securely backed format and can be passed, peer-to-peer, through many parties while retaining its value. You know, money."

9 Unless the cash has been duplicated (electronically counterfeited), in which case, as a fallout of the mathematics involved, a trail will lead automatically and unavoidably right back to the perpetrator.

computer.[9] It will cost as little as one-tenth of 1 cent per transaction. It works (Levy 1994). It does have some drawbacks. The digital cash can go through only a single transaction before it must be passed back through a bank. While counterfeiters will, by the very nature of the system, be exposed, little guarantee exists that a victimized bank will be able to recover the lost assets. Citibank has a proposal for a digital wallet that has many of the benefits of Chaum's scheme, but with the "advantage" that the person who eventually attempts to deposit the bogus digital cash with the bank, rather than the bank itself, is the one stuck for it. The banks like that.

Anonymous cash will facilitate at least some limited crime. As always, privacy versus law enforcement comes down to a question of balance. We have the option to have anonymous digital cash. We have the option to regain much of our lost privacy. In the next few years, the managers and designers of our digital money system and society at large will make a decision as to whether the conflicting desires of the IRS, or the privacy rights of our citizens will prevail.

Personal Anonymity

In Chapter 9 I spoke about experiments wherein the movie likes and dislikes of 291 people were tracked by a computer. Armed with the resulting data, the researchers were able to generate amazingly precise predictions about whether their subjects would or would not enjoy a movie they had never seen (Hill et al. 1995). One need not extrapolate far from this experiment to see direct-marketing firms turning this kind of technology to their own purposes. I know of one mail order firm that today is already tracking over 1,200 data points on each and every one of its millions of customers. I'm sure the company wouldn't mind tracking a few more.

Prediction methods of this sort show promise of being a valuable new service, but only if we can keep the resulting data out of the wrong hands. I see no way of doing that without a combination of policy, design, and legislation. Even then, it will be important that people retain full rights and ability to cut off data collection entirely, given that our best efforts at protecting privacy may fail.

Privacy in the Workplace

John Whalen (1995) recently wrote that an "ad for Norton-Lambert's Close-up/LAN software package tempted managers to 'look in on Sue's computer screen .... Sue doesn't even know you're there!'"

Macworld (Piller 1993a) conducted a survey of a broad spectrum of businesses, 301 in total, to find out from top managers how they feel about employee privacy, and how their policies reflect those feelings: 45.9 percent of them felt that electronic monitoring of employees is justifiable under at least some circumstances, and 21.6 percent of them reported that their employees' files are searched without court order. In 44.6 percent of the cases, the searches were conducted on the authority of the MIS director. In 66.2 percent of the cases, the employee was not warned. It is not enough for designers to build functionality and then expect others to set the rules. We must design in policy from the start—policy that will bring into balance the legitimate needs of business and the right to privacy of the individual.

> *Where corporate interests and personal privacy clash, ensure a minimum invasion of the user's space.*

Corporations have significant legal exposure if employees are ripping off software vendors through illegal copying, forcing them toward some form of monitoring. One organization is offering these corporations a program that wanders around on the network, looking for all software, illegally obtained or not, then offering up a list.

One employee I know of was humiliated when the people reviewing the list let the word out that this guy had a game with a most unsavory name. He had downloaded it as part of a collection of games and didn't even know he had it. It was not stolen but was public domain software, held in a folder labeled "personal." Some employers do not allow their workers to keep personal files. This employer did. The employee faced an embarrassing situation because the pirate software application was collecting and delivering information far beyond that necessary to accomplishing its task.

This program should be rewritten to check found applications against a list of published software and then against an inventory of applications purchased by the company. The program should report only those applications that were potentially stolen. This would require more work on the part of the developers of the searching application but would avoid the rather serious attack on privacy the current system makes.

Maintain individuals' right to control their own accessibility.

I first heard this guideline proposed by human interface guru William Buxton. In the past decade, several research groups have tried out employee smart cards that track the whereabouts of workers. The idea seemed a good one at the time: an employee walking down a hallway could receive phone calls by the simple expedient of having the tracking computer ring the nearest phone. In return for this somewhat unnerving service (having phones ring in one office after another as you walk down a hallway is spooky), workers gave up all semblance of privacy.

This same effect can be achieved by giving people radio-telephones, as was done at Chiat/Day (see Chapter 1). Chiat/Day people maintain full access while at the same time enhancing their privacy. (Before, people could tell whether employees were out of their offices, potentially important data for the dedicated snoop. Now callers have no idea where people are.)

Smart cards that report your whereabouts are inherently dangerous. The researchers who have put these systems together work in team-oriented environments with modern, enlightened bosses. Many other workers do not. If such systems are marketed, they will be abused.

Incorporate circles of disclosure in potentially privacy-invasive technologies.

As people are further distanced socially, they should be able to access less and less potentially private information. For example, I want my administrative assistant, when looking at my calendar, to know I'm at a doctor's appointment and can be reached at 555-3946. I want my immediate work groups to learn only that I'm off-campus and will be back by 3:00. I want everyone else to find out nothing except that I'm not available between 1:30 and 3:00. Many calendar applications today offer this kind of capability as an option. It should become the default policy.

Make disclosure reciprocal.

Collaborative computing is a blending of computation and communication that often includes audio and video links. Starfire's viewports enabled members of Julie's work group to look in on each other if for no other reason than to maintain a sense of community. This same technology could, however, be used by managers for spying on their employees to see if they "look busy." While power users might soon learn to run 15-minute digital loops of themselves seated at their desk looking busy, we still need to consider the more naive users among us. In the Starfire world, you can't see anyone else without your picture's being simultaneously displayed on their screen, and viewports can't be opened without mutual consent.

Cover the lens; put a switch on the mike.

Telephones from the beginning had mechanical switchhooks that positively prevented others from listening in on conversations in the room. Today more and more cameras are shipping without lens covers, and microphones are shipping without switches. The hardware engineers, saving a good 15 cents per piece, tell us to handle it in software.

If you want to listen in on your neighbor's chit-chat via the phone, you have to break into your neighbor's house and modify his or her phone (instructions available on the Internet). If you want to break into your neighbor's video conference link, all you need to do is download a little software onto his system. So much more convenient, don't you think?

In Starfire, we placed Molly's "glance camera" outside her office door. Once she realized what was going on, all she had to do was close the door—proof positive of her subsequent privacy.

Make an open voice channel obvious.

If we walk into a room with an open phone line, we don't recognize it by sensing someone is hearing us; we recognize it by the sight of a phone handset lying elsewhere than on the phone. In Starfire, Julie can open a voice channel in a viewport only by touching the other person's image at the same time as the other person touches hers.[10]

....
10 That's the way it would usually be done. People unable to use their hands could use an alternative method.

(While we didn't show Julie establishing such a contact, we did show a hint of how it would work. At the beginning of the third scene, just as Julie is returning with her sandwich and glass of milk, Natalie looks up to see if it is her. Natalie then touches Julie's viewport, and the image jumps to a close-up of Natalie, instead of the view from her office door glance camera. When she releases her touch, the picture springs back. When she touched Julie's picture, she also opened up a one-way audio link between the two. If she'd wanted to talk via video instead of just confirm Julie's return, Natalie would have then said, "Hey, Julie, let's talk," or some other equally deathless prose, at which point Julie would have touched Natalie back, locking open a two-way voice channel and locking in the close-up images.)

The close-up camera in the Starfire design is hard-wired to opening up an audio link between people: no close-up, no sound; no sound, no close-up. The close-up view takes the place of the handset lying beside the phone.

Make an open video channel equally obvious.

Several years ago, two research centers separated by some 3,000 miles tied together two conference rooms with 24-hour-a-day video. Into one of those rooms crept a young couple who, unaware of their coworkers' watching from the opposite coast, engaged in what has been described to me as "a career-limiting activity." In Starfire, we echoed that incident in the engagement scene. Our system also failed, though we built in the best policy and feedback we could think of. After all, during the (soundless) engagement scene, all Molly had to do at any time was to close the door to cut off the picture. She even had images of all the looky-loos right on the face of her screen. Unfortunately, she wasn't looking at the face of her screen; she was looking at the face of her on-again, off-again boyfriend. Emotions were running high, and thoughts of technology were finishing a close third.

We thought of adding all kinds of active feedback mechanisms to Molly's office, like having several monitors scattered around the room or a floor-to-ceiling display outside in the hall with a bunch of people looking in, waving, but all seemed too distracting under normal use. We need to develop better solutions.

Offer employees the ability to privately encrypt, ensuring their right to limit access to potentially private information.

It is becoming difficult to tell where work stops and private life begins. In Starfire, Julie's husband calls her from the restaurant, asking her to please affix her digital signature to the truth-in-lending form. Today, that task would take perhaps an hour or two, involving a trip to the bank or title company during "normal business hours," meaning time taken off work. Companies will benefit by enabling their employees to spend 30 seconds on the job instead of 90 minutes away from their work, but no employee will want to have private personal documents appear on their display if they know that someone down the hall may be recording them for later examination.

Some companies today make the legal argument that it is okay for them to read their employees' personal e-mail if the company paid for the provider's services (Pillar 1993a). Will this extend into the home, for those millions of workers who will soon telecommute? Will employers have the right to root around the hard disk in their employees' living rooms just because they lent them the system?

Today's systems lack security as well as privacy. Both problems can be alleviated by enabling personal encryption. Corporations will benefit visibly from increased protection of corporate information, and everyone will benefit from a return to privacy. Our encryption technology need not be mindless and anarchistic. For example, if an employee steals a vital corporate document, encrypts it, then sends it on its way to a company's competitor, that document should now bear the digital fingerprint of the culprit who sent it—a digital fingerprint that can be raised in case of a court suit. The particulars of such a system are beyond the scope of this book, but this example represents the kinds of approaches we must take if we are to balance the legitimate needs of business against the rights of a (still) free people.

Choices

Huxley is dead, but his nightmare of the future lives on. It is we who are devising Huxley's technological advances. It is we who will decide whether we continue downward on the path toward restrictive social order or turn toward the light of increased personal freedom.

At Apple in 1990, I was asked to consult on the "Marketplace: Households" product. It became apparent to me almost immediately that the product represented a serious invasion of people's right to privacy, and I refused to work on it any further. I did so with not a little fear, but happily I discovered my managers were willing to back me up.

We will all be faced with much more difficult and important choices in the coming years. Privacy and anonymity are under full-scale attack from government, business, and individuals. Sometime, somewhere, each of us may come face to face with a deep moral decision. Will we take the easier, softer way toward order and expediency, or tough it out by fighting for solutions that promote privacy and freedom? The future of our society is at stake. Choose well.

The First Step

The Starfire vision is not based on wishful thinking, at least when it comes to the technology. Most of what you've read about in this book could already be in place if we had only learned to work together as an industry instead of spending most of our time at cross-purposes.

Free enterprise, with all its sound and fury, has built the greatest economy in the history of the world, and competition has been the key to its success. However, humankind has never in history tried to build a single product with the sweeping scope of the millions of computers scattered around the world, all tied together into a single cyberspace whole.

This industry must continue to compete vigorously, but it must temper that competition with cooperation if we are to have any chance of fulfilling the promise of interpersonal and ubiquitous computing. We must cancel the twenty-seventh rerun of the VHS versus Betamax wars. We have to work together.

Camels, Carriages, and Compromise

The computer industry has seen several examples of attempts at multi-company cooperative ventures. Most begin with the greatest of enthusiasm. Then they break down as each side tries its utmost to gain the most from the partnership while contributing the least.

An ancient Arabian legend offers the story of a rich merchant whose will called for a race among his three sons. The race would span a thousand miles of desert, from the merchant's village to Mecca. According to the provisions of the will, whosoever's camel would be the *last* to reach Mecca would receive the merchant's entire fortune.

After 6 months or a year of mourning their father's death, the three young men enthusiastically set off on their dash to Mecca. Within the month, they had covered almost a full mile. They then spotted an oasis to which they retired to rest and recuperate from their labors.

Computer people involved in cooperative ventures have also spent a lot of time resting, with each party expending an inordinate amount of effort ensuring they don't expend an inordinate amount of effort. As each partner has tried to outdo the other in their lack of dedication, the resulting product has grown weaker and weaker.

This outcome may seem the inevitable result of the free enterprise system, based as it is on competition, selfishness, and greed. After all, gaining the greatest possible advantage with the least amount of work is the very underpinning of our economic system. I would not be one to change the system. Competition, selfishness, and greed are powerful motivators, absolutely responsible for building the greatest economies in the history of the world. The trick is to channel these motivators so they achieve a more practical result.

One morning at the oasis, the three brothers arose at the first glimmer of light, saddled the camels, and galloped off toward Mecca at full tilt, eyes aglow and camels a-spittin'. What had happened? Did they suddenly each decide they really didn't want to be burdened with the responsibility of all that money? Did they hire a clever lawyer who changed the rules of the game? No. They traded camels. Now each brother had the incentive to get his brother's camel to Mecca as fast as possible, in hopes that his own would get there last. Same game. Same rules. Same goal. Different game plan. Different results.

With the computer industry, we aren't really on different camels. A better analogy might be a single carriage pulled by different camels. For quite a few years, we had our camels spotted around the entire perimeter of the carriage, all pulling in whatever direction seemed to offer each company's camel a temporary (90-day) advantage. The result has been that the industry has stood still for the better part of a decade, with everyone pulling against each other. More recently, the UNIX sector of the industry has made some headway in its private race against Microsoft and Apple by actually attaching all its camels on the front of the carriage, thereby achieving a certain Motif. However, even though the camels are all in front, they are still being driven in different directions. As a result, the carriage is moving forward, but in fits and starts. Meanwhile, Apple and Microsoft continue pulling in their own directions.

We cannot get to the Starfire vision without switching from today's grudging collaboration to genuine cooperation. We must find a way to shrug off today's 90-day mentality, to stop taking temporary advantage of the competition at the expense of long-term rewards that will benefit everyone, ourselves included. If we don't build a brighter future, someone else will.

Which brings me to the fourth and most powerful corporate motivator: fear. Fear was the motivator that finally got the American automobile industry moving when the Japanese began looming over the horizon. I personally am not nearly as fond of fear as I once was. I would like to see us move forward before the advent of a new "common enemy."

Christo and the Fine Art of Cooperation

Can people in Western society cooperate without some outside force breathing down our necks? Yes. The artist Christo has proved repeatedly that people with the most widely disparate backgrounds, interests, and goals can be drawn into a single, tightly integrated, cooperative venture.

Christo is known not so much for the beauty of his art as for its sheer audacity. He is the man who, in 1991, simultaneously unfurled hundreds of gigantic yellow and blue umbrellas in California and Japan. He's the man who skirted the islands off Miami with bright magenta bloomers. The man who wrapped up the Pont Neuf in Paris like some giant child's Christmas toy. The man who serpentined a 24.5-mile-long, 20-foot-high, gossamer curtain across the rolling hills of Northern California and into the sea.

The real beauty of Christo's art lies not so much in the product—those fleeting glimpses of fabric outrage—but in the process that envelops its production. Christo is, in a very real sense, a performance artist, and the importance of his work lies in the passionate involvement of people in its creation. Consider the Northern California Running Fence Project.

In the fall of 1972, Christo decided that a 24-mile-fence was just the thing needed to brighten up the landscape in Sonoma and Marin counties, just north of San Francisco. On September 10, 1976, some 4 years, 15 government agencies, 17 public hearings, 60 easement contracts, 2,015 steel poles, and 165,000 yards of fabric later, the fence was completed. Eleven days after that, it was dismantled forever.

During those 11 days, thousands of people traveled to Marin and Sonoma counties to see the miles of brilliant white drapery shimmering as, in Christo's words, "it describe[d] the wind." Millions more people viewed the spectacle on television, wondering what could drive people to construct such a thing. But the drive—and the art—lay not so much in the fence as in the immersion of thousands of local people, many of whom had never so much as stepped into an art museum, in an art project on a scale so mammoth it required an environmental impact report.

When Christo and his wife, Jeanne-Claude, began the project, they were warned that the local, archconservative ranchers would never allow them to fence their properties. And for a while they were chased away by rancher after rancher who were unconvinced that giant telephone poles hung with surplus General Motors air bag material stretching across their property was art. But Jeanne-Claude persevered, driving to ranch house after ranch house during the day, drinking gallons of coffee, and talking to the ranchers' wives about life, love, art, and her irrepressible husband. Soon, one by one, the ranchers came over—all the way over—becoming Christo's and Jeanne-Claude's biggest supporters.

A small group of local artists were infuriated by what they saw as rich out-of-towners' stretching fabric to make a quick buck, an unfounded charge.[1] They joined with a band of environmentalists and stormed the Sonoma County Board of Supervisors meeting on March 18, 1975, ready to demand an end to this foolishness. When they arrived, however, they found a chamber packed with those same ultraconservative local ranchers, there to defend with all their heart and soul this great work of art they had come to accept as their own.

The protesters went down to defeat, but not before Christo left them writhing in fury when he defended the essence of his art to the supervisors: "It's hard to explain that the work is not only the fabric, steel poles, or Fence. Everybody here is part of my work. Even those who don't want to be are part of my work" (Christo 1978).

....
1 The fence cost Christo more than $3 million, which he raised, as is his tradition, by creating and selling somewhat smaller pieces of art to his patrons around the world.

Integration of Effort

What can we adopt from Christo's success? What might work for our industry? The central tenet of Christo's great works is the total integration of people—engineers, artists, politicians, landowners—all working in concert to build one great explosion of art. The massively scaled singular works of art that result are a direct reflection of the process that creates them. That process grows from a certain level of selflessness.

Those farmers who descended on the supervisors did have a small self-interest: Christo, in return for running his fence across their land, was to give them the surplus automobile air bag fabric, steel cables, and telephone poles that made up their section of the fence. (It's always nice to have a couple of thousand yards of air bag material around the house.) I think it safe to say that when they walked into those meetings they weren't thinking about their own small, selfish prize. They were thinking about a greater good. A nonprofit greater good.

We have our own running fence today. It's called the World Wide Web. Tens of thousands of people—young people predominantly—are giving up their time and energy to build the structures and tools that will improve the Web for all. They have made no demands and ask for no reward. Contrast this outpouring of selflessness with the story of the businessman who heard at a conference in early 1994 that the Internet was growing at the rate of 15 percent per year. Did he inquire, "What can we do to help?" Did he even try to figure out how his company might begin to position itself in this new market? No. According to the story, he rushed to the phone, called his broker, and yelled, "Buy Internet!" The story may be true, it may be apocryphal, but I have yet to hear anyone who has heard it respond, "Gee, that sounds unlikely."

Idealistic, selfless outpourings tend to lack focus, and they do not last. I've been through three of them: the San Francisco Summer of Love in 1967, the birth of the personal computer industry in 1977, and now the World Wide Web. Lots of enthusiasm and energy with little direction. In both of the earlier cases, something rather cynical took over. We cannot afford, out of purely selfish reasons, to allow that to happen today. Computer software is only as interactive as the process that created it. Software assembled alone stands alone. To build a tightly integrated, *kansei* interface, we will need to pull together, to display the same unity of purpose, direction, and goal found in Christo's efforts.

No more can system software be built to the lowest common denominator. No longer can applications exist in isolation. No longer can any one company, no matter how giant, no matter how well financed, do the job alone. The Starfire world can arise only if everyone, from hardware manufacturers to system software houses to applications developers to in-house engineers, joins together to construct a single, unified user experience.

Cross-platform operating systems must be aware of and make use of the features of each hardware configuration, from high-end workstations to low-end portables. System software and applications must degrade gracefully as they find themselves in progressively more limited circumstances. Twenty-four-bit color must automatically become 8-bit-color or monochrome on limited machines. In an absence of sufficient memory, video must transform itself to sound-tracked snapshot stills.

Today we have a hard line of demarcation between that which is system software and that which is not. To build systems and applications capable of a far higher level of communication, we will need to raise our own level of communication. No longer will it be sufficient for a system software house to finish a new system, then "throw it over the wall" to independent developers and volume end users, along with a couple of manuals and maybe some tools.

We need standards, standards, and more standards. Never before have we had a machine that can benefit as much from close coupling. For you to send me a document requires compatibility and communication between hardware and hardware, system software and system software, and application and application. Any failure anywhere means that when I try to open that document, either it won't be there or I won't be able to see what is inside.

Perhaps this is an ideal time for "government interference." For the price of a single modern fighter, the government could fund the development of rich text, rich graphics, and rich multimedia tools and formats, placing the results in the public domain to begin to chip away at the enclaves of profit that are separating us today. Perhaps it is time for a computer Christo to step forward, to harness and direct that idealistic outpouring of talent and energy directed toward the World Wide Web today. Surely it is time that computer companies redouble their efforts to work together toward common goals.

Phillips and Sony developed the exact specifications for audiocassettes more than 20 years ago, then gave their invention away rent free to anyone who would follow the specs. It caused a revolution from which Phillips and Sony profited handsomely, even if their competitors made a few bucks too. Phillips and Sony learned that if you have a consistent, easy-to-use pie, that pie will grow so much larger that you will make more money than had you owned all of a smaller pie. They put that lesson to work again in their development of the audio CD, causing a second revolution, from which they similarly profited.

The record for video is a lesson in how not to do things. Matsushita figured it could outmarket Sony, and it did, but at a terrible cost for the industry and for consumers, who ended up stuck with an inferior system. RCA execs were so intent on outmarketing Sony and Phillips in the videodisk market that they completely forgot that their product had to achieve any technical level of refinement at all. They not only failed with their own product, but dragged the entire videodisk industry down with them. Those in the consumer electronics industry apparently learned their lesson: with government insistence, they cooperated on a single high-definition TV standard. With no outside pressure, they closed in on a single red-laser optical disk standard, one that will replace both VHS and videodisks.

Software today is expensive to produce and, by future standards, remains primitive. None of us can build a second-generation visual interface system alone. The only way we can push this industry forward is to come together into a tightly knit movement, a juggernaut worthy of Christo, working relentlessly toward the single goal of building a tightly integrated system that will produce a new leap forward in human–computer productivity.

At the end of *Tog on Interface* I said, "Treat your users with love. Seek to help them grow, thrive, and succeed, and you cannot fail." The time is here to turn that same spirit toward the building of that greatest of machines called cyberspace. If we will each give just a little toward the common good, we will usher in an era of opportunity, productivity, and happiness that will be truly breathtaking. We have the talent. We have the technology. Let's do it. Now. May we have the heart, the drive, and the will.

Behind the Scenarios

*F*ollowing is a glimpse into some of the process and work product that led up to Starfire. Appendix B, "Designing with Video Prototypes," gives extensive detail on the Starfire film process itself.

The Starfire vision team consisted of marketers, engineers, human factors people, and graphic designers, from both coasts and from both SunSoft and Sun Labs. For several months, we met every other week for three-to-four day face-to-face sessions, augmented with frequent video conferences.

With the help of the marketing folks, we came to understand Sun's current customer base, as well as our future customers and direction. We then proceeded to lay the groundwork for a new interface, responsive to the needs of the millions of new customers to whom we wanted to appeal, while at the same time supportive of the traditional Sun-installed base.

The team had a healthy mixture of traditional Sun engineers and designers, as well as people who trace back to the heyday of Xerox PARC and the beginnings of the Lisa and Macintosh. We attempted to achieve a design direction that would, first and foremost, increase user productivity, while at the same time result in far higher user satisfaction. We also aimed for a look and feel with flash.

The software design community adopted the scenario process because it forces designers to broaden their view of their target audience when developing new software. Before scenarios, software had a tendency to be so specialized that it not only made it impossible for marketers to carry it to new audiences, it often failed to fulfill the needs of even the current audience. Software was often designed around a single user: a mysteriously average person who worked in an equally mysteriously average business, carrying out mysteriously average tasks.[1] Compare this single point of reference to the building of a "user space," as sketched below:

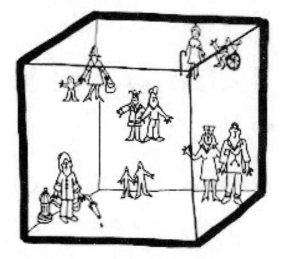

The dimensions of such a space typically represent classes of users, tasks, and environments. During the Starfire exercise, we began by generating lists of these classes. (These lists are, as intended, rough. The scenario process starts from the most informal group-think down through progressive layers of more formalized codification.)

Users

Clerical versus executive
Individual versus supervisor
Designer versus data enterer
Child versus young adult versus seniors
Blue collar versus white collar
Novice versus expert
Current PC users versus new users
Teachers versus learners
Learners versus users
Explorers versus stay-at-home types
Non-dolts versus dolts

....

1 Several years ago, the Air Force carried out a test to find out how many cadets could fit into what were statistically the average-size clothes. They assembled 680 cadets in a courtyard and slowly called off the average sizes—plus or minus one standard deviation—of various items, such as shoes, pants, and shirts. Any cadet not in the average range for a given item was asked to leave the courtyard. By the time they finished with the fifth item, there were only two cadets left; by the sixth, all but one had been eliminated.

Occasional versus regular users
Task domain expertise (high versus low)
Early adopters versus tree huggers
People who talk to other people
Children
Disabilities, special needs, handedness
Programmers
Multilingual/multicultural
Developers
Multiple users on one machine

Environments

Home versus office
Outside versus inside
Connected versus remote
Vehicle/portable versus stationary
Shop floor versus office
Work versus vacation/travel
Public versus private education versus industry
versus government
"Wherever I am"
All over your office
Meetings with other people
Classroom
Coffee shops, random meetings
Outer space
Law offices
In the executive suite
Construction site, hostile environment
On golf courses
Hotel rooms
Medical offices
Multivendor environments
Real estate agencies
Amusement park, rock concert
Museums/galleries/theaters
Post office
Bank
Financial traders

Artists' studios
Elevators/escalators
Sky diving
On a boat, camping, vacation
In a hospital
In a library
Fire station
In your kitchen
In bed
All over your house
In your car
On the beach
Under water
Vacations: Guidebook, exchange rates, disable everything that
relates to work

Tasks

Time management
Projects
Information management
Creative design versus data entry
Presentation
Writing/composition/drawing
Teaching/learning
Monitoring: trends/news/nuclear power
Time critical versus self-paced
Simulate things
Communicate with people
Listen in (note taking)
Gossip
Create documents
Share things
Manipulate images
Find things

This rather short list was fleshed out when we turned our attention
to creating the scenarios.

We also came up with the following list of strategies for what we
wanted our new designs to accomplish.

Strategies

Portables are a design center

Integration

Eliminate "computer" modes

Add support for user modes

Increase human productivity and happiness

Give back time to user

Make it visually compelling

Increase variation in standard objects (windows, containers, etc.)

User is faced with minimum number of obstacles

Make what must be visible

Hide everything else

Don't wait for the Return key, Apply button, or anything else

Instant interactive, not batch

We started with around 12 scenarios, then winnowed them down to 6.

1. The Growing Manufacturer
2. Higher Education
3. Home Services
4. Oilware
5. Real Estate, or "Have I Got a Deal for You!"
6. The New Builder

The first three have been presented earlier in the book. The rest follow.

Around midway through the scenario process, we turned our attention to designing the new objects and services that would populate the new interface, blending them into the stories as we went along. We eventually incorporated all the following technologies:

Hardware Technologies

High-reliability hardware/software systems

Portable workstation

    Multimedia-capable portables

Standard workstation

Video

    Video camera as peripheral

    Still digital camera as peripheral

Video and graphic overlays
Video input/output
Peripherals
Wall-size display
Secure card reader for authentication
Touch tablet clipboard, room estimator, and other cordless
peripherals
Image scanning
Mouse input
Stylus input
Laser pointer input
Movement-of-display input
Networking
Heterogeneous environment
Network connections extended to include infrared and cellular
communications
Wireless network within a building
Wireless outside network (ubiquitously available public
networks)
Public terminals become user's home desktop
Remote synchronization of identical (copies of) documents over
network to reduce latency

Software Technologies

High-reliability hardware/software systems
Automatic sensing of user's physical context: house versus car
versus subway.
Any computer becomes your computer on log-in
Shared work surfaces
ID cards/business cards to represent people
Simulation
Simulation of physical changes in material over time based on
experimental data
Collaboration
Eye-gaze awareness
Shared and private documents in same workspace
Video conferencing
Automatic scripting
Verbal commands (structured natural language)

New human interface objects/elements
  Active paper
  Scrapbooks
  Notebooks
  Permanent record books
  Automatic transmogrification from active paper to notebook
  Casual creation of an active paper document
  Casual creation of new regions inside a document
  ID cards/business cards to represent people
  Embedded regions
  Embedded icons/thumbnails
  Embedded controls, such as buttons and menus
  Voice annotation
  Graphic annotations converted to gestural commands
  "Live" gestural editing
  "Intelligent" graphics and other objects
  Animated objects
Custom mission-critical applications integrated into complete
    environments
Information
Standardized data formats interpretable by a multitude of
    applications
Widespread use of standard information formats
Live and stored access to lectures
Searching informal data and published data locally and over the
    wide area net
Registered queries
  Notification (interesting events like query results and class data)
Services
  Course registration
  Library information
  News wire service
  Video transfer
  Tailored filtering and processing of services
  Connection to public services (e.g., banks, weather service maps)
  Access to public services
  User-interface infrastructure for collecting and organizing infor-
    mation across applications
  Machine-"comprehensible" public information sources

Audio
    Verbal commands
    Audio recording (NoteTaker)
    Voice messaging
    Speech recognition of commands
    Audio/voice feedback
Video
    Video conferencing
    Video retrieval of the network (stored and live)
    Video editing
Multimedia
    Database
    Presentations
Graphics
    Large screen, power, information delivery
    Intelligent graphics
    Interactive 3D animation
    Image processing/summarizing/3D video software
    Combining synthetic 3D with real video images
Easy image scanning
Programming
Digital signatures
    Automated signature process
Watching
Computer "watches" user and doesn't interrupt reading until
    eyes rest

After several iterations, the initial project was done, and the team disbanded. I then turned my attention toward weaving many key technologies and messages into the Starfire story and eventual screenplay.[2]

Scenarios are not a marketing tool; they are a design tool. Although the tasks and environments should have some relationship to the actual tasks and environments of the target audience, we use scenarios to explore the edges of the user space, not just the center. As a result, part of our scenario discipline is to push those edges by purposefully creating characters and situations that, while they may not be typical of most target users, will cause us to focus on tasks many target users

....
2 You can read more about the scenario design process in greater depth in *Tog on Interface*. It is available at finer bookstores everywhere—or did I mention that before?

may occasionally want to accomplish. In addition, we purposely put our characters in situations where their ability to perform their work or access needed information in a timely and dependable way is critical, as you saw in Starfire, leading to designs that are fast and responsive.

Scenarios result in flexible, versatile software, and often lead to ideas that become vitally important in improving the productivity of the most central of the target audience, even when they have seemingly arisen at the edge of the user space.[3]

Oilware: A Scenario

It was early in the morning as Giles boarded the train that would take him from Tokyo to Fuchinobe, where he worked as a software engineer for Nippon Explora, KK, the Japanese subsidiary of Explora Ltd. Explora Ltd., is a multibillion dollar international company with engineering centers in four cities around the world. Its main source of revenue is from oil exploration, a service it performs for most oil companies worldwide.

As soon as Giles sat down for the 45-minute ride, he activated his Sun portable workstation and begun reading the morning's load of electronic mail. Explora is a large-volume end user of workstations. For data acquisition, Explora has a few thousand trucks and offshore units equipped with several workstations each. The final stages of data interpretation are done by Explora in a few dozen centers around the world, each containing a small network of workstations. All acquisition units, interpretation and engineering centers, as well as headquarters offices are networked together via a combination of satellite, terrestrial, and local radio links.

Giles was flipping the pen over the third message when a small notice popped up in the screen. This was a long-distance call from Karla Beckman, a field engineer he had met in the last Explora interpretation symposium. After he accepted the call, her face appeared on the screen greeting him. She informed him that she was in a well-testing job in Villahermosa, Mexico. The well

---

3 To study scenario building in exhaustive detail, read *Scenario-Based Design* by Carroll (1995).

was about to be capped, presumed dry, but there were some resistance patterns that looked somewhat promising. The problem was, their current software was unable to bring the added information out of the data stream. She needed help in proving conclusively whether this pattern was really a sign of oil or just spurious noise.

Giles asked her to send him her charts, and in a couple of seconds, he had them open on his display. Karla, her face still visible under the semitransparent charts, began pointing at the features she had found interesting. Giles promised to send her a new software module to improve the analysis.

An hour later, Giles was in his office in the midst of preparing the new interpretation module. He'd decided to use the large wall-mounted display, instead of continuing working on his portable. He stood next to the display, stylus in his hand, dragging a new chart-viewing region to the document he was preparing. The document contained several documents joined by arrows he had drawn. He drew one more arrow from the last one, labeled "merge" to the chart and via a simple dialog specified the ports from the merge box that would drive the X and Y channels of the chart. A few more gestures with the stylus, and he established how units would be converted and displayed and in what scale.

Just before testing, he opened the merge document and made sure the software specified was consistent with what the chart would expect. He had built the document (and all the other 20 or so documents in this "boxes and arrows" diagram) by mostly dragging code "clippings" he'd collected over the years. Upon his closing the program document, the system automatically produced machine language from it, extracted information for software browsing and debugging documents, and stood ready for him to connect its inputs and outputs (ports, as they called them) to other programs, by sketching the connections with the stylus.

With the connections drawn, Giles tried the new module on the data Karla had sent him earlier, finally satisfied with the results. He stripped the module of the documents he had used to test it and quickly moved back to his desk, pulling a keyboard from the drawer. He attached a note to Karla with directions to insert the module in the data stream coming from the truck, just before the final viewer. Having his book with business cards open in a corner with her card showing in the current page, he dropped the module with attached message into Karla's in-box.

A few days later he received a message from Karla saying that she had convinced the customer to keep the well open, based on the improved interpretation his module had allowed. After another 28 hours of drilling, they had hit a major oil pocket. They were fighting now to cap it.

Although the new module had worked, Karla was puzzled as to what exactly it was interpreting. She told Giles the well owner was willing to pay for a nice dinner for the two of them once she got back to Japan, but he was going to starve unless he coughed up the secret to the software. Giles smiled as he scribbled a few notes at the bottom of her message, attached a video clipping of a talk he had given on the new technique, added the name of his favorite Tokyo restaurant, and dropped the results on her business card, mailing it back to her.

Real Estate, or "Have I Got a Deal for You": A Scenario

It is 9:30 A.M., and Kevin McFee, the top salesperson at the Millennium 11 offices in Ann Arbor, Michigan, has just arrived at his office. As he starts to drink his coffee, he runs his ID card by his portable computer. His in-box appears on his display, showing that Gloria Sanchez, an old client, left him a voice message sometime last evening. She is retiring to Arizona and is interested in having Kevin sell the house she had bought from him many years ago.

Kevin can't remember exactly when he sold Gloria her house, so he requests a search of the client archives going back 15 years by dropping Gloria's client card on the archive service. (The archives are periodically updated with official property transaction reports from the local registry of deeds, so even if Gloria had moved in the meantime, the client archive should still be current.) While Kevin's portable is connecting with other systems to find the information, he also has it dial Gloria's number so he can set up a meeting later in the day. Gloria is not at home so he leaves her a voice message saying he can come by that evening. By the time he finishes the message, the archive server has returned with the available information on Gloria's house.

Kevin arrives at Gloria's house just after lunch, carrying his portable, which resembles an attaché case. After passing pleasantries, he opens his "portable office," then starts verifying with Gloria the information needed to list her house. Most of the information, such as number of bedrooms and current valuation, are already recorded. Kevin notes any changes or updates on a touch-tablet clipboard, connected via infrared beam to the portable. He walks through the various rooms, recording a video image as he goes. Since Gloria has added a sun room since she purchased the house, he also uses a miniature radar room estimator to measure and record the room's size. These measures are also sent from the estimator back to the portable.

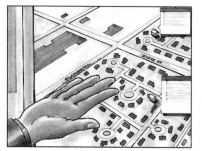

Once Kevin is confident he has collected and verified the necessary information, he presses a button to send it (by radio link) to his office. Within seconds, he receives in return a competitive analysis listing the prices and displaying a street map of the locations of comparable houses, some of which have recently sold and some of which are still on the market. In the past, such a competitive analysis would have taken Kevin several hours to pull together and format appropriately. This ability for instant analysis not only saves both the seller and the broker valuable time, it has become a centerpiece in the brokerage firm's advertising—a real competitive advantage.

Gloria recognizes some of the properties as homes in her neighborhood and shows concern over how hard it might be for Kevin to sell her house. Kevin can respond to that, because the analysis has also determined the optimal asking price and even estimated the number of days on the market expected for a range of asking prices.

Even with his explanation, Gloria is still a little unsure as to the asking price, given the competition. Kevin understands how traumatic selling a house can be, so he downloads video information for the competitive houses, so Gloria can see on the screen exactly what sold and what her competition is. Having a close look at the actual competitive houses, including their interiors convinces Gloria that the

asking price suggested by Kevin is reasonable, so she signs the listing contract.

At this point Kevin confirms Gloria's listing, which allows the information to be entered into the multiple listing service database. Other brokers who expressed interest in this type of house, location, and price range are now automatically notified. The video footage he shot is stored in his portable, with only representative stills forwarded for now. It is just too much information and would take too long to send over the radio connection, but it will automatically be sent to the MLS database upon his return to his office. The video will then also be accessible by any participating real estate office.

Back in the office later that day, Kevin meets Bobby Danford from Austin, Texas. Bobby has just accepted a job in the area and is looking to buy a house for himself, his wife, Betty, and the three little Danfords. Bobby is a little cautious about selecting a particular house, for Betty is an interior decorator with a clear notion of what she does and does not like. However, they need to purchase a house as soon as possible to get the kids settled in before school begins.

Kevin assures Bobby that he will, through Kevin's computer, be able to evaluate neighborhoods and even walk though houses without ever taking a step outside. By physically inspecting only the most promising houses, Bobby will be able to zero in on promising houses very quickly. More important, Betty will be able to view the same images of the neighborhoods and houses, and though she is 1,500 miles away, she will be able to participate in the discussions with Bobby and Kevin. Kevin sets up an appointment with Bobby in Ann Arbor and Betty at the Austin Millennium office for the following morning.

Meanwhile Kevin begins his information gathering by helping Bobby determine the price range of houses the Danfords might consider. Kevin suggests to Bobby that he has the option of going to a bank to get prequalified for a mortgage, or he can do it right in Kevin's office. Since Bobby is under a tight schedule, he chooses to do it right there. Kevin slides a touch screen toward Bobby and tells Bobby to slide his bank card though the card reader and follow the directions. He, Kevin, will be right back.

Sliding the bank card through the reader causes the touch screen to connect with the local bank network to verify Bobby's account balances and outstanding loans. Since his annual salary is available from the relocation information, Bobby need only specify from which account the down payment will come, after which the system comes back with an estimated range of house prices the Danfords can afford, as well as a range of mortgage options varying in down payment, payback period, points, and monthly payment.

When Kevin returns, he takes the house price range as the first piece of data needed to narrow the house search. He also collects from Bobby some basic house features such as number of bedrooms, degree of privacy, presence of a swimming pool, and neighborhood child concentration by age. Knowing the location of Bobby's new employer, average commuting time can be automatically determined based on the system's knowledge of optimal routes.

The next morning, video and audio contact is established with Betty at one end and Kevin and Bobby at the other. Bobby can see one of his children tied up in the background, the two others running around him whooping and screaming, and Betty frantically trying to get them all to sit down for a moment. Finally, someone at the Austin end offers to take the darling children out for an ice cream cone so Betty can focus on buying a house. It takes Betty a few moments to calm down, all the while muttering under her breath about just how well she figures Bobby would cope if she were the one house hunting and he was home with the kids.

With things settled down, they're ready to look at some houses. As Bobby looks on, Kevin recapitulates what he and Bobby have discussed thus far. Betty and Kevin then discuss a set of additional features Betty considers important in a home, and Kevin adds these to the ideal-house specification he has been building.

Based on the input, Kevin presses a button, and a street map showing locations of possible houses is returned. The richness of the descriptions varies over a wide range, depending on listing office, house price, newness of the listing, and other factors. The descriptions come in one of four possible resolutions:

- Single front image with description (Polaroid picture)
- Outside and inside still pictures

- Video walk-through (hard-wired)
- Synthetic video fly-through (for homes under construction).

As each house is displayed in turn, floor plans, neighborhood descriptions, and other pertinent information are displayed alongside.

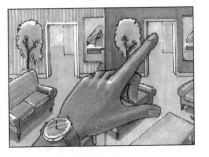

Betty and Bobby, who are viewing the same images at the same time, trade comments and compare notes. Betty prefers one particular type of house, so Kevin does a similarity search and identifies two other houses to look at. In one video fly-by, Betty is concerned that the carpet and wall colors would clash with their furniture. Betty is amazed when Kevin shows her how she can change the carpet and wall colors and even patterns by selecting options from a palette.

Of course, Bobby differs from his wife in his favorite set of colors, but at this instant, the kids return with a vengeance. Luckily, by this time they had already flown though a good number of houses and evaluated floor plans, closet space, and lawns, and had decided on four houses to visit.

That afternoon Bobby and Kevin drive around to the various houses. As they approach each house, Kevin displays the floor plans of the house on his portable.

At one point, Bobby is concerned that a house might be sited too near a pig farm that appears on their map. Kevin is able to display a

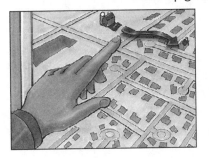

weather map with wind patterns for the area, with the house lot boundaries and pig farm clearly indicated. This quick analysis shows Bobby that unless Betty and Kevin enjoy the aroma of pig farms, they should eliminate this house from consideration.

By the end of the day Bobby and Kevin have narrowed down the choices to three houses. Bobby calls Betty, and she agrees to fly to Ann Arbor the next day. When she arrives, they spend a day revisiting the three houses under consideration. With Kevin's help, they prepare an offer strategy that evening and make the offer the next day.

The Danfords are happy. Mrs. Sanchez is amazed: that nice real estate man, Mr. McFee, sold her house to those Texas folks in only three days.

The New Builder: A Scenario

Today Bill Harris received the "final" plans for a 500-unit housing development that will occupy one of the last large empty plots of land in the town of San Fernando. Tonight he will be defending his company's position at a packed hearing of the city council. He's got less than 5 hours to check the plans, develop his report, and prepare to respond to some expected hard questions, not only from the members of the council, but from some of the more outspoken members of the community.

Bill has recently been hired into his first job working for the state's largest builder at a site in San Fernando. When he arrived at his new office less than 6 weeks ago, he found a new computer waiting for him. He'd stumbled through using some pretty powerful computers in college, but he'd always been in somewhat in terror of the unfriendly beasts with their cryptic operating systems. Bill immediately noticed the new computer was different: the folders and other items had understandable names (he remembered the short cryptic names required by the UNIX environment he used at college). Soon he found that objects throughout the system worked in consistent, predictable ways. He had felt comfortable almost immediately.

But he wasn't comfortable this Tuesday afternoon—not with his first crowded public hearing on the way. In the past, his company's plans had consisted of large rolls of drawings and reams of paper, but with international data standards now becoming universal, developers could instead submit their plans to local planning boards electronically.

Bill brings up a 3D visualization of the development and moves about it. Since the last draft, reviewed by his predecessor, they've squeezed in another 12 units, and Bill wants to check the additional load the new units will place on the town's infrastructure: sewers, power grid, roads, and schools. He's aided in this by an electronic town model supplied by the planning department. Developed as part of the town's general plan, it includes specifications for the current infrastructure, along with a residential impact model.

When Bill drops the specification for the new development onto the model, it automatically generates a large table of numbers indicating the load at various points and at various times of the day. He then asks the computer to visualize this information, and it generates false-color geographic displays showing the sewers, the power grid, and other displays. Each has sliders for time and load. As he adjusts the time slider, the colors change to show the load at each point. Adjusting the load slider, markers appear adjacent to the time slider showing the various times of the day when some part of the system exceeds that load. Adjusting the sliders, he gets a good sense for how the loads on the various systems change over the day. It is clear that the increased loads can be accommodated. So far so good.

Even fresh out of college, Bill knows how quickly plans can change, and so he opens the session history window, selects the set of actions he used to check the infrastructure impact, and saves the script for possible later use.

Meanwhile, Marion Friedlander at the town's plan checking department has received and begun pouring over the same set of plans. She needs to check conformance with existing regulations, so she accesses the town, county, and state online databases using the verbal query "retrieve existing and proposed regulations for housing developments." She is at first overwhelmed by the number of regulatory documents but soon ferrets out one that is an electronic synopsis of local and state regulations, maintained by her own department. (She faintly remembers being told about it on her first or second day, but she had long forgotten it.)

Running this synopsis against the proposed development, she finds that although the development is close to meeting the mandated requirement for low-cost housing units, it will still be four units short. Since the developer has already agreed in principle to bring the town up to conformance, Marion calls the firm to negotiate additional units. When Bill's face shows up on the screen, they both smile in recognition. Bill and Marion took some classes together in college, and it turns out that Marion has also recently landed her job with the town.

After spending a few minutes exchanging pleasantries, they get down to business. Bill, after checking briefly with his management, is able to agree to four more low-cost units, which he quickly adds by replacing two more deluxe units along the outside of the development.

The plans are automatically updated, and Bill reruns the earlier infrastructure checks using the script he saved earlier. They both see

immediately that with the net increase of two new units, the sewer line on that side of the development has exceeded full capacity. A good rain, and it will be a real mess.

Bill notices that while this sewer line is full, one on the other side of the development is still quite a bit under capacity. He swiftly switches one row of houses from their current line to the other line, and both watch as the numbers drift down to safe levels. With Marion now satisfied that the new plans meet requirements, the two ring off.

Following a few other checks, Bill has all the information he needs for his presentation. Now it's time to plan strategy. He has been to enough of the council meetings to get a general idea of the kinds of queries likely from the council members, but the general public is a different matter. Fortunately, Bill even has a way to anticipate their questions too.

Prior to Bill's hiring, the planning department had held several community meetings scattered around town to solicit input on a revision to the town's general plan. Figuring the same issues that came up then are likely to be brought up at his presentation, he queries for citizen comments on the general plan. He narrows down the large retrieval by drawing a circle on the town map to restrict retrieval to comments received at hearings that took place in the same general area as his company's project.

After sorting the response by content, he notes the high frequency of traffic complaints. Flipping through the traffic comments (using a flicking motion of his finger on the combination mouse/touch pad), he notes down several questions and arguments that occur repeatedly. He mentally prepares ad-lib answers to their expected questions. He also gets on the phone to a friend who works in the video archives at the local TV station.

The city council chambers seat about 200, and tonight it is packed. Bill gets up to present his argument for why his company's development would be good not only for future residents of the development but for current residents of the town. Using a projector to display output from the computer on a large wall, he shows the 3D presentation of the development, first from overhead, then moving along the bounding streets as if from a passing car. As this is running, he describes the overall impact on the town's infrastructure, noting among other things that the sewers (with his change) will be well within capacity. He describes the adjustments for low-cost housing from the previous draft. He concludes the report stating that the development will be a major economic boon for the community, resulting not only in jobs but a raise in the tax base with no need for major outlays to expand the infrastructure.

The council opens the meeting for comments from the floor. As expected, someone is quick to complain about the terrible impact the development will have on the traffic flow. Bill starts up the town's existing traffic simulation model, presented as an overhead view of the undeveloped areas and surrounding streets. At this relatively close view, cars are discernible moving along the streets. A clock in the corner shows 7:30 A.M., the heaviest traffic time. Numbers next to the traffic signals display the average number of cars and wait time.

Explaining that he is using anticipated trip-origination volumes derived from the town's general plan, he adds the proposed development to the view, which increases the number of cars and signal numbers somewhat but not nearly to the volume the citizen has described. When the speaker suggests that the town's existing traffic simulation model understates the true volume, Bill removes the proposed development, reducing the number of moving cars to their original levels. He then overlays the simulation with video footage taken by the local TV station a couple of mornings earlier. It is clear that the trip figures used in the simulation reasonably match the real-

ity of the morning's traffic.

Bill continues well into the evening, responding to questions about increased school enrollment, water usage, and a myriad of other issues. By the end of the long evening, his own preparation, along with his easy, instant access to the large-screen multimedia display of compelling information, leaves even the harshest critics nodding silently in agreement. He has won the day.

Designing with Video Prototypes

*D*eveloping a new working computer system can cost hundreds of millions of dollars, all expended at great risk. Company managers who must take responsibility for making development decisions are loath to do so without being able to see and understand the system they will be buying.

When SunSoft launched the Starfire project, we turned to video prototyping, enabling us to show in mature form many key specifics of our new interface design and to communicate a strong sense of the resulting overall user experience. What follows are observations and guidelines we developed during the early stages of the film, along with our experiences when we applied them.

Why a Video Prototype?

Computer prototypes offer a relatively inexpensive way to visualize at least parts of future systems but may fail to communicate the overall sense of a new user experience, either because key hardware that will support the new system does not exist or because of the difficulty of creating a fluid, interactive mock-up of a large system (Nielsen 1989, 1993; Tognazzini 1992).

Film or video enables one to build the ultimate demo out of pure "unobtanium." Gone are hardware limitations and computer artifacts. Everything works perfectly, no matter how many times the spectator looks at the tape, and messages both subtle and explicit can move the user toward any conclusions the filmmaker had in mind. These are both the advantage and curse of video prototyping. Will you end up with a prototype of a system that can be built, or only a slick piece of propaganda?

Starfire Observations and Guidelines

Starfire was under the technical and creative control of SunSoft Engineering from the beginning. It was to be a video prototype of an actual proposed system, capturing enough detail of the interaction methodology to display the concepts. The software interface had to be capable of reaching maturity within a decade, specifically by November 16, 2004, when the story in the film takes place.

"Knowledge Navigator" (Dubberly and Mitch 1987), its Apple successors, and Hewlett-Packard's "HP 1995" video demonstrated technologies, such as highly skilled anthropomorphic agents, that may not be approachable for 100 years. AT&T's "Connections" video featured videophones that could not only perform flawless live translations, but could rearticulate the caller's lip, throat, and facial movements to track the new words perfectly.

In attempting to create a believable ten-year vision, we wanted to avoid such leaps into the future, but soon found both the film and video media inexorably pulling on us to make radical compromises of our own. Over the course of the project we developed the following set of observations and guidelines to keep us from straying into fantasy.

Observation: Interaction techniques most easily accomplished on film may be difficult or even impossible to implement on the computer.

Video prototyping at once eliminates all software limitations. Want an anthropomorphic agent capable of carrying out your most softly whispered voice command? No problem. Want a 30-frame-per-second, real-time fly-through of an extremely complex 3D shaded model? No problem. Want instant translation with computed reanimation of mouth and lip positions? No problem.

Such seeming technological feats are easily accomplished in film. After all, to make it appear that a translator is not only converting the words but the mouth position, you need only film the actor speaking in the second language. The remarkably correct mouth position then comes for free. To do a more realistic simulation of live translation, you must go to extra trouble to not "correct" the mouth position, by filming the actor saying the words in the original language, then overdubbing the dialog in the second language.

Our Guideline: In translating the interface vision into film, continually question whether each object or action can be accomplished in ten years on a real computer.

Result: We were repeatedly tempted to lower the cost of the film by pushing the time line out "just a little." We ended up eliminating some of the interactivity when the only other choice was to take some impossible leap into the future.

At the same time, we tried not to overlook the film's "suggestions" too quickly. The level of detail shown in the computer graphics during the brief fly-over of Julie's information is well beyond today's technology and may be beyond workstation technology in 2004. However, as with the curved workspace display, we felt that such an information environment was worthy of introduction. It could well be that ten years from now, we won't have the polygon count to produce quite as high-quality graphics as we show in the film, but we will have a count high enough to make effective use of the metaphor.

Observation: The "users" (actors) in a video prototype will show no distress in using the interface, regardless of its quality.

Video prototypes, while costing a tiny fraction of robust full-system prototypes, tend to be off-budget. They are not a matter of gathering together a few or a few dozen engineers together for a year or three, working kind of over in a corner. They require actual cash.

When at Apple, several Starfire team members worked on a project to develop a series of vignettes showing future users accomplishing tasks with experimental interfaces. The final results were shot in-house in video with practically no budget. Managers and outsiders were unable to look past the dearth of production values and appreciate the ideas expressed. The project had virtually no impact on Apple's future direction.

"Knowledge Navigator" was produced by Apple's creative services department, the folks responsible for the corporate logo and the building signs. They had three things going for them: the creators, Hugh

Dubberly and Doris Mitch, are both talented individuals; they received good input from Alan Kay and several of his colleagues, and they had a high enough budget to produce a real film. "Knowledge Navigator" had a profound effect on Apple and on the industry.

We were interested in Starfire's having a profound effect. We launched a full-blown fund-raising effort, garnering support not only within engineering, but within marketing, sales, and public relations. These people do not intend to shell out money for a film showing people with dour expressions making errors while stumbling through a prototype system. They want happy people basking in the warm glow of a computer that always works. We wanted to do our best to ensure that those happy people would be just as happy ten years from now when they sat down at the real thing.

Our Guideline: The Starfire interface must be designed, tested, and iterated the same way any other interface would.

Result: We fooled the marketers. Starfire may be the first video prototype to show an actual bug, seen when the computer attempts to "read" Julie's ham on rye sandwich. Outside of this single glitch, however, Starfire is indeed the story of a woman finding fame, fortune, and happiness through the good graces of her perfectly functioning machines.

Most of the interactions seen in the film were built and tested in isolation to ensure that they would work. A few, including the most advanced one, the second-person virtual reality SunPad display, could not be built within our time constraints. (We did later build it, and it worked.) In these cases, we relied on a lot of feedback from Sun's senior designers and other industry leaders.

Observation: In real life, things don't always work as planned. In film, they will unless you're very careful.

It's much easier to write a story where everything goes as planned rather than one where things go wrong and people must react instantaneously. In the case of a video prototype, however, such a plan will safely insulate a slow and ineffective computer design from displaying its obvious flaws. (One also has the problem of the spectators' falling asleep.)

We could have ended the Starfire story in the boardroom, at the end of Julie's opening presentation, with lots of hearts and flowers and pats on the back for what a swell job Julie had done, except for the following guideline:

Our Guideline: *Use time pressure and plot twists to discipline design.*

We used the following scenario development cycle:

1. Write story.
2. Build solutions.
3. Tighten story.
4. Build better solutions.
5. Tighten story.

We first emphasized time by forcing Julie to develop a multimedia presentation in only 5 hours, instead of the week she had allotted. We then really turned the screws when she was in the boardroom. When Julie finished her report, O'Connor offered an effective rebuttal, based on a 5-year-old *Auto Week* report on a different car. Armed with today's technology, Julie would have been sunk.

Writing a story line like this forced us to look at the real needs of presenters. Things don't always go as planned. Anyone who has ever been in an executive staff meeting at a large corporation knows that it is rare to get even halfway through a formal presentation before the questions and shouting begins.

Our story line forced us to develop a design for Starfire that would enable people to reach their information space quickly and smoothly, that would enable Julie, when O'Connor waves around his copy of *Auto Week*, not only to pull up within 30 seconds the same issue—with annotations—but to retrieve subsequent materials that would help her negate everything in O'Connor's central argument.

Result: *Having to write the story as it would likely happen in real life, rather than in a perfect world, forced us to explore some very real issues, such as ubiquitous information space access with fast, intelligent retrieval, that we might otherwise have ignored.*

Observation: *Hardware in video prototypes can be complex to the point of impossibility and still appear to be easy to fabricate.*

"Knowledge Navigator" featured a fold-in-half display that, once unfolded and started up, became a seamless, continuous surface. For engineers to build such a display would border on the impossible. For the filmmakers compositing screen animations over a still image of the opened "Knowledge Navigator" model, showing a seam would have required them to take the extra step of superimposing the image of a seam over the animation.

Guideline: Avoid impossible hardware designs and reintroduce hardware artifacts where needed.

Results: We developed a wide range of computing devices for Starfire. Since we were showing a mature system in only ten years, we stuck to hardware designs that were either working in laboratories or had been actually implemented, though perhaps on a smaller scale. For example, many of our portable models had an HDTV aspect ratio of 16:9, with an implied increase in resolution. It does not require much of a leap of faith to see such portables being widely available in ten years.

The primary display device in Starfire was Julie's high-definition (300 dpi or better) 24-bit color, 2-square-meter curved panel that acts as both an input device (touch, stylus, and digitizing) and display.

For purposes of the film, we assumed we would be able to fabricate such a surface out of a solid-state matrix, as described in Chapter 8, "The Shape of Tomorrow's Computers." This allowed us the greatest freedom in creating a photogenic industrial design. It could well be that in 2004, we would have to build the device using projection technology, as explored by Kreuger (1991) and by Newman and Wellner (1992).

Observation: In the film medium, the simpler and less direct the physical interaction with the interface is, the less expensive it is to film it.

The problem with film is that it is too good. In Starfire, we show Julie producing a really slick presentation over the course of 5 hours. We could have had her walk into her office, announce to the computer, "Whip me up a hot presentation by 4:00," and then leave for a long lunch. Five hours later, an anthropomorphic agent could have "handed" her the report, and we would have saved tens of thousands of dollars on special effects.

"Knowledge Navigator" used apparently flawless continuous-speech voice and context recognition as extensively as it did to save money. Nothing had to be animated on the screen. No visible commands needed to be accepted and acknowledged.[1]

Our Guideline: First design the interface. Then make filming decisions based on budget limitations.

Result: In Starfire, we show three classes of input: gestural and stylus (with the actors' hands visible in the shots), mouse, and voice. In addition, we had

....
1 From a private conversation with Doris Mitch, co-creator of "Knowledge Navigator."

two film techniques open to us to help reduce costs: the reverse angle shot and conversion of action to monologue.

Direct Physical Interaction: Gestural and Stylus Input

Gestural and stylus input are by far the most expensive to film, requiring complex animations synchronized to the actors' movements. This type of shooting entailed a considerable amount of special effects processing later on to make the final composite look real. The cost would have been considerably higher had we not created the animations in-house.

Indirect Physical Interaction: Mouse Input

The mouse turned out to be a real money saver. Once we had established through a long shot that an actor was holding the mouse, we were able to cut away to an insert shot that showed only the animation. We still had the time and expense of producing the animations themselves, but the hand-synchronization and special effects compositing costs went away. An insert shot cost around one-third as much as a gestural or stylus shot to produce, again based on our developing the animations in-house.

Fortunately, we felt we needed a mouse (or other indirect pointing device) for our giant, curved display. Using the hands on the horizontal part of such a display, with the wrists and arms resting on the surface, would be quite natural. Occasionally reaching up to the vertical surface to slide an object or two would be more productive than searching for the mouse (Dillon, Edey, and Tombaugh 1990; Potter, Weldon, and Schneiderman 1992). However, having to suspend one's hand and arm in the air to really accomplish work on the vertical surface would be torturous (Potter, Weldon, and Schneiderman 1988).

Over the course of preproduction, we moved several key sequences to the vertical part of the display, primarily to save the money that hand or stylus interaction would have cost us. In real life, Julie would have probably spent more time working on the flat part of her desk than we have shown.

Voice Recognition

Voice recognition was a real money saver, costing one-tenth the price of hand and stylus interaction. Voice fit in well with our interface strategy of enabling a wide range of overlapping input methods, and we assumed a fairly mature voice recognition technology by 2004.

We did not assume that voice recognition would be backed up by a robust contextual recognition capability that would allow the computer to "know" whether it or another human was being spoken to. We developed a set of rather simple voice guidelines. The primary rule was that if no one else was in the room or on the videophone, the computer would assume anything the protagonist said to be directed toward the computer. That meant that the user could not talk very loudly to herself, but it did eliminate the need for any preface to communication. When someone else was in the room or on the screen, the user had to initiate an instruction with a predefined command word.

Reverse Angle Shots

Reverse angle shots are a standard part of film technique (Katz 1991; Mamet 1991). They can be seen in their most blatant form on TV news magazines, such as "60 Minutes" or "20/20," wherein periodically we switch from watching the interviewee to looking at the interviewer nodding sagely in response (the latter shot having been filmed afterward, then cut, often awkwardly, into place).

In Starfire, we used reverse shots not only during human-to-human dialog but during human-to-computer dialog. By switching our spectators from a shot of the screen to a shot of the actress reacting to the screen, for seconds at a time our special effects budget fell to practically zero. Instead of costly and complex animations of screen elements whizzing around, we were able to substitute some simple sound effects, along with movements of the actors' eyes, to convey motion in the spectator's mind.

Our reverse shots also cost one-tenth the price of hand and stylus interaction. Thus, at the price of voice recognition, we were able to deliver the impact of far more expensive physical interaction.

Monologue

Monologue is the bargain basement of video prototyping. In this technique, an actor delivers a soliloquy on some complex series of interactions that were accomplished off-screen at a previous time. Monologue not only costs a minimum amount, it can compress a series of interactions that might take an hour or two into the space of a few seconds. It can also put an audience to sleep if it runs much more than 15 or 20 seconds (an eternity in film; Katz 1992; Mamet 1991).

We avoided monologue in Starfire.

Observation: The first goal in a video prototype is to communicate a vision to the viewing audience. The second goal is to design a usable system.

Our Guideline: Ensure that the viewing audience can see and understand the stages in complex computations, even if that requires making things visible that might be quite invisible in the actual product.

Result: Throughout the course of writing the screenplay, blocking the action, shooting, and editing, we were constantly aware of our two sets of "users": the fictional users parked in front of their fictional computers and our very real spectators watching the final Starfire film.

Every time a new decision point arose in the project, we looked at our options from the perspective of both our future users and our immediate spectators. This process did not result in our changing the basics of the interface but did result in our increasing the visibility of our interactivity.

User Input

Anyone who has ever been given a demonstration of a visual interface product by someone using shortcut keys knows what happens when, as a spectator, you can't see every step the user is following. Things start popping up and disappearing from the screen as though by magic. We found it necessary to ensure that our spectators could see or hear every communication from user to computer.

We also found it necessary sometimes to limit the number of movements that actors had to make to accomplish a task. Too much flailing around was just as disconcerting as hidden movements. In one case, I had to come up with a simplified interaction while standing on the stage in North Hollywood while 20 highly paid people stood around waiting. The result was a much simpler gesture that not only made the film more watchable but made the interface itself cleaner and more productive to use.

Computer Feedback

Both users and spectators will need to see the ultimate result of a calculation or process, but in many cases, users would be confused by seeing the underlying algorithms that drive the process (see Chapter 34). For us to communicate our vision to our spectators, however, we had to ensure that every concept was faithfully transmitted.

We developed our most complex animation strictly so that the viewing audience could understand our algorithms. In the scene with

Natalie, Julie wants to place a male model beside a 3D model of her car in order to dress up her presentation. She first asks for a 3D mannequin from her Vellum 3D tool set, then chooses a male model from an existing 2D film as the source of a texture map. The system maps the male model onto the mannequin form.

We wanted to show each step of what might be the internal process by which this 2D to 3D modeling might happen. To show how the male model is picked out of the film, we have her use a future version of the Photoshop wand on the model. The wand tool jogs the film back and forth, demonstrating that it is finding the edges of the object not by color or value but by movement in time against the background. It then selects the object. Originally we showed the selected object by removing the color from everything else in the image. Test viewers could identify the object as being special but didn't understand he was selected. We had to add the familiar marquee of moving black lines for viewers to understand. (And, of course, we increased the thickness of the marquee, so VHS viewers would be able to see what is going on.)

Once Julie approves the selection, a system tool takes control, running the film forward, taking snapshots of different views of the man as he walks through the commercial and developing them into a bottled texture map of the man that Vellum can then pour out onto the articulated mannequin Julie will place beside the new car.

In a real product, the computer could carry out all its work without showing the film moving at all, and, indeed, if it could capture the texture map quickly enough, that would probably be the correct interface. For the sake of the movie, however, we wanted people to understand that we were not using magic; we were using a specific set of algorithms that communicate an even more specific message: in systems like Starfire, applications—and their developers—will work in close cooperation with each other and the system to reduce the work burden on the user and to enable results that would otherwise be difficult or impossible to achieve.

Observation: *Video prototyping offers the opportunity to explore social as well as technical issues.*

Because video prototypes show systems operating *in situ*, they present the opportunity to explore potential impacts, negative as well as positive, on the daily lives of their users.

Our Guideline: Showcase an unresolved social issue that Starfire will raise or exacerbate.

Starfire has the characteristics of a media space, defined by Mantei et al. (1993) as "a system that uses integrated video, audio, and computers to allow individuals and groups to work together despite being distributed spacially and temporally." Such systems immediately raise the specter of violations of the right to privacy (Barrett 1993; Fish, Kraut, and Root 1992; Gaver et al. 1992; Mackay 1993; Mantei et al. 1993). We wanted to explore the ramifications of media spaces not by solving the privacy problem but by demonstrating it.

Result: We assumed our system would have such built-in safeguards as no one being able to see into your private space without your being able to watch them (Root 1988). We also assumed that the mechanism for turning off the cameras showing your space would be tied to the physical structure of your space. For example, the glance camera, used by others to see if you are in, might be mounted in your door frame: close the door, and it would be impossible for outsiders to see in.

The privacy invasion we wanted to show in the film would not be based on a design stressing functionality over privacy or on someone "getting around" the system to spy. Rather, we wanted to show the result an unexpected event could have even with a well-protected system.

We considered several unexpected events. The event would have to thrust a character suddenly into an intimate moment, inadvertently shared by everyone on the network. It would have to make the film's spectators feel that they had ceased being viewers and had suddenly crossed over to being voyeurs. At the same time, we didn't want a lot of letters of complaint coming in after the film was released.

We finally settled on the scene surrounding the character, Molly, on Julie's design team. Her boyfriend quite unexpectedly arrives at her office and proposes. We thus broadcast a tender and private scene that Molly might not have chosen for her coworkers to be watching, had she had the time to consider. We expect that some spectators may extrapolate to the possibility of less tender and more startling interactions initiated by a young lover, interactions inadvertently hurled at 186,000 miles per second around the world, leading to the necessity of updating resumés. Others may consider the less career-threatening embarrassment of being seen a continent away while hiking up one's pantyhose or cleaning one's nose. With or without such extrapolations, we hoped the scene would engender discussion.

Film is a powerful medium, capable of showing either perfection, thereby stifling discussion, or imperfection, thereby promoting debate. In building a video prototype, we felt an ethical imperative to show the limitations of our designs.

Conclusion

Video prototyping is a powerful medium for communicating not only the functionality but the spirit and personality of a new application or computer. It eliminates all the limitations of computer prototyping, but at the expense of introducing a number of seeming advantages that can work together to lure the prototyper away from the possible toward the land of fantasy.

We found that by adhering to the guidelines we developed, we were able to produce a drama with a strong story line, a large number of clear and definite messages, and a sprinkling of controversial elements, all wrapped in a video prototype that demonstrated the fundamentals of an implementable new architecture.

High-budget video prototyping is a new field, and we are confident that those who come after us will improve greatly upon what we have done. We offer these observations and guidelines as a platform from which they can begin.

R E F E R E N C E S ◆

"Apple Information Manager, MultiMedia Reference and Learning" (1989). Video disk. Apple Computer.

Barker, K., Kimbrough, W., and Heller, W. (1966). *A Study of Medication Errors in a Hospital.* Fayetteville, AR: University of Arkansas.

Barrett, Phil (1993). "Ubiquitous Computing in Action." *Wired* (September–October): 24–25.

Bergman, Hans; Brinkman, Albert; and Koelega, Harry S. (1981). "System Response Time and Problem Solving Behavior." *Proceedings of the Human Factors Society,* 25th Annual Meeting, Rochester, NY, October 12–16, pp. 749–753.

Berne, Eric (1964). *The Games People Play.* New York: Ballantine Books.

Bias, Randolph G., and Mayhew, Deborah J. (1994) *Cost-Justifying Usability.* Boston: Academic Press.

Bloch, Hannah; Cole, Wendy; and Epperson, Sharon E. (1995). "On a Screen Near You: Cyberporn." *Time,* July 3, pp. 38–45.

Booth, William (1993). "Catfish Grabbing: Divers Hook Giant Prey with Bare Hands." *Washington Post,* August 31.

Boston Globe (1995). "Sidebar: Profiles of the New Schools." March 26.

Boyer, Earnest L., and Carnegie Foundation (1995). *The Basic School: A Community for Learning.* New York: Carnegie Foundation.

Boyett, Joseph H., and Conn, Henry P. (1991). *Workplace 2000: The Revolution Reshaping American Business.* New York: Plume.

Bulkeley, William M. (1992). "Study Finds Hidden Costs of Computing." *Wall Street Journal,* November 2.

Bulkeley, William M. (1994). "A Tool for Women, a Toy for Men." *Wall Street Journal,* March 16.

Burger, Eugene (1991). *Strange Ceremonies, Bizarre Magick for the Modern Conjuror,* published by Richard Kaufman and Alan Greenberg.

Cameron, Charles (1974). *Invocation* magazine (July), as quoted by Burger, Eugene (1991), in *Strange Ceremonies, Bizarre Magick for the Modern Conjuror,* published by Richard Kaufman and Alan Greenberg.

Carlson, Richard, and Goldman, Bruce (1994). *Fast Forward: Where Technology, Demographics, and History Will Take America and the World in the Next 30 Years.* New York: HarperCollins.

Carroll, John M. (1995). *Scenario-Based Design: Envisioning Work and Technology in System Development.* New York: Wiley.

Cavazos, Edward A., and Morin, Gavino (1994). *Cyberspace and the Law: Your Rights and Duties in the On-Line World.* Cambridge, MA: MIT Press.

Christo (1978). In Edith Pavese (ed.), *Christo: Running Fence.* New York: Harry N. Abrams.

Clinton, William J. (1994)."Remarks by the President at Goals 2000 Event, The South Lawn." White House Forum, America Online.

"Connections" (1993). AT&T video.

Consumers Union (1991). "What Price Privacy." *Consumer Reports* (May).

Crichton, Michael (1993). *Disclosure.* New York: Ballantine Books.

Davidow, William H., and Malone, Michael S. (1992). *The Virtual Corporation, Lessons from the World's Most Advanced Companies.* New York: HarperBusiness.

Dawes, Edwin A., and Setterington, Arthur (1986). *The Encyclopedia of Magic.* New York: W. H. Smith Publishers.

De Mente, Boye Lafayette (1993). *Behind the Japanese Bow: An In-Depth Guide to Understanding and Predicting Japanese Behavior.* Lincolnwood, IL: Passport Books.

Diggins, John Patrick (1988). *The Proud Decades: America in War and Peace, 1941–1960.* New York: Norton.

Dillon, Richard F.; Edey, Jeff D.; and Tombaugh, Jo W. (1990). "Measuring the True Cost of Command Selection: Techniques and Results." In *Proceedings of CHI'90.* Reading, MA: Addison-Wesley.

Dillon, Tim (1986). "Milestones: Steps Along the Path of Computer Progress." *USA Today,* September 22.

Dobyns, Lloyd, and Crawford-Mason, Clare (1991). *Quality or Else.* Boston: Houghton Mifflin.

Dubberly, Hugh, and Mitch, Doris (1987). "The Knowledge Navigator." Video. Apple Computer.

Fish, Robert S.; Kraut, Robert E.; and Root, Robert W. (1992). "Evaluating Video as a Technology for Informal Communication." In *Proceedings of CHI'92.* Reading, MA: Addison-Wesley.

Fiske, Edward B. (1992). *Smart Schools, Smart Kids.* New York: Touchstone

Fitzkee, Dariel (1943). *Showmanship for Magicians.* Pomeroy, OH: Lee Jacobs Productions. (© Copyright 1943, 1945 Dariel Fitzroy. Used by permission of the publisher.)

Fitzkee, Dariel (1944). *The Trick Brain.* Pomeroy, OH: Lee Jacobs Productions. (© Copyright 1944, 1976 Dariel Fitzroy. Used by permission of the publisher.)

Fitzkee, Dariel (1945). *Magic by Misdirection.* Pomeroy, OH: Lee Jacobs Productions.(© Copyright 1944, 1975 Dariel Fitzroy. Used by permission of the publisher.)

Gaver, William; Moran, Thomas; MacLean, Allan; Lövstrand, Lennart; Dourish, Paul; Carter, Kathleen; and Buxton, William (1992). "Realizing a Video Environment: EuroPARC's RAVE System." *Proceedings of CHI'92.* Reading, MA: Addison-Wesley.

Gerstner, Louis V. Jr.; Semerad, Roger D.; Doyle, Denis Philip; and Johnston, William B. (1994). *Reinventing Education: Entrepreneurship in America's Public Schools.* New York: Dutton.

Gibson, Walter B., and Young, Morris N. (1953). *Houdini on Magic.* New York: Dover Publications.

Gleick, James (1987). *Chaos, Making of a New Science.* New York: Viking Penguin.

Graham, Marty (1992). "Nerds Get Revenge—But They Pay a Price." *San Francisco Examiner,* August 30.

Gross, Ken (1989). "Back to the Future! Mazda Beats Ford to the Inexpensive Sports Car Niche with Its Miata MX-5 — a slicker Lotus Elan Than Colin Chapman's." *Automotive Industries* 169, no. 4, pp. 92–95.

Grossberg, Mitchell; Weisen, Raymond A.; and Yntema, Douwe B. (1976), "An Experiment on Problem Solving with Delayed Computer Responses." In *IEEE Transactions on Systems, Man, and Cybernetics* (March), pp. 219–222.

Hale, Ellen (1995). "Numerous Hackers Toying with Super Info Highway." *San Jose Mercury News*, March 11.

Harris, Thomas A. (1969). *I'm OK—You're OK*. New York: Harper & Row.

Heckel, Paul (1991). *The Elements of Friendly Software Design*. Alameda, CA: Sybex.

Henning, Doug (1986). "Houdini." Video. New York: Congress Video Group.

Hetzner, Amy (1994). "Wiring into Work." *San Francisco Chronicle*, October 3, p. C–1.

Hill, William C.; Hollan, James D.; Wroblewski, Dave; and McCandless, Tim (1992). "Edit Wear and Read Wear." In *Proceedings of CHI'92*. Reading, MA: Addison-Wesley.

Hill, Will; Stead, Larry; Rosenstein, Mark; and Furnas, George (1995). "Recommending and Evaluating Choices in a Virtual Community of Use." In *Proceedings of CHI'95*. Reading, MA: Addison-Wesley.

Hotakainen, Rob (1993). "In Baltimore, a Radical School Experiment Seems to Be Working." *Minneapolis–St. Paul Star Tribune*, December 8.

Howard, Philip K. (1994). *The Death of Common Sense: How Law Is Suffocating America*. New York: Random House.

"HP 1995" (1989). Video. Hewlett-Packard.

Huxley, Aldous (1965). *Brave New World and Brave New World Revisited*. New York: Harper & Row.

Ignelzi, R.J. (1995). "Computerized Medical Information May Be Hazardous to Your Privacy." *San Diego Union-Tribune,* July 2, pp. D2–3.

Jeffries, Robin; Miller, James R.; Warton, Cathleen; and Uyeda, Kathy M. (1991). "User Interface Evaluation in the Real World: A Comparison of Four Techniques." In *Proceedings of CHI'91.* Reading, MA: Addison-Wesley.

Jillette, Penn, and Teller (1989). *Cruel Tricks for Dear Friends.* New York: Villard Books.

Katz, Steven D. (1991). *Film Directing: Shot by Shot: Visualizing from Concept to Screen.* Stoneham, MA: Focal Press.

Katz, Steven D. (1992). *Film Directing: Cinematic Motion: A Workshop for Staging Scenes.* Stoneham MA: Focal Press.

Kay, Alan (1991). "User Interface: A Personal View." In Brenda Laurel (ed.), *The Art of Human-Computer Interface Design.* Reading, MA: Addison-Wesley.

Koenig, David (1994). *Mouse Tales: A Behind-the-Ears Look at Disneyland.* Irvine, CA: Bonaventure Press.

Kreuger, M. (1991) *Artificial Reality II.* Reading, MA: Addison-Wesley.

Kroeger, Otto, and Thuesen, Janet M. (1988). *Type Talk: The 16 Personality Types That Determine How We Live, Love, and Work.* New York: Tilden Press.

Landauer, Thomas K. (1995). *The Trouble with Computers.* Cambridge, MA: MIT Press.

Laurel, Brenda (1991). *Computers as Theater.* Reading, MA: Addison-Wesley.

Legge, James (trans.) (1973). *I Ching Book of Changes.* New York: Causeway Books.

Levy, Steven (1994). "E-Money (That's What I Want)." *Wired* 2, no. 12 (December): 174.

Logitec Inc. (1992). "PC's and People Poll: A National Compatibility Study of the Human Experience with Hardware." Fremont, CA: Logitec.

Mackay, Wendy E. (1993). "Ethical Issues in the Use of Video: Is It Time to Establish Guidelines?" In *Proceedings of CHI'93*. Reading, MA: Addison-Wesley.

Main, Jeremy (1994). *Quality Wars*. New York: The Free Press.

Mamet, David (1991) *On Directing Film*. New York: Penguin Books.

Mander, Richard; Salomon, Gitta; and Wong, Yin Yin (1992). "A 'Pile' Metaphor for Supporting Casual Organization of Information." In *Proceedings of CHI'92*. Reading, MA: Addison-Wesley.

Mantei, Marilyn M.; Baecker, Ronald M.; Sellen, Abigail J.; Buxton, William A. S.; and Milligan, Thomas (1993). "Experiences in the Use of a Media Space." In *Proceedings of CHI'93*. Reading, MA: Addison-Wesley.

Miller, Robert B. (1968). "Response Time in Man-Computer Conversational Transactions." In *Proceedings Sprint Joint Computer Conference, 33*. Montvale, NJ: AFIPS Press.

Mingo, Jack (1994). *How the Cadillac Got Its Fins*. New York: HarperCollins.

Moskowitz, Robert (1994). "The State of Telecommuting." *San Jose Mercury News,* November 14.

Myers, Isabel Briggs, and McCaulley, Mary H. (1985). *A Guide to the Development and Use of the Myers-Briggs Type Indicator.* Palo Alto, CA: Consulting Psychologists Press.

Negroponte, Nicholas (1991). "The Noticeable Difference." In Brenda Laurel (ed.), *The Art of Human-Computer Interface Design*. Reading, MA: Addison-Wesley.

Negroponte, Nicholas (1995). *Being Digital*. New York: Alfred A. Knopf.

Nelms, Henning (1969). *Magic and Showmanship: A Handbook for Conjurers*. New York: Dover Publications.

Nelson, Theodor Holm (1980). "Interactive Systems and the Design of Virtuality." *Creative Computing* 6, no. 11, 12 (November and December).

Nelson, Theodor Holm (1991). "The Right Way to Think About Software Design." In Brenda Laurel (ed.), *The Art of Human-Computer Interface Design*. Reading, MA: Addison-Wesley.

Newman, William, and Wellner, Pierre (1992) "A Desk Supporting Computer-Based Interaction with Paper Documents. In *Proceedings of CHI'92*. Reading, MA: Addison-Wesley.

Newsday (1993). "As Clinton Got His Trim, the Planes Ran on Time." *San Francisco Chronicle*, June 30, p. A11.

Nielsen, Jakob (1989). "Usability Engineering at a Discount." In *Proceedings of the Third International Conference on Human-Computer Interaction*. Boston: Elsevier.

Nielsen, Jakob (1993). *Usability Engineering*. Boston: Academic Press.

Nielsen, Jakob (1995). *MultiMedia and Hypertext: The Internet and Beyond*. Boston: Academic Press.

Nolan, Norton & Company (1992). *Managing End-User Computing*. Boston: Nolan, Norton & Company.

Norman, Donald (1983). "Some Observations of Mental Models," In Dedre Gentner and Albert L. Stevens (eds.), *Mental Models*. Hillsdale, NJ: Lawrence Erlbaum Associates.

Norman, Donald (1986). "Cognitive Engineering." In D.A. Norman and S. W. Draper (eds.), *User Centered System Design*. Hillsdale, NJ: Lawrence Erlbaum Associates.

Norman, Donald (1988). *The Psychology of Everyday Things*. New York: Basic Books.

Ohanian, Thomas A. (1993). *Digital Nonlinear Editing: New Approaches to Editing Film and Video*. Boston: Focal Press.

O'Neill, Molly (1995). "The Lure and Addiction of Life On Line." *New York Times*, March 8, p. C1.

Perelman, Lewis J. (1992). *School's Out*. New York: Avon Books.

Perkins, Ed (ed.) (1993). *Consumer Reports Travel Letter* 9, no. 4 (April).

Peters, Tom (1994). *The Pursuit of Wow!* New York: Vintage Books.

Phlegar, Phyllis (1995). *Love Online*. Reading, MA: Addison-Wesley.

Piller, Charles (1993a). "Bosses with X-Ray Eyes." *Macworld Magazine* (July).

Piller, Charles (1993b). "Privacy in Peril." *Macworld Magazine* (July).

Plauger, P. J. (1990). "Technicolor and Cinemascope." *Computer Language Magazine* (August): 17–23.

Plotnikoff, David (1994). "Why Women Are On-Line Outsiders." *San Jose Mercury News,* July 24.

Popcorn, Faith (1991, 1992). *The Popcorn Report*. New York: Harper-Collins.

Potter, Richard L.; Weldon, Linda J.; and Shneiderman, Ben (1988). "Improving the Accuracy of Touch Screens: An Experimental Evaluation of Three Strategies." In *Proceedings of CHI'88*. Reading, MA: Addison-Wesley.

Quittner, Joshua (1995). "How Parents Can Filter Out the Naughty Bits," *Time,* July 3, p. 45.

Report of the Presidential Commission on the Space Shuttle Challenger Accident. Washington, D.C.: Government Printing Office.

Rheingold, Howard (1993). *The Virtual Community: Homesteading on the Electronic Frontier*. Reading, MA: Addison-Wesley.

Root, R. W. (1988). "Design of a Multi-media Vehicle for Social Browsing." In *Proceedings of the CSCW'88*. New York: ACM.

Rowland, Diana (1985, 1993). *Japanese Business Etiquette: A Practical Guide to Success with the Japanese*. New York: Warner Books.

Rubinstein, Richard, and Hersh, Harry M. (1984). "Design Philosophy." In *The Human Factor: Designing Computer Systems for People*. Burlington, MA: Digital Press.

Samuelson, Pamela (1993). "The Ups and Downs of Look and Feel." *Communications of the ACM* (April): 29–32.

Sellen, Abigail J. (1990). "Mechanisms of Human Error and Human Error Detection." Ph.D. dissertation, University of California.

Shneiderman, Ben (1988). "A Nonanthropomorphic Style Guide: Overcoming the Humpty Dumpty Syndrome." *Computing Teacher* (October) 9–10.

Shneiderman, Ben (1992). *Designing the User Interface: Strategies for Effective Human-Computer Interaction.* Reading, MA: Addison-Wesley.

Sitton, Sarah, and Chmelir, Gerard (1984). "The Intuitive Computer Programmer." *Datamation,* October 15.

Sproull, Lee, and Kiesler, Sara (1991). *Connections: New Ways of Working in the Networked Organization.* Cambridge, MA: MIT Press.

Starker, India and Bolt, Richard (1990). "A Gaze-Responsive Self-Disclosing Display." In *Proceedings of CHI'90.* Reading, MA: Addison-Wesley.

Suryaraman, Maya (1995). "Internet Access for Schools Is Near." *San Jose Mercury News,* March 21, p. 1.

Taguchi, Genichi, and Clausing, Don (1990). "Robust Quality." *Harvard Business Review* (January–February): 65.

Toffler, Alvin (1980). *The Third Wave.* New York: William Morrow.

Tognazzini, Bruce (1992). *Tog on Interface.* Reading, MA: Addison-Wesley.

Tufte, Edward (1983). *The Visual Design of Quantitative Information.* Cheshire, CT: Graphics Press.

Tufte, Edward (1990). *Envisioning Information.* Cheshire, CT: Graphics Press.

Tufte, Edward (1996). *Visual Explanations.* Cheshire, CT: Graphics Press.

Walton, Mary (1986). *The Deming Management Method.* New York: Putnam Publishing Group.

Walton, Sam, and Hey, John (1992). *Sam Walton: Made in America, My Story.* New York: Bantam Books.

Weiser, Mark (1991). "The Computer for the 21st Century." *Scientific American* (September).

Whalen, John (1995). "You're Not Paranoid: They Really Are Watching You." *Wired* (March): 76–85.

Wright, Brett (1994). "The SOHO Scenario." *21C: The Magazine of the Australian Commission for the Future,* no. 12 (Autumn): 64–69.

Wylie, Margie (1995). "No Place for Women: Internet Is a Flawed Model for the Infobaun." *Digital Media,* January 2.

Now available on videocassette . . .
In response to overwhelming demand . . .
The controversial film you've been waiting for . . .

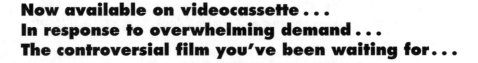

Starfire
The Directors' Cut

"With voice and gesture recognition, telepresence, VR, globally networked database retrieval driven by intelligent agents, and real-time image capture/manipulation techniques, Starfire is the logical extension of Apple's Knowledge Navigator vision of the mid-'80s—full of special-effects wizardry, layers of design, and obscured meanings."
— *Wired*, Sept., 1995

Julie was looking forward to a good day until Michael O'Connor tried to deep-six her sports car project. Now, only her team, scattered around the world, can save her . . .

Copyright © 1995, Sun Microsystems Inc. Closed-captioned for the hearing impaired. Not sold in stores.

ACT NOW! "Starfire: The Directors' Cut" is being sold at cost for a limited time. Free bonus: "The Making of Starfire" with the first 350,000 orders!

Video plus shipping and handling (4th class U.S. mail), contiguous states: US $13.50 per unit.* Video plus shipping and handling (1st class mail), AK/HI/Canada and other countries: US $14.50 per unit.

Call for information on faster shipping options.
*California residents, add 7.25% sales tax, for a total of US $14.22.

Credit card orders (AMEX, Mastercard, Visa) accepted by phone at **800-294-4404.** Credit card orders accepted by fax at **800-582-8000.** International orders (credit card only) accepted by phone at **916-939-1000.** (European versions available in PAL and SECAM.)

OR send check or money order (no p.o.'s or c.o.d.'s) with the following form to:
Sun Microsystems
P.O. Box 629000
El Dorado Hills, CA 95762

Please make check payable to *Sun Microsystems*.

Enclosed is $_____
Please send _____ copy/copies of *Starfire* to:

_____
Name

_____
Address

_____
City/State/ZIP